Explo
Constitution

A Study of America
&
Our Founding Documents

Independence Hall - McCabe, James D. The Pictorial History of the United States. Philadelphia. The National Publishing Company, 1877

Brian Harris

Liberty's Path – www.libertyspath.com

Libertatem et Veritas

We have no government armed with power capable of contending with human passions unbridled by morality and religion. Avarice, ambition, revenge, or gallantry, would break the strongest cords of our Constitution as a whale goes through a net. Our Constitution was made only for a moral and religious people. It is wholly inadequate to the government of any other.

– John Adams 1798

Liberty's Path - Fort Myers, FL - Printed in the United States of America
www.libertyspath.com - swflpatriot@gmail.com

Image credits - The images in this text are in the public domain and come from a single source, www.ushistoryimages.com.

ISBN (paper) 978-0-9892865-0-3, ISBN (electronic) 978-0-9892865-1-0
Library of Congress Control Number 2013907624

- Note: An asterisk (*) located next to a document title indicates that you will find the full text of that document in the Appendix.

- Note: Minor editorial liberties have been taken with regard to some "Old English" spellings where the original spelling may have been confusing.

Acknowledgements

This book has been a labor of love that I could have never completed without an understanding and patient wife, thank you Marion. I also have to thank our sons, Kenneth and Nathaniel, for going on many sign waves, doing neighborhood canvassing, and attending many meetings with their dad while he is doing what he can to save the republic. After all, this work is ultimately for them and their generation. Are we going to give our children the America of George Washington or the America of the progressive socialists who want to dictate every facet of their lives?

To all of my co-patriots in liberty that are actively engaged in the work that needs to be done I offer my thanks and encouragement. To my brothers and sisters in Christ who have realized that the path to liberty and the path to God are one in the same I thank you. "Therefore, my dear brothers, be steadfast, immovable, always excelling in the Lord's work, knowing that your labor in the Lord is not in vain." 1 Cor. 15:58 (HCSB)

Special thanks also goes out to Karen Hatzigeorgiou from ushistoryimages.com, for the extra help she provided with locating the image of Thomas Paine!

This work would have never made it to print without the wonderful assistance and expertise of Arthur Printing in Cape Coral, FL.

Contents

Appendix

1. Mayflower Compact – 1620
2. Fundamental Orders of Connecticut – 1639
3. Declaration of Rights and Grievances – 1765
4. Suffolk Resolves – 1774
5. Declaration and Resolves of the First Continental Congress – October 14, 1774
6. Give Me Liberty – Patrick Henry – 1775
7. Olive Branch Petition – July 1775
8. Declaration of the Causes and Necessity of Taking Up Arms – July 1775
9. Thomas Jefferson letter to Gideon Granger – Aug. 13, 1800
10. Thomas Jefferson First Inaugural Address – 1801
11. Essay on Property, James Madison – 1792
12. Virginia Declaration of Rights – June 1776
13. Summary View of the Rights of British America in 1774
14. Massachusetts Circular Letter – 1768
15. Address of the Annapolis Convention – 1786
16. Virginia Plan – 1787
17. New Jersey Plan – 1787
18. Ron Paul Congressional Speech 10/10/2001, text HR 3074, text HR 3076
19. NDAA section 1021
20. George Washington Farewell Address – 1796
21. Thomas Jefferson Second Inaugural Address – 1805
22. James Madison First Inaugural – 1809

Introduction

In 1607 a grand experiment was initiated on this continent. The seeds of liberty were planted and cultivated. When they were ripe they produced a harvest the likes of which had never been seen or harnessed in the history of the world. I am talking about the American experiment. This experiment is an experiment in liberty! After all, as Thomas Jefferson said, this is one of our unalienable rights. This experiment gave birth to a nation, a constitution, and an understanding that government is instituted, by the consent of the governed, to protect rights, not grant them or take them away.

America is at a tipping point and has been on a downward path to this junction for the last 100 years. Limited republican government has been replaced by excessive, intrusive, and abusive government. To substantiate what I am saying here it is worth noting that when our Constitution was written in 1787 it listed three crimes. As of 2010 there are over 4,500 crimes listed in the federal code. That is unacceptable!

The founding fathers did not intend for you and I to live in a police state. So, how do we restore our Republic? Answer, through education because there are millions of Americans that don't know that the Republic has been lost. They don't know that they aren't free. I count you as someone who has concern for their family and for their nation, or else you probably wouldn't have this book in your hands. You now have a tool to gain an understanding of the fundamental first principles that form the basis for the American experiment, our Declaration of Independence and our Constitution.

What started out as a simple project to develop an outline to conduct a home study group on the Constitution turned into a very time consuming affair as I became intimate with the founders and their writings. Concepts such as self-government, unalienable rights, separation of powers, sovereignty, taxation, and property rights deserve a thorough examination because they form the basis for you and I to exist in what used to be a nation that cherished and promoted liberty. This work attempts to walk through America's founding documents in a methodical fashion so that we can explore the true meaning of the concepts that form the basis of the American experiment. For the most part the founders and their role models speak for themselves throughout this work but you will see commentary from me regarding how some of these principles are relevant today. You will see in the first couple chapters a brief history of the colonies and their feud with mother England so that we can gain a historical context to our founding documents. I have undertaken to produce a document based on my own self-study that is backed by the best sources of all, the founding fathers and their mentors. I hope this work is useful to you and I hope too, that it will spur you on to seek out additional study in this area. We should never stop learning, examining, and questioning.

Thank you for taking time to equip yourself with VERITAS! We must be informed and we must pass on our knowledge to any and all that will listen. Let us not refrain from doing all that is in our power to save our blessed republic.

Early Colonial Background

Jamestown / Virginia

Jamestown - Stephens, Alex H. A Comprehensive and Popular History of the United States. Chattanooga: Hickman and Fowler, 1882

The first permanent English settlement in the Americas was established in 1607 by the Virginia Company of London. On April 26, 1607 Captain Christopher Newport, Captain John Smith, and three ships, the Susan Constant, Discovery, and Godspeed, make landfall in what we know today as Virginia. They chose a poor piece of land for their settlement that was swampy and mosquito infested. Over half of the original settlers were dead within six months. The British settlers were not accustomed to the hard work required to plant a colony and subsist off the land. John Smith implemented a policy of, "no work, no eat," because the settlers realized that in their communal system of sharing provisions they could get an equal ration for doing no work.[1] In 1619 we have the first establishment of representative government in the new world when the House of Burgesses or Virginia Legislature is established.

Plymouth Plantation / Massachusetts Bay

The Mayflower set sail on September 6, 1620 with 102 passengers including religious separatists commonly known today as the *Pilgrims*. The pilgrims were Christians who believed in freedom to worship according to the Scriptures and apart from the formalities of the Church of England. Prior to this momentous event the group had been living in Leyden Holland since 1607. Their early leaders were John Robinson, William Brewster, and William Bradford. While they enjoyed religious liberty in Leyden life was hard. According to William Bradford the group started to contemplate relocation to the new world. Reasons for this included the protection of their children from the influences and temptations of the surrounding community so that they would not "degenerate and become corrupt." Another reason provided by Bradford was to advance the gospel of the kingdom of Christ. He states, **"Last and not least, they cherished a great hope and inward zeal of laying good foundations, or at least of making some way towards**

it, for the propagation and advance of the gospel of the kingdom of Christ in the remote parts of the world, even though they should be but stepping stones to others in the performance of so great a work."[2] The pilgrims anchored at Cape Cod on Nov 11, 1620. They went ashore at Plymouth on December 21, 1620.

Prior to disembarking the Mayflower the passengers created the first written charter of government in America. It is known as the ***Mayflower Compact****. It begins, 'In the name of God, Amen."

Mayflower Compact - Ellis, Edward S. The History of our Country: From the Discovery of America to the Present Time. Cincinnati: The Jones Brothers Publishing Company, 1910

The story of the pilgrims is fascinating and deserving of further study in your spare time. Interestingly, the Pilgrims did not have permission to settle in the area now known as New England because their charter called for them to settle in the Virginia Colony. Their original destination was to be near the mouth of the Hudson River in what would be the area of New York City.[3]

Was it by divine intervention that the Mayflower was blown off course so that they could establish a settlement where they could partake of the religious freedom that they were seeking?

In 1629 Massachusetts got an infusion of Puritans that settled in the area of Boston under the guidance of John Winthrop who had said, "We shall be a city upon a hill, the eyes of all people are upon us."[4]

Over the next 80 years additional colonies came into existence. The Reverend Roger Williams founded the settlement of Providence in what would become Rhode Island. Williams believed in separation of church and state as well as freedom of worship and freedom of conscience. Exeter, New Hampshire was settled by a preacher named John Wheelwright in 1638.

In Connecticut a preacher named Reverend John Hooker was instrumental in writing their first governing document, the ***Fundamental Orders of Connecticut**** in 1639. This document included a representative legislature, separation of church and state, and voting rights regardless of particular faith. In 1681 Pennsylvania was founded by Quaker William Penn. The final colony to be planted was Georgia in 1733. General John Oglethorpe brought former prisoners of England's debtor's jails as his first settlers. Early missionaries to Georgia included John and Charles Wesley, who went on to found the Methodist Church.

Prior to 1763 the colonies were generally prosperous and there was little friction with Great Britain. Other than regulation of trade, parliament exercised little control over them. While the colonial governors were agents of the crown and had absolute veto powers the colonial assemblies were filled with elected colonists who controlled the purse strings. Other than taxation for the regulation of trade the colonial assemblies conducted their own taxation. By controlling the purse strings the assemblies controlled the governor's pay and influenced what he could or could not spend money on. The power of the purse was useful for keeping the colonial governors in check.

Three types of colonies:

In colonial America there were essentially three types of colonies:

(1) Royal colonies- under the direct control of the crown, ex. Georgia

(2) Proprietary colonies- the king grants land and political authority to a proprietor, ex. Pennsylvania

(3) Corporate colonies- founded by groups in conjunction with trading companies, ex. Massachusetts and Virginia.

Rumblings

The French & Indian Wars were fought over a period of 70 years (1688-1763) with the final "war" being waged from 1754 to 1763. This was called the Seven Years War. This had drained the resources of Britain and the king wanted the colonies to pay their share of defense costs. Going forward from here we will explore a series of actions by King George II, George III, and the British Parliament that will result in counter action on the part of the colonists.

Navigation Acts

Starting in 1650 England passed a series of laws that forbid foreign vessels from trading with the colonies. Goods being exported out of the colonies had to be on English ships. In 1660 goods such as sugar, cotton, rice, and tobacco had to be shipped to England first before they could be sold elsewhere. In 1696 England required that duties be paid before goods could be shipped. These acts were not strictly enforced but they did propel colonial merchants to engage in smuggling and they had an effect of increasing the self sufficiency of the colonies to some extent.

Molasses Act of 1733

High duties were placed on sugar and molasses not bought from the British West Indies. These were openly violated and also increased smuggling.

Proclamation of 1763

Westward expansion past the Appalachians was restricted. Fur trading was also restricted by the crown.

Sugar Act 1764

New duties on sugar were not as high as the Act of 1733 but these laws were enforced with patrols, inspections, and searches of property. There were new duties placed on popular items such as Madeira wine, coffee, and pimento.

Currency Act 1764

Colonies can't print currency and must pay debt in gold and silver.

Quartering Acts of 1765

Required colonial authorities to provide barracks and supplies for British troops.

Stamp Act of 1765

Stamps must be purchased for items such as legal documents, dice, playing cards, newspapers, and almanacs. This was viewed as a *direct tax* on the people by parliament, where they had no representation.

Declaratory Act 1766

The Stamp Act was repealed in 1766 but Britain replaced it with the Declaratory Act which upheld that Britain has full power and authority to make statutes and laws to bind the colonies in all cases whatsoever.

Townshend Acts 1767

These were a series of acts designed to raise revenue. Duties were levied on items of everyday use such as tea, lead, paint, and glass. The British mistakenly thought that the colonists would not resist a tax on these items because it was not a *direct tax*. This act also legalized *writs of assistance*, which were searches of private property for smuggled goods. Revenues raised from these taxes would now go to paying the salaries of colonial governors and judges. As we recall, this "power of the purse" was a tool that the colonists had used to keep the governors in line. These acts also established the American Board of Customs Commissioners and placed its headquarters in Boston. In 1768 the Vice Admiralty Court was expanded to punish smugglers. These courts did not use juries. Widespread resistance in the colonies occurred and caused Britain to send troops to Boston. A clash was becoming inevitable.

Tea Act of 1773

The British East India Company had 17 million pounds of tea stored in warehouses and had no way selling all of it. In steps the British Parliament, of which, many members had a personal interest in the success of the East India Company. This tea was piling up in Great Britain because the colonies were consuming cheaper smuggled tea from the Indies. They were also shunning company tea because of the tax placed on it under the Townshend Acts. The Tea Act allowed "the company" to import tea directly into the colonies without middle man markup and without duty. This drove the price down to where it would be cheaper than smuggled tea. The company tea had to be consigned by designated merchants in the colonies who had ties to the British government. Britain thought the colonies would purchase this tea because it was cheaper and by doing so validate their claims to tax the colonies. Smugglers, merchants, and colonists alike, were outraged by this act. These events led to the Boston Tea Party, Dec 16, 1773.

Coercive (or Intolerable) Acts of 1774

A series of four punitive acts by Parliament to punish Massachusetts for the Boston Tea Party and to make an example out of them to demand obedience from the other colonies. 1. The Port of Boston was ordered closed. 2. The Massachusetts Colony charter was effectively revoked and government officers were placed under control of the crown. 3. British agents will be tried in Great Britain, not in colonial courts. 4. The quartering acts were revived.

Responses

The colonies were denied direct representation in Parliament and therefore held that the aforementioned Acts were in violation of their rights and colonial charters. Taxation without representation was a major issue but it was not the only one. The colonists believed in their right to trial by jury and their right to be secure from unlawful searches and seizures. These rights would eventually be protected in the Bill of Rights. The offenses perpetrated on the colonies led to the formation of organizations such as the Sons of Liberty and Committees of Correspondence throughout the colonies. These committees would communicate from colony to colony to share ideas, news, and methods of resistance.[5]

Non-importation agreements were also an effective method of resistance. Local groups also resorted to destructive and violent action.

Resistance to the Stamp Act

May 29, 1765 Patrick Henry introduces the **Virginia Resolves**, which were a response to the Stamp Act. These asserted the rights of the colonies to tax themselves and that the colonists had the same rights as Englishmen. These were printed in newspapers throughout the colonies. In August 1765 the home and property of stamp distributor Andrew Oliver were destroyed. Oliver was also hung in effigy from the Liberty Tree.[6] Oliver was made to resign his post in a public display under the Liberty Tree the next day. Lt. Gov. Hutchinson's house was also ransacked and destroyed by angry Bostonians. The **Stamp Act Congress** was convened in New York during October 1765. Representatives from nine of the thirteen colonies met and drafted the **Declaration of Rights and Grievances**.* These affirmed the rights of the colonists including right to trial by jury and no taxation without representation. The Stamp Act Congress is viewed as the first major example of unified resistance to British violations of colonial rights. The Stamp Act was repealed in 1766 but the Declaratory Act was passed on the same day.

Boston Massacre

Boston Massacre - Bryant, William Cullen and Sydney Howard Gay. A Popular History of the United States. New York: Charles Scribners' Sons, 1881

Outside of the Custom House on March 5, 1770 five Bostonians were killed by British soldiers after a confrontation that involved several hundred townspeople and a handful of redcoats. This event was dramatized ingeniously by Paul Revere when he created this engraving. The soldiers were defended at trial by patriots John Adams and Josiah Quincy.

Gaspee Affair June 1772

The British customs schooner Gaspee ran aground in shallow water off the coast of Rhode Island on June 9, 1772. A group of the Providence Sons of Liberty boarded the ship and burned it to the water line. British authorities pondered trying the offenders in England which sparked outrage in the colonies. This incident re-awakened colonial resistance after a brief lull.

Boston Tea Party Dec 16, 1773

During September and October 1773 over 600,000 lbs. of tea was sent over on seven ships. Four would land in Boston, one in New York, one in Philadelphia, and one in Charleston. Tea Consignees were forced to resign in Charleston and New York and in Philadelphia the tea was refused and sent back to Britain. In Boston there would be an ultimate act of glorious resistance against tyranny, now known as the Boston Tea Party. Patriot leaders had urged Gov. Hutchinson to send the boats back to Britain without unloading their tea. On Dec 16, 1773 several thousand townspeople gathered at the Old South Meeting House. After receiving word that the governor would not allow the ships to leave a group of patriots dressed as Indians boarded the three ships (the other never made it to port) and disposed of all the tea by tossing it overboard. In retaliation, as indicated above, the Parliament responded with the Coercive Acts.

Continental Congress

The first Continental Congress was held in Philadelphia as a response to the Coercive Acts. Congress was in session from September 5, 1774 to October 26, 1774. Every colony except for Georgia sent delegates to this meeting. Congress agreed to resist violations of their rights as Englishmen however there were divisions within the body as some were more inclined toward independence while others were hopeful of restoration of their position with Britain. Congress endorsed the **Suffolk Resolves***, which had been drafted by Dr. Joseph Warren and the Suffolk County Convention of the Committees of Correspondence on Sep. 6, 1774. Paul Revere delivered a copy of the resolves to the Continental Congress in Philadelphia. The resolves identified grievances and methods of resistance that would be utilized to restore their rights. On October 14, 1744 the congress drafted the **Declaration and Resolves of the First Continental Congress*.** This document outlined congress' formal position regarding the rights that had been violated as well as certain measures, such as non-importation, that would be followed to bring about a restoration of the rights and liberties of the colonists. Congress also formed the **Continental Association,** which would be a coordinated non-importation and non-exportation effort throughout the colonies. The King was petitioned by Congress and their grievances were ignored.

Patrick Henry's Speech 3/23/1775

Within a discourse on the events leading up to independence it would be negligent not to discuss the event that took place on March 23, 1775 at St. Johns Church in Richmond, Virginia. The "Orator of Liberty" offered up a fiery speech, without notes or script, to the Virginia House of Burgesses, which was in favor of putting the colony into a posture of defense and for forming a militia. The speech ended with the lines below.

Patrick Henry - Bryant, William Cullen and Sydney Howard Gay. A Popular History of the United States. New York: Charles Scribners' Sons, 1881

Is life so dear, or peace so sweet, as to be purchased at the price of chains and slavery? Forbid it, Almighty God! I know not what course others may take; but as for me, give me liberty, or give me death!*

Lexington & Concord April 19, 1775

British General Gage ordered 700 redcoats to Lexington to seize John Hancock and Samuel Adams who were staying at the home of the Reverend Jonas Clarke, a Hancock relative. They were then to march to Concord to destroy military supplies being stored by the colonials. Paul Revere and William Dawes were ordered by Dr. Warren to ride out and alert Adams,

Hancock, and the townspeople that the British were on the move. Revere ordered two lanterns hung in the spire of the Old North Church to signal that the British were moving by sea, "one if by land, two if by sea". The next morning a confrontation occurred on Lexington Green. It is still debated as to who fired the first shot, however this was the "shot heard round the world". Eight colonials under the command of Capt. John Parker were dead as a result of the skirmish. The redcoats then marched to Concord but most of the supplies had already been moved to other places. As more colonial militia responded to Concord a sizable force had formed to harass the British on their march back to Boston. The Siege of Boston had now begun as the colonials established a perimeter around the city. The war was now underway!

The Stone at Lexington - Pratt, Mara L. America's Story for America's Children: The Early Colonies. Boston: D.C. Heath & Company 1901

2nd Continental Congress

The Congress reconvened in Philadelphia on May 10, 1775. Many of the same delegates were present. New additions included Benjamin Franklin and Thomas Jefferson. Georgia eventually sent delegates in July 1775. John Hancock was elected to preside over the congress. They created the **Continental Army** on June 14, 1775 and named **George Washington** as Commanding General. The nucleus of the army would consist of the Massachusetts militia that were already laying siege to Boston. More blood was spilled at the **Battle of Bunker Hill**, which occurred on June 17, 1775. Dr. Joseph Warren was not only a leader of the Sons of Liberty; he was also a general in the militia and was killed atop Bunker Hill.

The Continental Congress drafted the ***Olive Branch Petition**** on July 5, 1775 and sent it to King George. This document was primarily the work of Pennsylvania delegate John Dickinson, who was a proponent of reconciliation with the crown. In August the King flatly refused to even read the petition and declared the colonies to be in a state of rebellion. On July 6, 1775 Congress published the ***Declaration of the Causes and Necessity of Taking up Arms****, in which they resolve to die free men, rather than live as slaves.

Battle of Bunker Hill - Pratt, Mara L. American's Story for America's Children: The Early Colonies. Boston: D.C. Heath & Company, 1901

Philosophy of the Founders

As we draw nearer to the drafting and signing of the Declaration it is important to briefly look at some of the political philosophers that influenced the likes of Jefferson, Adams, Madison, and the others.

Baron Charles Montesquieu (1689-1755)

French legal scholar that is most well-known for his work *The Spirit of the Laws*, which was produced in 1748. Montesquieu was cited more frequently by the founders than any other source except for the Bible.[7] Montesquieu's main contribution to the founders' political ideology was separation of powers between a legislative, executive, and judiciary branch of government.[8]

John Locke (1632-1704)

English political philosopher and physician who produced *Two Treatises of Government* and other writings that greatly influenced the founders. Locke espoused property rights, separation of powers and expounded on the laws of nature. Locke also expounded on social compact theory:

> *"If man in the state of nature be so free, as has been said; if he be absolute lord of his own person and possessions, equal to the greatest, and subject to nobody, why will he part with his freedom? Why will he give up his empire, and subject himself to the dominion and control of any other power? To which it is obvious to answer, that though in the state of nature he hath such a right, yet the enjoyment of it is very uncertain, and constantly exposed to the invasion of others; for all being kings as much as he, every man his equal, and the greater part no strict observers of equity and justice, the enjoyment of the property he has in his state is very unsafe, very unsecure. This makes him willing to quit a condition, which, however free, is full of fears and continual dangers: and it is not without reason, that he seeks out, and is willing to join in society with others, who are already united, or have a mind to unite, for the mutual preservation of their lives, liberties and estates, which I call by the general name, property."*[9]

Sir William Blackstone (1723-1780)

English jurist, judge and lecturer. He is most well-known for writing *Commentaries on the Laws of England* in 1766. This treatise on the common law formed the basis for the American legal system. By 1775 his *Commentaries* had sold more copies in America than in England.[10] Blackstone identified God as the source of all law, natural and revealed, and also identified God as the source of natural or unalienable rights.

Regarding the law of nature Blackstone said, "Man, considered as a creature, must necessarily be subject to the laws of his creator, for he is entirely a dependent being. A being, independent of any other, has no rule to pursue, but such as he prescribes to himself; but a state of dependence will inevitably oblige the inferior to take the will of him, on whom he depends, as the rule of his conduct: not indeed in every particular, but in all those points wherein his dependence consists. This principle therefore has more or less extent and effect, in proportion as the superiority of the one and the dependence of the other is greater or less, absolute or limited. And consequently, as man depends absolutely upon his maker for everything, it is necessary that he should in all points conform to his maker's will. This will of his Maker is called the law of nature."[11]

Regarding revealed law Blackstone said, "This has given manifold occasion for the interposition of divine providence; which, in compassion to the frailty, the imperfection, and the blindness of human reason, hath been pleased, at sundry times and in divers manners, to discover and enforce its laws by an immediate and direct revelation. The doctrines thus delivered we call the revealed or divine law, and they are to be found only in the Holy Scriptures. These precepts, when revealed, are found upon comparison to be really a part of the original law of nature as they tend in all their consequences to man's felicity."[12]

Of the natural and revealed law Blackstone said, "Upon these two foundations, the law of nature and the law of revelation, depend all human laws; that is to say, no human law should be suffered to contradict these."[13]

Regarding the subject of natural rights, which can also be called unalienable rights, Blackstone said, "Those rights, then, which God and nature have established, and are therefore called natural rights, such as are life and liberty, need not the aid of human laws to be more effectually invested in every man than they are; neither do they receive any additional strength when declared by the municipal laws to be inviolable. On the contrary, no human legislation has power to abridge or destroy them, unless the owner shall himself commit some act that amounts to a forfeiture."[14] Just like Locke before him, Blackstone identified the three principal rights as, "the right of personal security, the right of personal liberty, and the right of private property."[15]

These men had profound influence on the founders of America. In the first two paragraphs of the Declaration of Independence we see Jefferson utilizing the philosophy of Locke and Blackstone when he references "the Laws of Nature and of Nature's God", and that among our unalienable rights are, "Life, Liberty, and the pursuit of Happiness."

Common Sense

"O! ye that love mankind! Ye that dare oppose not only the tyranny but the tyrant, stand forth!"[16]

January 1776 was a time when the colonies and the continental congress, were struggling with indecision. Should they stay loyal and hope for reconciliation or declare independence and attempt self-government? Seemingly at the most perfect and opportune moment a pamphlet titled *Common Sense* was published in Philadelphia. Published anonymously, this work made the case that the time for separation was now! Covering subjects such as the laws of nature, the purpose of government and the absurdity of the doctrine of divine right of kings this pamphlet lays out a clear and convincing case for independence! Emphasizing that the opportunity for a nation to implement self-government and make laws for themselves only arises once and should not be squandered, this work seems to have moved the needle from indecision to support for a declaration of independence. Common Sense sold more than 150,000 copies in the first year, which is remarkable considering that the number of readers in the colonies was probably no more than 700,000.[17] Imagine one in five people being involved in the political affairs of today!

Thomas Paine

Thomas Paine - page 471 Scribner's History of the United States, Volume III by William Cullen Bryant, Sydney Howard Gay and Noah Brooks. New York. Charles Scribner and Sons, 1898.

Common Sense is broken into four parts. We shall examine each section briefly.

Part 1

On the Origin and Design of Government in General

"For were the impulses of conscience clear, uniform and irresistibly obeyed, man would need no other law-giver."[18]

In the quote above Thomas Paine notes the fallen nature of man. In Federalist No. 51 Madison affirms Paine when he asks, "But what is government itself but the greatest of all reflections of human nature? If men were angels, no government would be necessary. If angels were to govern men, neither external nor internal controls on government would be necessary."[19] Unfortunately we live in a fallen world and each have a sin nature. Therefore governments are instituted among men, as Paine points out, to "restrain our vices."[20] John Locke, as well as other notable thinkers such as James Madison and John Adams identify a primary purpose of government being the protection of property.[21] Essentially man's desire is to accumulate property and be secure in his possessions. Government is needed to protect what we have acquired. This correlates with what Paine identifies as the design and end of government, "freedom and security."[22] Government should protect the freedom to acquire property and allow man to be secure in his property.

"Government, even in its best state, is but a necessary evil; in its worst state an intolerable one: for when we suffer, or are exposed to the same miseries by a Government, which we might expect in a country without government, our calamity is heightened by reflecting that we furnish the means by which we suffer."[23] This statement by Paine rings as true today as it did in 1776. When government becomes intolerable, and it sure feels that way today to many people, we have no one to blame but ourselves because we have created the monster that is abusing us. Under a republican system of government such as we have in the United States there is no excuse for intolerable government because the government derives its power and existence from you and me. Proverbs 29:2 is also clear what happens when we have evil leaders, **"When the righteous flourish, the people rejoice, but when the wicked rule, people groan."-** HCSB

In this first section of his essay Paine gives us his model of government, "I draw my idea of the form of government from a principle in nature which no art can overturn, viz. that the more simple anything is, the less liable it is to be disordered, and the easier repaired when disordered." Thomas Jefferson was in agreement with Paine. In a letter to Gideon Granger, dated August 13,

1800* he said, “Let the general government be reduced to foreign concerns only, and let our affairs be disentangled from those of all other nations, except as to commerce, which the merchants will manage the better, the more they are left free to manage for themselves, and our general government may be reduced to a very simple organization, & a very unexpensive one; a few plain duties to be performed by a few servants.”[24] Have we followed the common sense of Thomas Paine and Thomas Jefferson? I think not!

Part 2

Of Monarchy and Hereditary Succession

“Of more worth is one honest man to society, and in the sight of God, than all the crowned ruffians that ever lived.”[25]

Paine had much to say concerning the King of England and the monarchial government. As an Englishman that had immigrated to America in 1774, Paine was well acquainted with the crown. In this section he thoroughly examines scripture and makes a compelling and factual argument that there is no biblical authority for a king or hereditary succession. “But there is another and greater distinction for which no truly natural or religious reason can be assigned, and that is the distinction of men into KINGS and SUBJECTS.”[26] Jefferson referred to this fact as a “self-evident” truth, that all men are created equal. Paine references Judges 8: 22-23 where Gideon has delivered the Israelites from the hands of the Midianites. The Israelites ask Gideon, as well as his sons and grandsons, to rule over them and he declines, saying “the Lord will rule over you.” In 1Samuel chapter 8 the Israelites again clamor to have a king appointed to rule over them. 1Samuel 8:6 says that Samuel considered this request sinful. In 1Samuel chapter 12 Samuel reiterates that the Israelites committed a great evil by requesting a king. In verse 19 the Israelites came to acknowledge that their request for a king was an evil sin.

Paine goes on to use quite descriptive terms for the king which surely must have been fuel to a receptive fire in the colonies. The king was referred to as a worm and a ruffian among other names in the rest of the pamphlet. Finally, “One of the strongest natural proofs of the folly of hereditary right in kings, is that nature disapproves it, otherwise she would not so frequently turn it into ridicule, by giving mankind an *Ass for a Lion*.”[27]

Part 3

Thoughts on the Present State of American Affairs

"Tis not in the power of Britain or of Europe to conquer America, if she doth not conquer herself by delay or timidity."[28]

In this section Paine makes the case that reconciliation is impossible and that this struggle affects all posterity to the end of time. The commencement of hostilities at Lexington and Concord changed everything according to Paine and all prior plans, proposals, petitions, etc. are now useless. To reconcile with Britain would bring nothing but injuries and disadvantages without number upon the continent. Dependence and submission to Britain will naturally make her enemies, our enemies, says Paine. "It is the true interest of America to steer clear of European contentions, which she never can do, while, by her dependence on Britain, she is made the make-weight in the scale of British politics."[29]

Paine lays out a foreign policy that is quite Jeffersonian, and "Paulian", and was America's modus operandi in dealing with foreign nations for the first 100 years of her existence. He points out that our goal should be commerce because it is in the interest of all Europe for America to be a free port. Paine indicates that commerce will secure the peace and friendship of Europe if well attended to. Recall Jefferson's words from his first inaugural address*, "Peace, commerce, and honest friendship with all nations, entangling alliances with none."[30]

In our current era former Congressman and presidential candidate Ron Paul reiterates what American foreign policy should be; "A proper foreign policy of non-intervention is built on friendship with other nations, free trade, and open travel, maximizing the exchanges of goods and services and ideas. Nations that trade with each other are definitely less likely to fight against each other. Unnecessary bellicosity and jingoism is detrimental to peace and prosperity, and incites unnecessary confrontation."[31]

In this section Paine also makes a Providential case for separation and independence. He states that the distance God has placed between England and America, "is a strong and natural proof that the authority of the one over the other, was never the design of Heaven."[32] Paine also observes that the timing of the discovery of this continent along with the method in which it was peopled, preceded the Reformation, which appears as if God, "graciously meant to open a sanctuary to the persecuted in future years, when home should afford neither friendship nor safety."[33] When reading the preceding quote do the Pilgrims come to mind? He concludes that prayer and petitioning have been ineffectual, "Wherefore, since nothing but blows will do, for God's sake let us come to a final separation, and not leave the next generation to be cutting throats under the violated unmeaning names of parent and child."[34] The only way to stand is with arms and Paine is making the case again that the time is now! He warns, "Ye that oppose independence now, ye know not what ye do: ye are opening a door to eternal tyranny."[35] And the rallying cry, "O! ye that love mankind! Ye that dare oppose not only the tyranny but the tyrant, stand forth!"[36]

Part 4

Of the Present Ability of America: With Some Miscellaneous Reflections

"Tis not in numbers but in unity that our great strength lies: yet our present numbers are sufficient to repel the force of all the world."[37]

Paine identifies that the present time is a once in a lifetime opportunity. A nation may only have one opportunity to form its own government and make its own laws. This time should not be squandered. All of the resources of this continent are in favor of independence. The colonies are of a youthful age and have all suffered the same distress therefore their unity is stronger at this time than it ever may be. We are also just the right size according to Paine, for if trade is a consequence of population, the increased commerce of an increased population will diminish both patriotic and military spirit. "The more men have to lose, the less willing are they to venture. The rich are in general slaves to fear, and submit to courtly power with the trembling duplicity of a spaniel."[38]

Not only are the colonies at the most opportune population and level of unity they have natural resources in abundance such as tar, timber, iron and cordage. These are all needed to build a navy and we need not go abroad for anything according to Paine. Saltpeter, cannon, gunpowder and small arms are available as well. Most important of all, "resolution is our inherent character, and courage hath never yet forsaken us."[39]

The Declaration of Independence

"It is the will of heaven that the two countries should be sundered forever"[40]

On June 7, 1776 Richard Henry Lee of Virginia presented a resolution to the congress calling for a declaration of independence. It was immediately seconded by John Adams. Significant opposition still existed within the delegations so the matter was tabled for a month. In the meantime a committee was appointed to draft a declaration in the event that the Lee motion would pass.

Committee of Five - Pratt, Mara L. American's Story for America's Children: The Early Colonies. Boston: D.C. Heath & Company, 1901

The responsibility for writing our national birth certificate was given to a **"committee of five"**. Thomas Jefferson, John Adams, Benjamin Franklin, Roger Sherman and Robert Livingston were assigned the task. Within this group Jefferson was called on to develop the draft.

On July 2, 1776 the Continental Congress formally voted to declare independence with twelve in favor and one abstention (New York). The congress then made some final edits to the declaration and approved the formal wording on July 4, 1776. Interestingly, John Adams initially believed that the 2nd of July would be the day that we would celebrate as Independence Day. In a letter to his wife on July 3, 1776 Adams said this,

> "***The second day of July, 1776, will be the most memorable epoch in the history of America. I am apt to believe that it will be celebrated by succeeding generations as the great anniversary Festival. It ought to be commemorated, as the Day of Deliverance, by solemn acts of devotion to God Almighty. It ought to be solemnized with pomp and parade, with shows, games, sports, guns, bells, bonfires and illuminations, from one end of this continent to the other, from this time forward forever.***
>
> ***You will think me transported with enthusiasm, but I am not. I am well aware of the toil and blood and treasure that it will cost to maintain this Declaration, and support and defend these States. Yet through all***

the gloom I can see the rays of ravishing light and glory. I can see that the end is worth more than all the means; that posterity will triumph in that day's transaction, even though we may regret it, which I trust in God we shall not."[41]

As we work our way through the declaration we will examine each sentence and provide notes and details. Webster's 1828 Dictionary will be referenced for defining many words used in the document to give us a closer understanding of the words and their true meanings. A copy of Black's Law Dictionary will also be utilized for some of the legal terminology.

Shall we begin?

Introduction

IN CONGRESS, July 4, 1776.

The unanimous Declaration of the thirteen united States of America,

When in the Course of human events, it becomes necessary for one people to dissolve the political bands which have connected them with another, and to assume among the powers of the earth, the separate and equal station to which the Laws of Nature and of Nature's God entitle them, a decent respect to the opinions of mankind requires that they should declare the causes which impel them to the separation.

1. Note the small "u" in united States. At this point we have thirteen sovereign and independent States that were uniting for a common cause. We will see that upon establishing the Articles of Confederation and the Constitution this "u" becomes a capital U.

2. "**the separate and equal station**", as in all men are created equal and have the right to self-government. This condition is from God, i.e. Laws of Nature and of Nature's God

3. **Law of nature**- a rule of conduct arising out of the natural relations of human beings established by the Creator, and existing prior to any positive precept. Thus it is a law of nature, that one man should not injure another, and murder and fraud would be crimes, independent of any prohibition from a supreme power. (Webster 1828)

- **Law of Nature according to John Locke**- "The law of Nature stands as an eternal rule to all men, legislators as well as others. The rules that they make for other men's actions, must, as well as their own and other men's actions, be conformable to the law of Nature, i.e. to the will of God, of which that is a declaration, and the fundamental law of nature being the preservation of mankind, no human sanction can be good, or valid against it."[42]

- **Law of Nature according to William Blackstone**- "Man, considered as a creature, must necessarily be subject to the laws of his Creator, for he is an entirely dependent being...as man depends absolutely upon his maker for everything, it is necessary that he should in all points conform to his maker's will. This will of his Maker is called the law of nature...This law of nature, being coeval with mankind, and dictated by God, Himself, is of course superior in obligation to any other. It is binding over all the globe in all countries, and at all times: no human laws are of any validity, if contrary to this."[43]

- We see right here in the introduction that the founders are making the "self-evident" case that the Law of Nature is none other than the will of God. Man is a part of God's creation just as the water, air, animals and fish are part of God's creation. All of creation exists because of Him and for Him. He gives life and He can take it away, whether it be man or animal. The laws of Nature's God are established for man through revealed law (Holy Scriptures) and these are supreme to any man made laws. If man's law does not conform to God's natural and revealed law it is not valid. The applicable sense here is that God's will and God's law entitles men to separate and equal status.

- Evidence of the "Laws of Nature" being the will of God are expressed clearly in scripture. In Job 12:7-10 we see that the animals, fish and birds understand God's sovereignty. In Job 12:23 we see that God creates nations, makes them great and can also destroy them according to His will. Paul's sermon on Mars Hill in Acts 17 (vs. 24-31) clearly espouses God's hand in creation, as well as the fact that he not only gives life and breath to every man, but he also establishes the life span and boundaries of the nations. God's sovereignty over nations can also be seen in Jeremiah 18:6-11.

4. **Impel**- To drive or urge forward; to press on; to excite to action or to move forward, by the application of physical force, or moral suasion or necessity. A ball is impelled by the force of powder; a ship is impelled by wind; a man may be impelled by hunger or a regard to his safety; motives of policy or of safety impel nations to confederate. (Webster 1828)

- By use of the word impel the founders are letting King George, as well as the rest of the world know that this is not an optional course, it is a necessary avenue of last resort and they are urging and driving forward in their cause.

Preamble

We hold these truths to be self-evident, that all men are created equal, that they are endowed by their Creator with certain unalienable Rights, that among these are Life, Liberty and the pursuit of Happiness.--That to secure these rights, Governments are instituted among Men, deriving their just powers from the consent of the governed, --That whenever any Form of Government becomes destructive of these ends, it is the Right of the People to alter or to abolish it, and to institute new Government, laying its foundation on such principles and organizing its powers in such form, as to them shall seem most likely to effect their Safety and Happiness. Prudence, indeed, will dictate that Governments long established should not be changed for light and transient causes; and accordingly all experience hath shewn, that mankind are more disposed to suffer, while evils are sufferable, than to right themselves by abolishing the forms to which they are accustomed. But when a long train of abuses and usurpations, pursuing invariably the same Object evinces a design to reduce them under absolute Despotism, it is their right, it is their duty, to throw off such Government, and to provide new Guards for their future security.--Such has been the patient sufferance of these Colonies; and such is now the necessity which constrains them to alter their former Systems of Government. The history of the present King of Great Britain is a history of repeated injuries and usurpations, all having in direct object the establishment of an absolute Tyranny over these States. To prove this, let Facts be submitted to a candid world.

1. **"We hold these truths to be self-evident"** - Evident without proof or reasoning; that produces certainty or clear conviction upon a bare presentation to the mind; as a *self-evident* proposition or truth. That two and three make five, is *self-evident.* (Webster 1828). Jefferson is telling us that what he is about to write is truth in and of itself, it needs no proof or reasoning.

2. **"that all men are created equal"-** see Genesis 1:27: God created man in His own image, in the image of God He created him; male and female He created them. (NASB)

3. **"that they are endowed by their Creator with certain unalienable Rights"-**

- **UNA'LIENABLE-** Not alienable; that cannot be alienated; that may not be transferred; as unalienable rights. (Webster 1828) Notice where the break is placed for pronunciation.

- What is a **Right**? When Webster's 1828 Dictionary is reviewed we find several entries for this word. Here are three of the entries under the word as a noun:

- Just claim; legal title; ownership; the legal power of exclusive possession and enjoyment. In hereditary monarchies, a right to the throne vests in the heir on the decease of the king. A deed vests the right of possession in the purchaser of land. Right and possession are very different things. We often have occasion to demand and sue for rights not in possession.

- That which justly belongs to one. Born free, he sought his right.

- Just claim; immunity; privilege. All men have a right to the secure enjoyment of life, personal safety, liberty and property. We deem the right of trial by jury invaluable, particularly in the case of crimes. Rights are natural, civil, political, religious, personal, and public.

4. **"that among these are Life, Liberty and the pursuit of Happiness"**- Life, Liberty and the pursuit of Happiness are just three of our God given, unalienable, exclusive, and non-transferable rights. Life, being the most important of our God given rights because He made us in His own image. We cannot have Liberty or the pursuit of Happiness if we do not have Life.

- John Locke on unalienable rights and their source, "The state of Nature has a law of Nature to govern it, which obliges everyone: and reason, which is that law, teaches all mankind, who will but consult it, that being all equal and independent, no one ought to harm another in his life, health, liberty or possessions: for men being all the workmanship of one omnipotent and infinitely wise maker; all the servants of one sovereign master, sent into the world by His order, and about His business; they are His property, whose workmanship they are, made to last during his, not one another's pleasure: and being furnished with like faculties, sharing all in one community of Nature, there cannot be supposed any such subordination among us, that may authorize us to destroy one another."[44]

- William Blackstone on unalienable rights: "Those rights, then, which God and nature have established, and are therefore called natural rights, such as are life and liberty, need not the aid of human laws to be more effectually invested in every man than they are; neither do they receive any additional strength when declared by the municipal laws to be inviolable. On the contrary, no human legislation has power to abridge or destroy them, unless the owner shall himself commit some act that amounts to a forfeiture."[45]

- John Adams on unalienable rights, "All men are born free and independent, and have certain natural, essential, and unalienable rights, among which may be reckoned the right of enjoying and defending their lives and liberties; that of acquiring, possessing, and protecting property; in fine, that of seeking and obtaining their safety and happiness."[46]

- Adams on the importance of property rights: "The moment the idea is admitted into society that property is not as sacred as the laws of God, and that there is not a force of law and public justice to protect it, anarchy and tyranny commence. Property must be secured or liberty cannot exist."[47]

- Frederic Bastiat said this concerning life, liberty and property, "And in spite of the cunning of artful political leaders, these three gifts from God precede all human legislation, and are superior to it. Life liberty, and property do not exist because men have made laws. On the contrary, it was the fact that life, liberty, and property existed before-hand that caused men to make laws in the first place."[48]

- Civil liberty, as defined by Webster, "is the liberty of men in a state of society, or natural liberty, so far only abridged and restrained, as is necessary and expedient for the safety and interest of the society, state or nation. A restraint of natural liberty, not necessary or expedient for the public, is tyranny or oppression. Civil liberty is an exemption from the arbitrary will of others, which exemption is secured by established laws, which restrain every man from injuring or controlling another. Hence the restraints of law are essential to civil liberty." (Webster 1828)

-"pursuit of happiness" - notice that happiness itself is not an unalienable right, but the pursuit of it is. Government cannot make a man happy, no matter how much redistribution and leveling takes place.

- Pursuing happiness is not license to do whatever one wants. With liberty, comes responsibility. Bible references such as Galatians 5:1 indicate that Liberty is not license, it is through Christ: "Stand fast therefore in the liberty wherewith Christ hath made us free, and be not entangled again with the yoke of bondage. (KJV) Other verses indicating the same include 2Corinthians 3:17 and James 1:25.

5. **"That to secure these rights, Governments are instituted among Men"-**

- According to Locke, the reason that men enter into society is the preservation of property. See quotation under heading number seven, as Locke's quote from *Two Treatises*, gives us both, the reason for entering into society and the justifications for altering or abolishing the government.

- In his essay on Property*, James Madison said, "Government is instituted to protect property of every sort; as well that which lies in the various rights of individuals, as that which the term particularly expresses. This being the end of government, that alone is a just government, which impartially secures to every man, whatever is his own."[49]

6. **"deriving their just powers from the consent of the governed"-** We have seen that all men are created equal and that natural and unalienable rights come from God. We have seen that government is instituted to protect these rights. And, now Jefferson identifies the source of government power, "the consent of the governed.

- Alexander Hamilton concurs with Jefferson, "The fabric of American empire ought to rest on the solid basis of THE CONSENT OF THE PEOPLE. The streams of national power ought to flow immediately from that pure, original fountain of all legitimate authority."[50]

- James Madison defines a republican form of government in Federalist #39, and in doing so identifies the source of government power; "we may define a republic to be, or at least may bestow that name on, a government which derives all its powers directly or indirectly from the great body of the people, and is administered by persons holding their offices during pleasure for a limited period, or during good behavior."[51]

7. **"That whenever any Form of Government becomes destructive of these ends, it is the Right of the People to alter or to abolish it, and to institute new Government, laying its foundation on such principles and organizing its powers in such form, as to them shall seem most likely to effect their Safety and Happiness."** - As we learned in the introduction to the declaration, Locke and Blackstone both indicate that government actions and laws must conform to the Laws of Nature or they are invalid. Therefore, if government is obstructing the unalienable rights of man it has become destructive of man's natural rights and he has a Right to alter, abolish, or institute new government.

- John Locke, in his Second Treatise on Civil Government, says this concerning altering, abolishing and instituting new government:

> The reason why men enter into society, is the preservation of their property; and the end why they chuse and authorize a legislative, is, that there may be laws made, and rules set, as guards and fences to the properties of all the members of the society, to limit the power, and moderate the dominion, of every part and member of the society: for since it can never be supposed to be the will of the society, that the legislative should have a power to destroy that which every one designs to secure, by entering into society, and for which the people submitted themselves to legislators of their own making; whenever the legislators endeavour to take away, and destroy the property of the people, or to reduce them to slavery under arbitrary power, they put themselves into a state of war with the people, who are thereupon absolved from any farther obedience, and are left to the common refuge, which God hath provided for all men, against force and violence. Whensoever therefore the legislative shall transgress this fundamental rule of society; and either by ambition, fear, folly or corruption, endeavour to grasp themselves, or put into the hands of any other, an absolute power over the lives, liberties, and estates of the people; by this breach of trust they forfeit the power the people had put into their hands for quite contrary ends, and it devolves to the people, who have a right to resume their original liberty, and, by the establishment of a new legislative, (such as they shall think fit) provide for their own safety and security, which is the end for which they are in society.[52]

8. **"Prudence, indeed, will dictate that Governments long established should not be changed for light and transient causes"** - Should a government be changed because one person or a minority of persons have believed that their rights have been violated? What is the threshold for altering, abolishing, or implementing new government?

- The Virginia Declaration of Rights* was drafted by George Mason and adopted by the Virginia Constitutional Convention on June 12, 1776. In section three the subject of government alteration is discussed, "That government is, or ought to be, instituted for the common benefit, protection, and security of the people, nation, or community; of all the various modes and forms of government, that is best which is capable of producing the greatest degree of happiness and safety and is most effectually secured against the danger of maladministration. And that, when any government shall be found inadequate or contrary to these purposes, a majority of the community has an indubitable, inalienable, and indefeasible right to reform, alter, or abolish it, in such manner as shall be judged most conducive to the public weal."

- Locke said this about "disturbing the government"-

> "But if the unlawful acts done by the magistrate be maintained (by the power he has got), and the remedy which is due by law, be by the same power obstructed; yet the right of resisting, even in such manifest acts of tyranny, will not suddenly, or on slight occasions, disturb the government: for if it reach no farther than some private men's cases, though they have a right to defend themselves, and to recover by force what by unlawful force is taken from them; yet the right to do so will not easily engage them in a contest, wherein they are sure to perish; it being as impossible for one, or a few oppressed men to disturb the government, where the body of the people do not think themselves concerned in it, as for a raving mad-man, or heady malcontent to overturn a well settled state; the people being as little apt to follow the one, as the other.
>
> But if either these illegal acts have extended to the majority of the people; or if the mischief and oppression has lighted only on some few, but in such cases, as the precedent, and consequences seem to threaten all; and they are persuaded in their consciences, that their laws, and with them their estates, liberties, and lives are in danger, and perhaps their religion too; how they will be hindered from resisting illegal force, used against them, I cannot tell."[53]

9. "**But when a long train of abuses and usurpations, pursuing invariably the same Object evinces a design to reduce them under absolute Despotism, it is their right, it is their duty, to throw off such Government**"

- **USURPA'TION-** The act of seizing or occupying and enjoying the property of another, without right; as the usurpation of a throne; the usurpation of the supreme power. (Webster 1828)

- **DESPOTISM-** 1. Absolute power; authority unlimited and uncontrolled by men, constitution or laws, and depending alone on the will of the prince; as the despotism of a Turkish sultan. (Webster 1828)

- **DUTY-** That which a person owes to another; that which a person is bound, by any natural, moral or legal obligation, to pay, do or perform. Obedience to princes, magistrates and the laws is the duty of every citizen and subject; obedience, respect and kindness to parents are duties of children; fidelity to friends is a duty; reverence, obedience and prayer to God are indispensable duties; the government and religious instruction of children are duties of parents which they cannot neglect without guilt. (Webster 1828)

10. **"and such is now the necessity which constrains them to alter their former Systems of Government."** - The entire focus of the declaration to this point has been justification for declaring independence. Jefferson has used words throughout such as, ***necessary, declare, impel, right and duty.*** Now he adds, ***necessity and constrains.*** As if to leave no doubt Jefferson and the delegates are telling the world that they must do this, as there is no other remedy left to pursue.

- **NECESSITY-** Irresistible power; compulsive force, physical or moral. If man's actions are determined by causes beyond his control, he acts from necessity, and is not a free agent. Necessity compelled the general to act on the defensive. (Webster 1828) Webster also notes unavoidableness and inevitableness.

- **CONSTRAIN-** In a general sense, to strain; to press; to urge; to drive; to exert force, physical or moral, either in urging to action or in restraining it. Hence,

> 1. To compel or force; to urge with irresistible power, or with a power sufficient to produce the effect.

The spirit within me constraineth me. Job 32.

I was constrained to appeal to Caesar. Acts 28.

For the love of Christ constraineth us. 2 Corinthians 5. (Webster 1828)

11. **"all having in direct object the establishment of an absolute Tyranny over these States."**

- **TYR'ANNY-**

> 1. Arbitrary or despotic exercise of power; the exercise of power over subjects and others with a rigor not authorized by law or justice, or not requisite for the purposes of government. Hence tyranny is often synonymous with cruelty and oppression.
>
> 2. Cruel government or discipline; as the tyranny of a master.
>
> 3. Unresisted and cruel power.
>
> 4. Absolute monarchy cruelly administered. (Webster 1828)

Indictment

The following indictment levels 27 charges against King George

1. He has refused his Assent to Laws, the most wholesome and necessary for the public good.

- The King had authority over the laws in the colonies and could withhold assent. The Declaratory Act of 1766 signaled that the King was going to bring the colonies in line. Parliament had also been passing all of the offensive acts that we have previously addressed without colonial representation.

2. He has forbidden his Governors to pass Laws of immediate and pressing importance, unless suspended in their operation till his Assent should be obtained; and when so suspended, he has utterly neglected to attend to them.

- Jefferson had addressed this complaint previously in his Summary View of the Rights of British America in 1774*. This essay provided instructions for the Virginia delegation to the Continental Congress and gave a very extensive historical context to this grievance as well as events leading up to the point of declaring independence. Interestingly Jefferson notes in *Summary View* that the colonies detested the practice of slavery and wanted to eliminate it but the King refused his assent to measures attempting to reduce the import of slaves.

3. He has refused to pass other Laws for the accommodation of large districts of people, unless those people would relinquish the right of Representation in the Legislature, a right inestimable to them and formidable to tyrants only.

- Multiple colonies such as New Hampshire, New York, South Carolina and Virginia had passed laws for establishing new communities and the methods for elective representation. These laws were disallowed by the king.

4. He has called together legislative bodies at places unusual, uncomfortable, and distant from the depository of their public Records, for the sole purpose of fatiguing them into compliance with his measures.

- In Massachusetts no town meetings were allowed without the approval of the governor as part of the Coercive Acts. The capital was also moved to Salem.

5. He has dissolved Representative Houses repeatedly, for opposing with manly firmness his invasions on the rights of the people.

-The Virginia House of Burgesses was dissolved in 1769 and 1774. The NY legislature was suspended as part of the Townshend Acts of 1767 for not complying with the Quartering Acts. The Massachusetts General Court was dissolved in 1768 for not rescinding the 1768 Circular Letter*.

6. He has refused for a long time, after such dissolutions, to cause others to be elected; whereby the Legislative powers, incapable of Annihilation, have returned to the People at large for their exercise; the State remaining in the meantime exposed to all the dangers of invasion from without, and convulsions within.

- In Massachusetts Governor Gage refused to convene another assembly after they had voted in favor of convening a continental congress.

7. He has endeavoured to prevent the population of these States; for that purpose obstructing the Laws for Naturalization of Foreigners; refusing to pass others to encourage their migrations hither, and raising the conditions of new Appropriations of Lands.

- The Proclamation of 1763 had prohibited westward expansion which was viewed as being an impediment to additional population.

8. He has obstructed the Administration of Justice, by refusing his Assent to Laws for establishing Judiciary powers.

- Laws for establishing courts and their proceedings in the Carolinas were disallowed by the King because the crown held that it was their right to establish the courts.

9. He has made Judges dependent on his Will alone, for the tenure of their offices, and the amount and payment of their salaries.

- Revenue generated through the Townshend Acts would be used to pay the salaries of judges and governors. This took the "power of the purse" away from the popularly elected assemblies. In 1774 the Massachusetts Government Act also placed these appointments in the control of the crown.

10. He has erected a multitude of New Offices, and sent hither swarms of Officers to harrass our people, and eat out their substance.

- Townshend Acts created the American Board of Customs Commissioners. The Stamp Act allowed for the appointment of stamp distributors by the prime minister.

11. He has kept among us, in times of peace, Standing Armies without the Consent of our legislatures.

- Since the conclusion of the French and Indian War the British kept between 6,000 and 10,000 troops within colonial America. The English Bill of Rights of 1689 prohibited standing armies during time of peace without the consent of parliament.

The colonists had no representation in parliament and had definitely not consented through their popular assemblies to have a standing army in America.

12. He has affected to render the Military independent of and superior to the Civil power.

- 1774 General Gage appointed governor in Massachusetts and attempts to enforce the Intolerable Acts. This was essentially what we would consider martial law.

13. He has combined with others to subject us to a jurisdiction foreign to our constitution, and unacknowledged by our laws; giving his Assent to their Acts of pretended Legislation:

- Others being the British parliament. "our constitution" being the charters and laws of the colonies, as well as the right to self-government. The colonies had not acknowledged parliament because parliament afforded them no representation. King George assented to "Acts of pretended Legislation" when he did not veto the laws coming from parliament.

14. For Quartering large bodies of armed troops among us:

- As stated above, there was a large body of British troops that remained after the French and Indian War. The Quartering Acts of 1765 and 1774 were implemented.

15. For protecting them, by a mock Trial, from punishment for any Murders which they should commit on the Inhabitants of these States:

- Coercive Acts of 1774 provided that British soldiers and officials will be tried in England instead of the colonies.

16. For cutting off our Trade with all parts of the world:

- Navigation Acts 1650-1696 restricted colonies from trading with foreign vessels. Molasses Act of 1763 placed high duties on sugar and molasses not bought from the British West Indies. Intolerable Acts closed the port of Boston.

17. For imposing Taxes on us without our Consent:

Sugar Act, Stamp Act, Townshend Acts

18. For depriving us in many cases, of the benefits of Trial by Jury:

- The Sugar Act and Townshend Acts expanded the use of Courts of Admiralty for cases involving customs, duties, and taxes. Admiralty Court was without jury.

19. For transporting us beyond Seas to be tried for pretended offences:

- The 1774 Intolerable Acts were designed to punish Massachusetts and allowed for "disturbers of the Kings peace" to be sent to England for trial.

20. For abolishing the free System of English Laws in a neighbouring Province, establishing therein an Arbitrary government, and enlarging its Boundaries so as to render it at once an example and fit instrument for introducing the same absolute rule into these Colonies:

- Quebec Act of 1774 extended boundaries south into territories that had been claimed by other colonies. It also allowed for the use of French civil law for private matters and English common law for public administration. There was no system for elected assemblies and the colonials felt that this Act also favored Catholicism over protestant Christianity.

21. For taking away our Charters, abolishing our most valuable Laws, and altering fundamentally the Forms of our Governments:

- Coercive Acts revoked the Massachusetts charter. Governors throughout the colonies were abolishing elected assemblies on a whim and were making it difficult for any form of government to function.

22. For suspending our own Legislatures, and declaring themselves invested with power to legislate for us in all cases whatsoever.

- Declaratory Act 1766 Parliament has complete power to govern colonies. In 1767 the NY legislature had also been suspended for noncompliance with the Quartering Act.

23. He has abdicated Government here, by declaring us out of his Protection and waging War against us.

- Prohibitory Act of 1775 created a blockade of all colonial ports and declared all trade and commerce prohibited. This was essentially a declaration of war by Great Britain on America as ships were to be treated by the British Navy as the enemy.

24. He has plundered our seas, ravaged our Coasts, burnt our towns, and destroyed the lives of our people.

- Boston Port Act 1774, Prohibitory Act of 1775, Lexington and Concord 4/19/1775 (destroyed lives), Falmouth Mass was burned 4/18/1775, Charlestown, Mass was burned 6/17/1775, and Norfolk, VA was burned 1/1/1776.

25. He is at this time transporting large Armies of foreign Mercenaries to compleat the works of death, desolation and tyranny, already begun with circumstances of Cruelty & perfidy scarcely paralleled in the most barbarous ages, and totally unworthy the Head of a civilized nation.

- King George contracted German soldiers to fight in the war. They landed July 2, 1776 and participated in many major battles beginning with the Battle of Long Island Aug 1776. Up to 30,000 German troops were estimated to have participated in the war.

26. He has constrained our fellow Citizens taken Captive on the high Seas to bear Arms against their Country, to become the executioners of their friends and Brethren, or to fall themselves by their Hands.

- Prohibitory Act of Dec 1775 allowed for capture of vessels trading with the colonies, including American ships. They were to be treated as the enemy and their sailors were to be pressed into service in the British navy.

27. He has excited domestic insurrections amongst us, and has endeavoured to bring on the inhabitants of our frontiers, the merciless Indian Savages, whose known rule of warfare, is an undistinguished destruction of all ages, sexes and conditions.

- Governor Dunmore in Virginia made a proclamation in Nov 1775 to free any slaves who would fight with the British. He also declared martial law and threatened to leave the colony unprotected from Indian attacks. Great Britain also sought Indian service to raid colonial settlements and it was rumored in the summer of 1775 that the royal governor in Canada desired to set the Indians on a war path against the colonies.

Petition

In every stage of these Oppressions We have Petitioned for Redress in the most humble terms: Our repeated Petitions have been answered only by repeated injury. A Prince whose character is thus marked by every act which may define a Tyrant, is unfit to be the ruler of a free people.

Nor have We been wanting in attentions to our British brethren. We have warned them from time to time of attempts by their legislature to extend an unwarrantable jurisdiction over us. We have reminded them of the circumstances of our emigration and settlement here. We have appealed to their native justice and magnanimity, and we have conjured them by the ties of our common kindred to disavow these usurpations, which, would inevitably interrupt our connections and correspondence. They too have been deaf to the voice of justice and of consanguinity. We must, therefore, acquiesce in the necessity, which denounces our Separation, and hold them, as we hold the rest of mankind, Enemies in War, in Peace Friends.

1. **In every stage of these Oppressions We have Petitioned**- As we have seen the colonies had made repeated formal petitions to the King George and Parliament and such as the Declaration of Rights and Grievances (1765) that were submitted by the Stamp Act Congress, the Declaration and Resolves of the First Continental Congress (1774), and the Olive Branch Petition in the Second Continental Congress (1775). These were ignored or met with more tyranny by the crown.

2. "**Our repeated Petitions**"- The colonists had also made numerous pleas formally and informally to their brethren via colonial agents, pamphlets, and declarations.

3. - **Tyrant-** A monarch or other ruler or master, who uses power to oppress his subjects; a person who exercises unlawful authority, or lawful authority in an unlawful manner; one who by taxation, injustice or cruel punishment, or the demand of unreasonable services, imposes burdens and hardships on those under his control, which law and humanity do not authorize, or which the purposes of government do not require. (Webster 1828)

Declaration

We, therefore, the Representatives of the united States of America, in General Congress, Assembled, appealing to the Supreme Judge of the world for the rectitude of our intentions, do, in the Name, and by Authority of the good People of these Colonies, solemnly publish and declare, That these United Colonies are, and of Right ought to be Free and Independent States; that they are Absolved from all Allegiance to the British Crown, and that all political connection between them and the State of Great Britain, is and ought to be totally dissolved; and that as Free and Independent States, they have full Power to levy War, conclude Peace, contract Alliances, establish Commerce, and to do all other Acts and Things which Independent States may of right do. And for the support of this Declaration, with a firm reliance on the protection of divine Providence, we mutually pledge to each other our Lives, our Fortunes and our sacred Honor.

1. **"appealing to the Supreme Judge of the world"**- appealing to God

2. **"for the rectitude of our intentions"**- According to Webster the word **rectitude** means: In morality, rightness of principle or practice; uprightness of mind; exact conformity to truth, or to the rules prescribed for moral conduct, either by divine or human laws. Rectitude of mind is the disposition to act in conformity to any known standard of right, truth or justice; rectitude of conduct is the actual conformity to such standard. Perfect rectitude belongs only to the Supreme Being. The more nearly the rectitude of men approaches to the standard of the divine law, the more exalted and dignified is their character. Want of rectitude is not only sinful, but debasing.

-There is a sublimity in conscious rectitude - in comparison with which the treasures of earth are not worth naming. (Webster 1828)

3. **"That these United Colonies are, and of Right ought to be Free and Independent States; that they are Absolved from all Allegiance to the British Crown, and that all political connection between them and the State of Great Britain, is and ought to be totally dissolved; and that as Free and Independent States"** This is a reiteration of Richard Henry Lee's resolution in congress from June 7, 1776, which was seconded by John Adams.

4. **"And for the support of this Declaration, with a firm reliance on the protection of divine Providence, we mutually pledge to each other our Lives, our Fortunes and our sacred Honor."** In this final sentence of the declaration we see that this document is not only a declaration of independence but it is also a **declaration of dependence.** The signers are not just relying on God's protection; rather they are firmly relying on it! They pledge their lives, fortunes and sacred honor. What are we sacrificing today to maintain what they gave us?

Signers of the Declaration - McCabe, James D. The Pictorial History of the United States. Philadelphia. The National Publishing Company, 1877.

ARTICLES OF CONFEDERATION

Background

In July 1776 Congress began debating the draft of what would become the *Articles of Confederation.* There were several purposes to be served by creating this document. It would provide a formal constitutional identity to the union of states and it would identify the boundaries of authority between the union and the states. America also needed to present itself as a formal nation state to seek alliances and commerce. Congress was unable to agree on and approve the Articles until Nov 15, 1777. Some of the issues of contention included how votes would be cast, rules for apportioning expenses and how to control unsettled lands west of Pennsylvania and north of the Ohio River. It would take another three years for the Articles to be ratified by all of the states, the last being Maryland on March 1, 1781.

Articles

To all to whom these Presents shall come, we the undersigned Delegates of the States affixed to our Names send greeting. Whereas the Delegates of the United States of America in Congress assembled did on the 15th day of November, in the year of our Lord One thousand Seven Hundred and Seventy seven, and in the Second Year of the Independence of America, agree to certain articles of Confederation and perpetual Union between the States of New Hampshire, Massachusetts-Bay, Rhode Island and Providence Plantations, Connecticut, New York, New Jersey, Pennsylvania, Delaware, Maryland, Virginia, North- Carolina, South-Carolina, and Georgia in the Words following, viz. "Articles of Confederation and perpetual Union between the States of New Hampshire, Massachusetts-Bay, Rhode Island and Providence Plantations, Connecticut, New-York, New-Jersey, Pennsylvania, Delaware, Maryland, Virginia, North-Carolina, South-Carolina, and Georgia.

- **Confederation:** The act of confederating; a league; a compact for mutual support; alliance; particularly of princes, nations or states. (Webster 1828)

Article I. The Stile of this confederacy shall be, "The United States of America."

- We see that "United" is now capitalized. A formal confederacy and government is being established.

Article II. Each state retains its sovereignty, freedom, and independence, and every Power, Jurisdiction and right, which is not by this confederation expressly delegated to the United States, in Congress assembled.

- Note that the states are retaining their sovereignty, freedom, and independence. They are not merging into one organism and they are not losing their identity. This is the basis for the 10th Amendment in the Bill of Rights.

Article III. The said states hereby severally enter into a firm league of friendship with each other, for their common defence, the security of their Liberties, and their mutual and general welfare, binding themselves to assist each other, against all force offered to, or attacks made upon them, or any of them, on account of religion, sovereignty, trade, or any other pretence whatever.

- The states are supreme. This document is creating a "firm league of friendship". Their reasons for entering into the league of friendship are listed, and they are few and clearly defined.

Article IV. The better to secure and perpetuate mutual friendship and intercourse among the people of the different states in this union, the free inhabitants of each of these states, paupers, vagabonds and fugitives from Justice excepted, shall be entitled to all privileges and immunities of free citizens in the several states; and the people of each state shall have free ingress and regress to and from any other state, and shall enjoy therein all the privileges of trade and commerce, subject to the same duties, impositions and restrictions as the inhabitants thereof respectively, provided that such restrictions shall not extend so far as to prevent the removal of property imported into any state, to any other State, of which the Owner is an inhabitant; provided also that no imposition, duties or restriction shall be laid by any state, on the property of the united states, or either of them.

If any Person guilty of, or charged with, treason, felony, or other high misdemeanor in any state, shall flee from Justice, and be found in any of the united states, he shall, upon demand of the Governor or executive power, of the state from which he fled, be delivered up and removed to the state having jurisdiction of his offence.

Full faith and credit shall be given in each of these states to the records, acts and judicial proceedings of the courts and magistrates of every other state.

Article V. For the more convenient management of the general interests of the united states, delegates shall be annually appointed in such manner as the legislature of each state shall direct, to meet in Congress on the first Monday in November, in every year, with a power reserved to each state to recall its delegates, or any of them, at any time within the year, and to send others in their stead, for the remainder of the Year.

- Delegates to Congress will serve one year terms and can be recalled by the state legislatures at any time. This is the ultimate in term limits and if the state is not satisfied with the performance of the delegate he can be recalled. During the constitutional convention Roger Sherman said, "Government is instituted for those who live under it. It ought therefore to be so constituted as not to be dangerous to their liberties. The more permanency it has the worse if it be a bad Government. Frequent elections are necessary to preserve the good behavior of rulers. They also tend to give permanency to the Government, by preserving that good behavior, because it ensures their re-election."[56]

No State shall be represented in Congress by less than two, nor by more than seven Members; and no person shall be capable of being delegate for more than three years in any term of six years; nor shall any person, being a delegate, be capable of holding any office under the united states, for which he, or another for his benefit receives any salary, fees or emolument of any kind.

Each State shall maintain its own delegates in a meeting of the states, and while they act as members of the committee of the states.

In determining questions in the united states, in Congress assembled, each state shall have one vote.

Freedom of speech and debate in Congress shall not be impeached or questioned in any Court, or place out of Congress, and the members of congress shall be protected in their persons from arrests and imprisonments, during the time of their going to and from, and attendance on congress, except for treason, felony, or breach of the peace.

Article VI. No State, without the Consent of the united States, in congress assembled, shall send any embassy to, or receive any embassy from, or enter into any conference, agreement, alliance or treaty, with any King prince or state; nor shall any person holding any office of profit or trust under the united states, or any of them, accept of any present, emolument, office or title of any kind whatever from any king, prince or foreign state; nor shall the united states in congress assembled, or any of them, grant any title of nobility.

No two or more states shall enter into any treaty, confederation or alliance whatever between them, without the consent of the united states in congress assembled, specifying accurately the purposes for which the same is to be entered into, and how long it shall continue.

- Here we see evidence of the states retaining sovereignty to enter into treaties with each other. This points to their sovereignty as independent republics as well.

No State shall lay any imposts or duties, which may interfere with any stipulations in treaties, entered into by the united states in congress assembled, with any king, prince or State, in pursuance of any treaties already proposed by congress, to the courts of France and Spain.

No vessels of war shall be kept up in time of peace, by any state, except such number only, as shall be deemed necessary by the united states in congress assembled, for the defence of such state, or its trade; nor shall any body of forces be kept up by any state, in time of peace, except such number only, as in the judgment of the united states, in congress assembled, shall be deemed requisite to garrison the forts necessary for the defence of such state; but every state shall always keep up a well regulated and disciplined militia, sufficiently armed and accoutred, and shall provide and constantly have ready for use, in public stores, a due number of field pieces and tents, and a proper quantity of arms, ammunition, and camp equipage.

No State shall engage in any war without the consent of the united States in congress assembled, unless such State be actually invaded by enemies, or shall have received certain advice of a resolution being formed by some nation of Indians to invade such State, and the danger is so imminent as not to admit of a delay till the united states in congress assembled can be consulted: nor shall any state grant commissions to any ships or vessels of war, nor letters of marque or reprisal, except it be after a declaration of war by the united states in congress assembled, and then only against the kingdom or state, and the subjects thereof, against which war has been so declared, and under such regulations as shall be established by the united states in congress assembled, unless such state be infested by pirates, in which case vessels of war may be fitted out for that occasion, and kept so long as the danger shall continue, or until the united states in congress assembled shall determine otherwise.

Article VII. When land forces are raised by any state for the common defence, all officers of or under the rank of colonel, shall be appointed by the legislature of each state respectively, by whom such forces shall be raised, or in such manner as such state shall direct, and all vacancies shall be filled up by the State which first made appointment.

Article VIII. All charges of war, and all other expenses that shall be incurred for the common defence or general welfare, and allowed by the united states in congress assembled, shall be defrayed out of a common treasury, which shall be supplied by the several states in proportion to the value of all land within each state, granted to or surveyed for any Person, as such land and the buildings and improvements thereon shall be estimated according to such mode as the united states in congress assembled, shall, from time to time, direct and appoint.

The taxes for paying that proportion shall be laid and levied by the authority and direction of the legislatures of the several states within the time agreed upon by the united states in congress assembled.

Article IX. The united states, in congress assembled, shall have the sole and exclusive right and power of determining on peace and war, except in the cases mentioned in the sixth article - of sending and receiving ambassadors - entering into treaties and alliances, provided that no treaty of commerce shall be made whereby the legislative power of the respective states shall be restrained from imposing such imposts and duties on foreigners as their own people are subjected to, or from prohibiting the exportation or importation of any species of goods or commodities, whatsoever - of establishing rules for deciding in all cases, what captures on land or water shall be legal, and in what manner prizes taken by land or naval forces in the service of the united states shall be divided or appropriated - of granting letters of marque and reprisal in times of peace - appointing courts for the trial of piracies and felonies committed on the high seas and establishing courts for receiving and determining finally appeals in all cases of captures, provided that no member of congress shall be appointed a judge of any of the said courts.

The united states, in congress assembled, shall also be the last resort on appeal in all disputes and differences now subsisting or that hereafter may arise between two or more states concerning boundary, jurisdiction or any other cause whatever; which authority shall always be exercised in the manner following. Whenever the legislative or executive authority

or lawful agent of any state in controversy with another shall present a petition to congress stating the matter in question, and praying for a hearing, notice thereof shall be given by order of congress to the legislative or executive authority of the other state in controversy, and a day assigned for the appearance of the parties by their lawful agents, who shall then be directed to appoint by joint consent, commissioners or judges to constitute a court for hearing and determining the matter in question: but if they cannot agree, congress shall name three persons out of each of the united states, and from the list of such persons each party shall alternately strike out one, the petitioners beginning, until the number shall be reduced to thirteen; and from that number not less than seven, nor more than nine names as congress shall direct, shall, in the presence of congress be drawn out by lot, and the persons whose names shall be so drawn or any five of them, shall be commissioners or judges, to hear and finally determine the controversy, so always as a major part of the judges who shall hear the cause shall agree in the determination: and if either party shall neglect to attend at the day appointed, without showing reasons, which congress shall judge sufficient, or being present shall refuse to strike, the congress shall proceed to nominate three persons out of each state, and the secretary of congress shall strike in behalf of such party absent or refusing; and the judgment and sentence of the court to be appointed, in the manner before prescribed, shall be final and conclusive; and if any of the parties shall refuse to submit to the authority of such court, or to appear or defend their claim or cause, the court shall nevertheless proceed to pronounce sentence, or judgment, which shall in like manner be final and decisive, the judgment or sentence and other proceedings being in either case transmitted to congress, and lodged among the acts of congress for the security of the parties concerned: provided that every commissioner, before he sits in judgment, shall take an oath to be administered by one of the judges of the supreme or superior court of the state, where the cause shall be tried, "well and truly to hear and determine the matter in question, according to the best of his judgment, without favour, affection or hope of reward: "provided, also, that no state shall be deprived of territory for the benefit of the united states.

All controversies concerning the private right of soil claimed under different grants of two or more states, whose jurisdictions as they may respect such lands, and the states which passed such grants are adjusted, the said grants or either of them being at the same time claimed to

have originated antecedent to such settlement of jurisdiction, shall on the petition of either party to the congress of the united states, be finally determined as near as may be in the same manner as is before prescribed for deciding disputes respecting territorial jurisdiction between different states.

The united states in congress assembled shall also have the sole and exclusive right and power of regulating the alloy and value of coin struck by their own authority, or by that of the respective states - fixing the standard of weights and measures throughout the united states - regulating the trade and managing all affairs with the Indians, not members of any of the states, provided that the legislative right of any state within its own limits be not infringed or violated - establishing and regulating post-offices from one state to another, throughout all the united states, and exacting such postage on the papers passing thro' the same as may be requisite to defray the expenses of the said office - appointing all officers of the land forces, in the service of the united states, excepting regimental officers - appointing all the officers of the naval forces, and commissioning all officers whatever in the service of the united states - making rules for the government and regulation of the said land and naval forces, and directing their operations.

The united states in congress assembled shall have authority to appoint a committee, to sit in the recess of congress, to be denominated "A Committee of the States," and to consist of one delegate from each State; and to appoint such other committees and civil officers as may be necessary for managing the general affairs of the united states under their direction - to appoint one of their number to preside, provided that no person be allowed to serve in the office of president more than one year in any term of three years; to ascertain the necessary sums of money to be raised for the service of the united states, and to appropriate and apply the same for defraying the public expences - to borrow money, or emit bills on the credit of the united states, transmitting every half year to the respective states an account of the sums of money so borrowed or emitted, - to build and equip a navy - to agree upon the number of land forces, and to make requisitions from each state for its quota, in proportion to the number of white inhabitants in such state; which requisition shall be binding, and thereupon the legislature of each state shall appoint the regimental officers, raise the men and cloath, arm and equip them in a soldier like manner, at the expence of the united states; and the officers and men so cloathed, armed and equipped shall

march to the place appointed, and within the time agreed on by the united states, in congress assembled: But if the united states in congress assembled shall, on consideration of circumstances judge proper that any state should not raise men, or should raise a smaller number than its quota, and that any other state should raise a greater number of men than the quota thereof, such extra number shall be raised, officered, cloathed, armed and equipped in the same manner as the quota of such state, unless the legislature of such state shall judge that such extra number cannot be safely spared out of the same, in which case they shall raise officer, cloath, arm and equip as many of such extra number as they judge can be safely spared. And the officers and men so cloathed, armed and equipped, shall march to the place appointed, and within the time agreed on by the united states in congress assembled.

The united states in congress assembled shall never engage in a war, nor grant letters of marque and reprisal in time of peace, nor enter into any treaties or alliances, nor coin money, nor regulate the value thereof, nor ascertain the sums and expenses necessary for the defence and welfare of the united states, or any of them, nor emit bills, nor borrow money on the credit of the united states, nor appropriate money, nor agree upon the number of vessels of war, to be built or purchased, or the number of land or sea forces to be raised, nor appoint a commander in chief of the army or navy, unless nine states assent to the same: nor shall a question on any other point, except for adjourning from day to day be determined, unless by the votes of a majority of the united states in congress assembled.

- On matters of significance a three-fourths majority will be required.

The congress of the united states shall have power to adjourn to any time within the year, and to any place within the united states, so that no period of adjournment be for a longer duration than the space of six Months, and shall publish the Journal of their proceedings monthly, except such parts thereof relating to treaties, alliances or military operations, as in their judgment require secrecy; and the yeas and nays of the delegates of each state on any question shall be entered on the Journal, when it is desired by any delegate; and the delegates of a state, or any of them, at his or their request shall be furnished with a transcript of the said Journal, except such parts as are above excepted, to lay before the legislatures of the several states.

Article X. The committee of the states, or any nine of them, shall be authorized to execute, in the recess of congress, such of the powers of congress as the united states in congress assembled, by the consent of nine states, shall from time to time think expedient to vest them with; provided that no power be delegated to the said committee, for the exercise of which, by the articles of confederation, the voice of nine states in the congress of the united states assembled is requisite.

Article XI. Canada acceding to this confederation, and joining in the measures of the united states, shall be admitted into, and entitled to all the advantages of this union: but no other colony shall be admitted into the same, unless such admission be agreed to by nine states.

Article XII. All bills of credit emitted, monies borrowed and debts contracted by, or under the authority of congress, before the assembling of the united states, in pursuance of the present confederation, shall be deemed and considered as a charge against the united states, for payment and satisfaction whereof the said united states and the public faith are hereby solemnly pledged.

Article XIII. Every State shall abide by the determinations of the united states in congress assembled, on all questions which by this confederation are submitted to them. And the Articles of this confederation shall be inviolably observed by every state, and the union shall be perpetual; nor shall any alteration at any time hereafter be made in any of them; unless such alteration be agreed to in a congress of the united states, and be afterwards confirmed by the legislatures of every state.

- Unanimous approval will be required from the states to amend the Articles of Confederation.

And Whereas it hath pleased the Great Governor of the World to incline the hearts of the legislatures we respectively represent in congress, to approve of, and to authorize us to ratify the said articles of confederation and perpetual union, Know Ye that we the undersigned delegates, by virtue of the power and authority to us given for that purpose, do by these presents, in the name and in behalf of our respective constituents, fully and entirely ratify and confirm each and every of the said articles of confederation and perpetual union, and all and singular the matters and things therein contained: And we do further solemnly plight and engage the faith of our respective constituents, that they shall abide by the determinations of the united states in congress assembled, on

all questions, which by the said confederation are submitted to them. And that the articles thereof shall be inviolably observed by the states we respectively represent, and that the union shall be perpetual. In Witness whereof we have hereunto set our hands in Congress. Done at Philadelphia in the State of Pennsylvania the ninth Day of July, in the Year of our Lord one Thousand seven Hundred and Seventy-eight, and in the third year of the independence of America.[57]

Shortcomings

Almost immediately, shortcomings with the Articles of Confederation were evident. The Congress could essentially make recommendations to the states for action and could make requests for funds but lacked the power to enforce any of these needs. Proposed amendments were doomed because they required unanimous approval by all thirteen legislatures for passage. As early as 1780 there was a movement afoot to replace the articles with a more powerful constitution that would centralize the government and give Congress more power. Of the shortcomings with the Articles of Confederation Alexander Hamilton would write in a letter to New York congressional delegate James Duane (delegate to Continental Congress from New York) 9/3/1780, that the "fundamental defect is a want of power in Congress." This is due to an "excess of the spirit of liberty which has made the particular states show a jealousy of all power not in their own hands." The method for amendments and seeking revenues places Congress in dependence on each of the states individually instead of collectively. Hamilton said specifically that "the confederation itself is defective and requires to be altered, it is neither fit for war, nor peace." In this letter Hamilton provides his recommendations. He tells Duane that Congress should resume its discretionary powers and that a convention should be called immediately to "conclude finally upon a general confederation." He also wants to see ownership of unoccupied lands vested in the Congress, establishment of a system of taxation to provide for perpetual revenue to the Congress, and also addresses his desire for a bank built on public and private credit.[58] Recall that Hamilton was the first Secretary of the US Treasury and was instrumental in the establishment of the First Bank of the United States.

On the brink!

The lack of power in Congress allowed the states to function like 13 individual countries. States were not upholding the obligations of the Treaty of Paris (peace agreement that ended the war), they were squabbling over land, and they were taxing each other. NY, NH and Connecticut were all claiming the land that would become Vermont. NY and NJ were imposing duties and taxes on each other. In the summer of 1786 through the winter of 1787 Massachusetts was on the verge of potential civil war. Taxation on farmers had become so burdensome that many were losing their farms to foreclosure and were being thrown in debtor's prisons. Massachusetts would not print paper money and had repealed legal tender laws. Therefore, debts had to be paid in specie (gold or silver coin), which was in short supply. Former revolutionary Captain Daniel Shays organized up to 2,000 farmers in at least five counties to march on courthouses in an effort to halt foreclosures, release prisoners, and initiate tax relief. This is known as **Shay's Rebellion.** The rebellion was finally suppressed in February 1787. Congress had been powerless to assist Massachusetts in suppressing the rebellion, which was a wake-up call to many Americans. This unfortunate event also highlighted the shortcomings with the current Articles of Confederation.

Annapolis Convention

As discussed above states were squabbling over land. Maryland and Virginia were involved in a running dispute over rights of navigation and commerce on the Potomac River. A convention was held at Mt. Vernon in the spring of 1785 to address this issue. An enlarged meeting was called for September 1786 to be held at Annapolis. Among those present were Alexander Hamilton and James Madison. The Annapolis Convention was to "take into consideration the trade and commerce of the United States."[59] While the convention was only attended by delegates from five states, those in attendance broadened their discussions to the general defects in the current federal system. These defects have rendered "the situation of the United States delicate and critical"[60] according to the commission's report[*], which was drafted by Hamilton. This report summarized the activity of the commission and was submitted to Congress. The commission recommended that all 13 states appoint delegates to convene at Philadelphia next May, "to take into consideration the situation of the United States"[61] and to, "to devise such further provisions as shall appear to them necessary to render the Constitution of the Federal Government *adequate to the exigencies of* *the Union."*[62] After two conventions, what had started out as a discussion concerning navigation of the Potomac had grown into the call for an evaluation of the entire federal system in existence at that time.

Convention Approved

Congress voted in favor of a convention at Philadelphia after debating the Annapolis Commission report. **The purpose of the convention was to meet *"for the sole and express purpose of revising the Articles of Confederation."***[63] It looks like Congress may have had one purpose in mind for a convention while some of the delegates like Hamilton, Madison and Washington had other intentions. Rhode Island was to stay away from the convention altogether. Jefferson and Adams would also be absent as they were serving overseas assignments. The "Orator of Liberty", **Patrick Henry** was appointed as a delegate but refused to attend because he **"smelt a rat."**[64]

Constitutional Convention

Philadelphia May 1787

The convention opened May 14, 1787 at the Pennsylvania State House but could do nothing as only two delegates were present, George Washington being one of them. It was not until May 25th that a quorum was in place. At that time delegates were present from seven states so activities could commence. George Washington is unanimously elected president of the convention. When all had arrived there were a total of 55 delegates. The age of the men present ranged from 26 (Jonathan Dayton of NJ) to 81 (Ben Franklin of PA). For the most part this was a young group by today's standards. James Madison, "Father of the Constitution" was 36, Virginia Governor Edmund Randolph was 33 and Alexander Hamilton was 30. Eight delegates were signers of the Declaration of Independence, seven had been state governors, and 21 had fought in the revolutionary war.

The proceedings of this convention were, for the most part, kept secret. While the public knew a big happening was underway in Philadelphia, they had no idea that the men present were going to develop an entirely new system of government. After all, the convention was supposed to be "revising the Articles of Confederation." Details of the intense debates that took place from May through September 1787 were largely unknown by the general public for many years. James Madison kept a meticulous journal of the proceedings but it was not released until 1836.

The Agenda

On May 29th Virginia delegate Edmund Randolph introduces ***The Virginia Plan (aka the Randolph Plan)*****. This plan consisted of 15 resolves that had been developed by the Virginian delegation in advance. They essentially outlined a new national government.[65] The resolves would provide the agenda, going forward, for the convention as they hammered out a new form of government. The Virginia Plan was favorable to large populous states and called for a bicameral legislature where one house would be filled based on the total number of free inhabitants of the states. The other house would be filled by members elected from the first house. The president would be chosen by the national legislature.

The Opposition

In opposition, William Paterson of New Jersey, submitted the ***New Jersey Plan****, on June 15, 1787. This would be the "small states" answer to the Virginia Plan which was favorable to the "large states". The New Jersey plan called for a "revision" of the Articles of Confederation. This approach seems like a novel concept since revision of the Articles was the original purpose of the convention as declared by congress. The New Jersey Plan would expand powers of the Congress in areas that had previously been deficient such as the laying of taxes and collecting revenues. The Congress would remain a unicameral body and the executive branch would be plural. This plan also outlined judiciary. This plan would be considered a federal form of government. Delegates such as Lansing, Yates, Bedford, Brearley, Luther Martin, Gerry, Sherman, Ellsworth, and George Mason supported the New Jersey Plan.

Federal vs. National

When debating the Virginia and New Jersey Plans the terms *federal* and *national* were reviewed and contemplated at length. The Virginia Plan uses the term national several times, such as when referring to the national legislature, the national executive and the national judiciary.

The New Jersey Plan, on the other hand, does not use the word national. The term federal is used when referring to the legislature and executive branches. We also see in section 6 of the plan that the states are "confederated".

Randolph had said on May 30th that, "a union merely federal will not accomplish the objects proposed."[66] The resolves that he proposed set forth a "national government". Gouverneur Morris of Pennsylvania described a federal government as a "mere compact" between parties while a national government had "complete and compulsive operation."[67] Madison told the delegates that federal governments operate on the states while national governments operate directly on the people.[68]

Webster's 1828 Dictionary defines these concepts:

Nation- A body of people inhabiting the same country, or united under the same sovereign or government; as the English nation; the French nation. It often happens that many nations are subject to one government; in which case, the word nation usually denotes a body of people speaking the same language, or a body that has formerly been under a distinct government, but has been conquered, or incorporated with a larger nation. Thus the empire of Russia comprehends many nations, as did formerly the Roman and Persian empires. Nation, as its etymology imports, originally denoted a family or race of men descended from a common progenitor, like tribe, but by emigration, conquest and intermixture of men of different families, this distinction is in most countries lost.

Federal- 1. Pertaining to a league or contract; derived from an agreement or covenant between parties, particularly between nations.

The Romans, contrary to federal right, compelled them to part with Sardinia.

2. Consisting in a compact between parties, particularly and chiefly between states or nations; founded on alliance by contract or mutual agreement; as a federal government, such as that of the United States.

3. Friendly to the constitution of the United States.

While each faction was using different verbiage, national vs. federal, the final product as we will see, ended up containing federal and national elements. Madison discusses the federal and national components at length in Federalist No. 39. Essentially, the House of Representatives is a national component because it derives its powers directly from the people. The original system for election of senators was a federal principle because the state legislatures had direct representation at the national or federal level. Hamilton described it best in Federalist No. 9 when he said, "The proposed Constitution, so far from implying an abolition of the State governments, makes them constituent parts of the national sovereignty, by allowing them a direct representation in the Senate, and leaves in their possession certain exclusive and very important portions of sovereign power. This fully corresponds, in every rational import of the terms, with the idea of a federal government."[69]

The 10th Amendment in the Bill of Rights affirms that powers not delegated to the United States government are retained by the states, or the people. This is a hybrid statement which contains both federal (the States) and national (the People) components. We ultimately ended up with a blending of the two concepts into our Constitution which created a type of government that the world had never seen before. It was federal and national.

Lastly, as a side note, Charles Kesler writes in the Introduction to the Signet Classic version of the Federalist Papers, that Hamilton and his like-minded framers had effectively stolen the name Federalist for their cause and left the true federalists (those who favored revision of the Articles of Confederation and opposed the new Constitution) in "political limbo". Those that opposed the Constitution were thereafter referred to Anti-federalists, which makes them sound uncooperative and rebellious.[70] After all, wouldn't the more appropriate term for Hamilton, Madison, and the strong central government men, have been "Nationalists"?

The Great Compromise

(aka Connecticut Compromise or Sherman Compromise)

Roger Sherman from Connecticut was a signer of the Declaration of Independence and one of the most prominent figures of this constitutional convention. In regard to the question of representation Sherman proposed proportional representation in the first branch (house) based on the number of free inhabitants and in the second branch (senate) each state would have one vote and no more. It would take another month until this matter was finally resolved. On July 16, 1787 The Great Compromise was approved. The House would have proportional representation with one representative for every 40,000 inhabitants and each state would have two members in the Senate. Prior to ratification by the states this number would be dropped to 30,000. The matter of representation nearly broke the convention apart and the Great Compromise saved the day.

Three-Fifths Compromise

Hamilton said that without the federal ratio "no union could possibly have been formed."[71] This federal ratio said that for the purpose of representation and taxes the proportion would be five slaves to three whites. The northern states also agreed that import taxes on slaves would not exceed more than ten dollars per head and that Congress could not pass navigation laws unless there was a two-thirds vote in each house. The southern states agreed that the importation of slaves would cease in 1808. Many of the delegates were opposed to slavery, including delegates from the south such as George Mason and Gouverneur Morris.

Tidbits

As it is not our intent to conduct a complete analysis of the convention we will depart from this discussion after looking at some interesting pieces of convention trivia.

- On June 18, 1787 Alexander Hamilton spoke for six hours in opposition of the New Jersey Plan, as well as the VA Plan for that matter. He called for a national executive that would be chosen by electors for life. Senators would also be chosen for life and the state governors would be appointed by the national government!![72]

- On June 30th Hamilton would leave the convention. The other two New York delegates, Yates and Lansing, would also leave on July 10th. They would not return. Hamilton eventually came back and was the sole delegate from New York to sign the Constitution.

- John Dickinson (of Olive Branch Petition and Letters from a Pennsylvania Farmer fame) said that a limited monarchy was one of the best governments in the world.[73]

- Edmund Randolph favored a plural executive and felt that a single strong executive would lead to monarchy. James Wilson supported a single executive because he felt that it was the best safeguard against tyranny. This is an example of how this convention was operating in totally uncharted territory. These men had strongly held beliefs based on knowledge and experience but what they were working to create in the Constitution had no exact blueprint for them to follow.

- George Mason had proposed that a Bill of Rights be added to the Constitution prior to completion. Elbridge Gerry seconded. The measure was defeated 10-0, although Massachusetts was not present to vote. This would cause much upheaval as the Constitution went to the states for ratification.

- Edmund Randolph, who had presented the Virginia Plan, refused to sign the final product.

- George Mason did not sign and theorized that the government produced by the Constitution would vibrate between a monarchy and a corrupt oppressive aristocracy.[74]

Signing and Ratification

On September 17, 1787 thirty-nine delegates signed the final draft of the constitution. Now it would be sent to the states where the ratification by nine states would be required for establishment. All thirteen, including Rhode Island, would eventually ratify.

Order of states- 1. Delaware (12/1787), 2. Pennsylvania (12/1787), 3. New Jersey (12/1787), 4. Georgia (1/1788), 5. Connecticut (1/1788), 6. Massachusetts (2/1788), 7. Maryland (4/1788), 8. South Carolina (5/1788), 9. New Hampshire (6/1788), 10. Virginia (6/1788), 11. New York (7/1788), 12. North Carolina (11/1789), 13. Rhode Island (5/1790)

There were five states where the vote for ratification was very close. A few votes against ratification in the states could have nullified the entire Constitution. In Massachusetts the margin was 19 votes. In New Hampshire and Virginia it was 10 votes. In New York 3 votes and in Rhode Island 2 votes. Assurance that a Bill of Rights would be added to the Constitution helped to assure successful ratification.

UNITED STATES CONSTITUTION

The Articles of Confederation had served as the first Constitution of the United States for eight years. After New Hampshire became the ninth state to ratify in June 1788 the new Constitution was established and became official. As we work our way through the constitution, article by article, we will attempt to dig in to the principles and philosophies that provide the foundation for our form of government. First, let us briefly examine some fundamental, overarching concepts that are ingrained in this document.

Republic vs. Democracy

Today America is most often described as a "democracy". This is untrue and unfortunate. Constitutional writer and teacher W. Cleon Skousen, discusses at length the corruption of the word "democracy" for the last 100 years in his book, *The 5000 Year Leap*. Socialist progressive groups such as the Intercollegiate Socialist Society, which was later renamed the League for Industrial Democracy, began using this word to describe their philosophy of a nationalized state where the central government controlled the economy (production and distribution).[75] While over the last 100 years the desires and aims of these types of groups have gained major headway in America (see bailouts of GM, AIG, etc.) their desires and aims are not democratic. They are socialistic.

Webster's definition of "republic" explains the concepts of a republic and a democracy:

> *A commonwealth; a state in which the exercise of the sovereign power is lodged in representatives elected by the people. In modern usage, it differs from a democracy or democratic state, in which the people exercise the powers of sovereignty in person. Yet the democracies of Greece are often called republics.* (Webster 1828)

In a republican form of government the people elect representatives to operate government on their behalf. A republican form of government is much more conducive to growth in population and in geographical expansion. A true democracy, where each person exercises their sovereignty in person, is not conducive to a large country such as ours. Democracy generally ends in anarchy, as every man is naturally inclined to look out for his own interests.

Madison in Federalist 10 states that, "democracies have ever been spectacles of turbulence and contention; have ever been found incompatible with personal security or the rights of property; and have in general been as short in their lives as they have been violent in their deaths."[76]

In Federalist 39 Madison defines and expounds on the term "republic":

> "We may define a **republic** to be, or at least may bestow that name on, **a government which derives all its powers directly or indirectly from the great body of the people, and is administered by persons holding their offices during pleasure for a limited period, or during good behavior**. It is *essential* to such a government that it be derived from the great body of the society, not from an inconsiderable proportion or a favored class of it; otherwise a handful of tyrannical nobles, exercising their oppressions by a delegation of their powers, might aspire to the rank of republicans and claim for their government the honorable title of republic. It is *sufficient* for such a government that the persons administering it be appointed, either directly or indirectly, by the people; and that they hold their appointments by either of the tenures just specified; otherwise every government in the United States, as well as every other popular government that has been or can be well organized or well executed, would be degraded from the republican character."[77]

We have now looked at four major terms that are used to describe American government in the last couple sections of this examination: federal, national, democracy and republic. All seem to be used almost interchangeably to describe some facet of the American system. This can be confusing. Prior to the establishment of the Constitution the thirteen states were essentially separate "republics" where the power of government was derived from the people. After establishment of the Constitution these republics were joined together as a "more perfect union" where the power of the government is still derived from the people. The states were joined together by delegating some of their sovereignty and powers to the new government, which could be defined as federal because the states still maintained numerous powers to themselves. In theory America's government was designed as a federal republic. It is arguable today that America is not operating as a federal republic anymore. If we are not careful we may slide into a unitary or socialist republic, whereby each state government is nothing more than an extension of the national government and can do nothing but administer the dictates of the centralized power.

Separation of Powers

As we shall see, the Constitution consists of seven articles. The first three articles deal with the three branches of American government, legislative (Article 1), executive (Article 2) and judicial (Article 3). The founders devised a system whereby these branches would provide a check on each other's power. The founders looked to Baron Charles de Montesquieu and his work, *The Spirit of Laws*, for guidance. Montesquieu warned that if the branches were not separated and able to provide a "check" on each other tyranny would ensue. He said, "When the legislative and executive powers are united in the same person, or in the same body of magistrates, there can be no liberty; because apprehensions may arise, lest the same monarch or senate should enact tyrannical laws, to execute them in a tyrannical manner."[78] Regarding the judiciary branch he said, "Again, there is no liberty, if the judiciary power be not separated from the legislative and executive. Were it joined with the legislative, the life and liberty of the subject would be exposed to arbitrary control, for the judge would then be the legislator. Were it joined to the executive power, the judge might behave with violence and oppression."[79]

Sovereignty

This word has fundamental meaning to man, his natural rights, and forms of government. It seems that today there is a misunderstanding of what sovereignty is and who possesses it. It is worthy to briefly explore its meaning and impact on our Constitution. Are you and I sovereign? Are governments sovereign? What is the definition of sovereign that our founders subscribed to?

As a starting point, let's take a look at how Webster defines "sovereign" in the 1828 dictionary-

> **SOVEREIGN,** a. suv'eran. [We retain this babarous orthography from the Norman sovereign. The true spelling would be suveran from the L. supernes, superus.]
>
> > 1. Supreme in power; possessing supreme dominion; as a sovereign ruler of the universe.
> > 2. Supreme; superior to all others; chief. God is the sovereign good of all who love and obey him.
> > 3. Supremely efficacious; superior to all others; predominant; effectual; as a sovereign remedy.
> > 4. Supreme; pertaining to the first magistrate of a nation; as sovereign authority.

SOVEREIGN, n. suv'eran.

> 1. A supreme lord or ruler; one who possesses the highest authority without control. Some earthly princes, kings and emperors are sovereigns in their dominions.
> 2. A supreme magistrate; a king.
> 3. A gold coin of England, value 20s or $4.44

From this definition we see that God is the ultimate Sovereign, as he is the ruler of the universe. We see this term used to describe God in Bible verses in various translations. For example:

- Psalm 103:19 (NASB)- The Lord has established His throne in the heavens, And His sovereignty rules over all.
- 1 Timothy 6:15 (HCSB)- God will bring this about in His own time. He is the blessed and only Sovereign, the King of kings, and the Lord of lords
- Jude 4 (NIV)- For certain men whose condemnation was written about long ago have secretly slipped in among you. They are godless men, who change the grace of our God into a license for immorality and deny Jesus Christ our only Sovereign and Lord.

This term is also used in the bible when referring to human rulers: "But as soon as he has arisen, his kingdom will be broken up and parceled out toward the four points of the compass, though not to his *own* descendants, nor according to his authority which he wielded, for his sovereignty will be uprooted and *given* to others besides them." Daniel 11:4 (NASB)

Webster uses words such as lord, ruler, magistrate, and king when defining sovereign. Are you a king or prince? Are you the supreme magistrate of your nation?

Samuel Adams, identified the Sovereign when giving a speech shortly after the colonies declared independence, "This day, I trust, the reign of political protestantism will commence. We have explored the temple of royalty, and found that the idol we have bowed down to has eyes which see not, ears that hear not our prayers, and a heart like the nether Millstone. — We have this day restored the Sovereign to whom alone Men ought to be obedient: He reigns in Heaven, and with a propitious eye beholds his subjects assuming that freedom of thought, and dignity of self-direction, which he bestowed on them, from the rising to the setting sun, may His Kingdom come."[80] It is interesting to ponder what Adams, known as the Father of the Revolution and The Last Puritan, is saying here. By declaring independence we have restored the true Sovereign, which is God, to His rightful place at the head of the states, versus living under a human, self-imposed sovereign. This goes against the grain of the secular humanist argument which teaches that America was created as a godless nation.

Dr. Benjamin Rush, signer of the Declaration of Independence, had this to say about sovereignty:

> "It is often said, that "the sovereign and all other power is seated *in* the people." This idea is unhappily expressed. It should be—"all power is derived *from* the people." They possess it only on the days of their elections. After this, it is the property of their rulers, nor can they exercise or resume it, unless it is abused. It is of importance to circulate this idea, as it leads to order and good government. The people of America have mistaken the meaning of the word sovereignty: hence each state pretends to be *sovereign*. In Europe, it is applied only to those states which possess the power of making war and peace – of forming treaties, and the like. As this power belongs only to congress, they are the only *sovereign* power in the united states."[81]

Dr. Rush hit the nail on the head when he said that you and I possess sovereignty on election days only. This is because we live in a republic with elected representatives. We grant them authority to govern on our behalf. You and I cannot declare war or enter into a treaty with a foreign nation but the government that we have established has sovereign authority to do those things.

William Blackstone echoes this understanding of sovereignty in his Commentaries on the Laws of England. Blackstone indicates that the sovereign power is the power to make and enforce laws.[82]

The founders were sure to point out that the States were included in the national sovereign power as well. Hamilton said in Federalist No. 9, "The proposed Constitution, so far from implying an abolition of the State governments, makes them constituent parts of the national sovereignty, by allowing them a direct representation in the Senate, and leaves in their possession certain exclusive and very important portions of sovereign power."[83]

In Federalist No. 32 Hamilton further identifies the specific areas of sovereignty that are retained by the States,

> "But as the plan of the convention aims only at a partial union or consolidation, the State governments would clearly retain all the rights of sovereignty which they before had, and which were not, by

that act (the Constitution, author note), *exclusively* delegated to the United States. This exclusive delegation, or rather this alienation, of State sovereignty would only exist in three cases: where the Constitution in express terms granted an exclusive authority to the Union; where it granted in one instance an authority to the Union, and in another prohibited the States from exercising the like authority; and where it granted an authority to the Union to which a similar authority in the States would be absolutely and totally *contradictory* and *repugnant*."[84]

Madison ties the sovereign power of the People and the States together in Federalist No. 39. He says, "assent and ratification is to be given by the people, not as individuals composing one entire nation, but as composing the distinct and independent States to which they respectively belong. It is to be the assent and ratification of the several States, derived from the supreme authority in each State—the authority of the people themselves."[85] This aligns with the statement from Dr. Rush that the people possess their sovereignty on election day, whether it be to send delegates to the continental congress, constitutional convention, or a state ratifying convention. Madison goes on to echo Hamilton when he discusses State sovereignty; "Each State, in ratifying the Constitution, is considered as a sovereign body independent of all others, and only to be bound by its own voluntary act."[86]

The extent of State sovereignty is important as well. As we just indicated, Hamilton outlined three areas where State sovereignty would be alienated. Madison tells us that under the Constitution the "States will retain …a very extensive portion of active sovereignty."[87] Madison also stated that the "States, in all unenumerated cases, are left to the enjoyment of their sovereign and independent jurisdiction."[88]

In summation, God is the Supreme Sovereign but aspects of sovereignty are delegated to earthly rulers for government. In a republic such as ours it is understood that men, not kings, have unalienable rights that come from God. These rights include self-government. Therefore, we as the supreme authority in our country can exercise our sovereignty to establish governments and elect representatives. As we have seen from the statements of Madison, Hamilton, and Rush it was the original intent of the Constitution to maintain portions of sovereignty for the people and the states. These parts comprise the national sovereignty. The people's sovereignty is exercised through electing representatives. The States retain sovereignty to make laws in areas not delegated to the federal government and also had assurance of their sovereignty at the federal level by electing senators. And finally, as

Blackstone summarized, the national sovereignty rests in Congress as it has the power to make and enforce laws at the federal level.

Does it appear that the States have any of their "active sovereignty" today? With the passage of the 17th Amendment to the Constitution in 1913 state sovereignty was effectively eliminated. This destroyed an important barrier that was meant to prevent federal overstep, usurpation, excessive spending, and unconstitutional activity. We need to exercise our sovereignty at the ballot box wisely and virtuously if we are to have a chance at restoring and repairing this great republic.

Preamble

We the People of the United States, in Order to form a more perfect Union, establish Justice, insure domestic Tranquility, provide for the common defence, promote the general Welfare, and secure the Blessings of Liberty to ourselves and our Posterity, do ordain and establish this Constitution for the United States of America.

1. The Preamble tells us that this Constitution is being established to do six things: form a more perfect Union, establish Justice, insure domestic Tranquility, provide for the common defense, promote the general Welfare, and to secure the Blessings of Liberty for the founders and future generations.

2. **"We the People of the United States"**- In Federalist No. 22, Hamilton describes the "CONSENT OF THE PEOPLE" as the "pure, original fountain of all legitimate authority"[89]. We the People have established this Constitution because, as Hamilton says, you and I are the source of all legitimate authority.

- Notice the "U" in United States is now capitalized. In the Declaration of Independence it was not. The States were formally "United" under the Articles of Confederation, and now they are forming a "more perfect Union".

3. **"in Order to form a more perfect Union, establish Justice, insure domestic Tranquility, provide for the common defence, promote the general Welfare, and secure the Blessings of Liberty to ourselves and our Posterity" -**

- **JUST'ICE-** The virtue which consists in giving to every one what is his due; practical conformity to the laws and to principles of rectitude in the dealings of men with each other; honesty; integrity in commerce or mutual intercourse. Justice is distributive or commutative. Distributive justice belongs to magistrates or rulers, and consists in distributing to every man that right or equity which the laws and the principles of equity require; or in deciding controversies according to the laws and to principles of equity. Commutative justice consists in fair dealing in trade and mutual intercourse between man and man. (Webster 1828)

- *"promote the general welfare"*- is one of the most abused concepts in American history. It has been used to justify everything from welfare to Social Security, Medicare, "free" cell phones and internet service, government healthcare, and never ending bureaucracy and burdensome regulations. According to the true definitions of these words we see that the constitution directs the federal government to "promote" the general welfare, not provide. And, "general" means all of us together, not as individuals. Therefore wealth redistribution through welfare checks to individuals, or tax breaks and subsidies to corporations is not "promoting" the "general" welfare, it is theft of property.

- **PROMO'TE-** To forward; to advance; to contribute to the growth, enlargement or excellence of any thing valuable, or to the increase of any thing evil; as, to promote learning, knowledge, virtue or religion; to promote the interest of commerce or agriculture; to promote the arts; to promote civilization or refinement; to promote the propagation of the gospel; to promote vice and disorder. (Webster 1828)

- **GEN'ERAL**- Public; common; relating to or comprehending the whole community; as the general interest or safety of a nation.

- Common to many or the greatest number; as a general opinion; a general custom.

- Not directed to a single object. (Webster 1828)

- **WELFARE:**

1. Exemption from misfortune, sickness, calamity or evil; the enjoyment of health and the common blessings of life; prosperity; happiness; applied to persons.

2. Exemption from any unusual evil or calamity; the enjoyment of peace and prosperity, or the ordinary blessings of society and civil government; applied to states. (Webster 1828)

-BLESS'ING-

1. Benediction; a wish of happiness pronounced; a prayer imploring happiness upon another.

2. A solemn prophetic benediction, in which happiness is desired, invoked or foretold.

This is the blessing wherewith Moses--blessed the children of Israel. Deut.33.

3. Any means of happiness; a gift, benefit or advantage; that which promotes temporal prosperity and welfare, or secures immortal felicity. A just and pious magistrate is a public blessing. The divine favor is the greatest blessing.

4. Among the Jews, a present; a gift; either because it was attended with kind wishes for the welfare of the giver, or because it was the means of increasing happiness.

Take, I pray thee, my blessing that is brought to thee. Gen.33. (Webster 1828)

- There are many today that will argue that the Constitution is a 'Godless" document. There are references to God in this document and this phrase, "secure the Blessings of Liberty" is the first. The framers are looking to secure the blessings, not create the blessings. It is evident that these "blessings of liberty" must come from a higher power.

-**POSTER'ITY-** Descendants; children, children's children, &c. indefinitely; the race that proceeds from a progenitor. The whole human race are the posterity of Adam. (Webster 1828)

Article I

Section. 1.

All legislative Powers herein granted shall be vested in a Congress of the United States, which shall consist of a Senate and House of Representatives.

1. The very first sentence in the meat of the constitution establishes a bicameral legislature. Made up of a senate and a house of representatives, this system originally protected dual sovereignty whereby the states had representation at the federal level through their ability to choose senators and the federal government had sovereignty provided by the people who directly elected their congressmen.

2. According to Joseph Andrews from the Center for Teaching the Constitution, Article 1 comprises over half the constitution.[90] Only Congress can make laws. The Supreme Court and Executive were given no power to create laws through executive order or judicial decree. The House is closest to the "fountain" that Hamilton spoke of in Federalist 22 and thus was intended by the founders to have the most power.

Section. 2.

The House of Representatives shall be composed of Members chosen every second Year by the People of the several States, and the Electors in each State shall have the Qualifications requisite for Electors of the most numerous Branch of the State Legislature.

1. Madison discussed the House of Representatives in Federalist 52. He said this regarding biennial elections, "As it is essential to liberty that the government in general should have a common interest with the people, so it is particularly essential that the branch of it under consideration should have an immediate dependence on , and an intimate sympathy with, the people. Frequent elections are unquestionably the only policy by which this dependence and sympathy can be effectually secured."[91] Madison also discussed the link between power and duration, "It is a received and well-founded maxim that where no other circumstances affect the case, the greater the power is, the shorter ought to be its duration; and, conversely,

the smaller the power, the more safely may its duration be protracted."[92] If we take his statement at face value it would mean that the framers intended for the Senate to wield less power than the House. After all, the term for a Senator is 6 years. Considering Madison's logic and original intent we can assume that the framers believed that the powers of the Senate were "small" and that it was "safe" for them to have a term of "protracted duration". At the time the Constitution was ratified the powers of the Senate were maintained by the States. Since passage of the 17th amendment we have regrettably turned Madison's logic upside down.

2. **ELECT'OR-** One who elects, or one who has the right of choice; a person who has, by law or constitution, the right of voting for an officer, In free governments, the people or such of them as possess certain qualifications of age, character and property, are the electors of their representatives, &c., in parliament, assembly, or other legislative body. In the United States, certain persons are appointed or chosen to be electors of the president or chief magistrate. In Germany, certain princes were formerly electors of the emperor, and elector was one of their titles, as the elector of Saxony. (Webster 1828)

-Those who can vote for state legislators according to the laws of each state, are guaranteed the right to vote for members of the House of Representatives. Madison said this in Federalist 52, "The definition of the right of suffrage is very justly regarded as a fundamental article of republican government. It was incumbent on the convention, therefore, to define and establish this right in the Constitution."[93] You and I would be considered an "elector" in the case of electing members of the House of Representatives.

No Person shall be a Representative who shall not have attained to the Age of twenty five Years, and been seven Years a Citizen of the United States, and who shall not, when elected, be an Inhabitant of that State in which he shall be chosen.

1. The qualifications for a Representative are very few! Does one need to be an attorney or have a PhD to go to Congress? The Constitution says not and we should as well! The people's house should be filled by people like you and I. The key is that society in general should have virtue and a proper understanding of civics and history. Samuel Adams indicates that wisdom and virtue are requisite qualifications for anyone who will hold office; "He therefore is the truest friend to the liberty of his country who tries most to promote its virtue, and who, so far as his power and influence extend, will not suffer a man to be chosen into any office of power and trust who is not a wise and virtuous man."[94] Says James Madison when discussing the qualifications for a Representative, "Under these reasonable limitations, the door of this part of the federal government is open to merit of every description, whether native or adoptive, whether young or old, and without regard to poverty or wealth, or to any particular profession of religious faith."[95]

Representatives and direct Taxes shall be apportioned among the several States which may be included within this Union, according to their respective Numbers, which shall be determined by adding to the whole Number of free Persons, including those bound to Service for a Term of Years, and excluding Indians not taxed, three fifths of all other Persons. The actual Enumeration shall be made within three Years after the first Meeting of the Congress of the United States, and within every subsequent Term of ten Years, in such Manner as they shall by Law direct. The Number of Representatives shall not exceed one for every thirty Thousand, but each State shall have at Least one Representative; and until such enumeration shall be made, the State of New Hampshire shall be entitled to chuse three, Massachusetts eight, Rhode-Island and Providence Plantations one, Connecticut five, New-York six, New Jersey four, Pennsylvania eight, Delaware one, Maryland six, Virginia ten, North Carolina five, South Carolina five, and Georgia three.

1. The constitution established that Representatives and direct Taxes would be apportioned among the States, according to their respective numbers. We will recall that the founders had fought a war for independence largely on the premise of "no taxation without representation." We saw earlier in this examination that the colonists were not totally adverse to indirect taxes, but direct taxes were another matter altogether because these were levied directly on the individual or his property and he had no direct representation in parliament. Now the powers of taxation would be levied by representatives chosen directly by the people.

2. The method of determining the numbers is the "federal ratio" or three fifths rule. This was held over from the Articles of Confederation.

3. Madison expounded on the need for a link between the apportionment of representatives and taxes in Federalist 54. He said, "Were their share of representation alone to be governed by this rule, they would have an interest in exaggerating their inhabitants. Were the rule to decide their share of taxation alone, a contrary temptation would prevail. By extending the rule to both objects, the States will have opposite interests which will control and balance each other and produce the requisite impartiality."[96]

When vacancies happen in the Representation from any State, the Executive Authority thereof shall issue Writs of Election to fill such Vacancies.

The House of Representatives shall chuse their Speaker and other Officers; and shall have the sole Power of Impeachment.

1. As part of the separation of powers we see that the House is given the power of impeachment.

Section. 3.

The Senate of the United States shall be composed of two Senators from each State, chosen by the Legislature thereof for six Years; and each Senator shall have one Vote.

1. Prior to the passage of the 17th amendment on May 31, 1913 Senators were chosen by each state legislature.

Madison states in Federalist 45, "States will retain under the proposed Constitution a very extensive portion of active sovereignty..." and that the "Senate will be elected absolutely and exclusively by the State legislatures."[97]

2. In Federalist 39 Madison says, "Each state, in ratifying the Constitution, is considered as a sovereign body independent of all others, and only to be bound by its own voluntary act." Madison then identifies that the Senate "will derive its powers from the States as political and coequal societies; and these will be represented on the principle of equality in the Senate, as they now are in the existing Congress."[98]

3. In Federalist 9 Hamilton states, "The proposed Constitution, so far from implying an abolition of the State governments, makes them constituent parts of the national sovereignty, by allowing them a direct representation in the Senate, and leaves in their possession certain exclusive and very important portions of sovereign power. This fully corresponds, in every rational import of the terms, with the idea of a federal government."[99]

4. From Madison and Hamilton's statements above we see how important and critical this issue of State sovereignty was. It was a vital piece of the federal system for the States to be directly represented at the federal level by the choosing of Senators. This protected their sovereignty and would act as a "check" against intrusions by the federal government into areas of State authority.

5. The passage of the 17th amendment has destroyed a vital piece of the original federal system so that now we are essentially operating under a purely "national" form of government whereby all representation is directly chosen by the people at large. The popular election of senators has taken away the ability of each state to stop the national government from expanding beyond its original enumerated powers. Many wonder today why Congress passes 1,000 page bills such as the Patient Protection and Affordable Healthcare Act, also known as "Obamacare". More than half of the state governments opposed "Obamacare"[100] and challenged this legislation in court, unsuccessfully I might add. If Senators had still been elected by the State legislatures it is possible that this bill would have never passed because the Senators would have taken their marching orders from the State legislatures, not from lobbyists and bribes (Google Cornhusker Kickback and Louisiana Purchase).

Immediately after they shall be assembled in Consequence of the first Election, they shall be divided as equally as may be into three Classes. The Seats of the Senators of the first Class shall be vacated at the Expiration of the second Year, of the second Class at the Expiration of the fourth Year, and of the third Class at the Expiration of the sixth Year, so that one third may be chosen every second Year; and if Vacancies happen by Resignation, or otherwise, during the Recess of the Legislature of any State, the Executive thereof may make temporary Appointments until the next Meeting of the Legislature, which shall then fill such Vacancies.

No Person shall be a Senator who shall not have attained to the Age of thirty Years, and been nine Years a Citizen of the United States, and who shall not, when elected, be an Inhabitant of that State for which he shall be chosen.

The Vice President of the United States shall be President of the Senate, but shall have no Vote, unless they be equally divided.

The Senate shall chuse their other Officers, and also a President pro tempore, in the Absence of the Vice President, or when he shall exercise the Office of President of the United States.

The Senate shall have the sole Power to try all Impeachments. When sitting for that Purpose, they shall be on Oath or Affirmation. When the President of the United States is tried, the Chief Justice shall preside: And no Person shall be convicted without the Concurrence of two thirds of the Members present.

1. More separation of powers. The House impeaches and the Senate conducts the trial.

Judgment in Cases of Impeachment shall not extend further than to removal from Office, and disqualification to hold and enjoy any Office of honor, Trust or Profit under the United States: but the Party convicted shall nevertheless be liable and subject to Indictment, Trial, Judgment and Punishment, according to Law.

Section 4

The Times, Places and Manner of holding Elections for Senators and Representatives, shall be prescribed in each State by the Legislature thereof; but the Congress may at any time by Law make or alter such Regulations, except as to the Places of chusing Senators.

1. The method of "chusing" Senators is affirmed to be within the authority of the states. The framers are protecting this piece of state sovereignty for a good reason, as we have seen.

The Congress shall assemble at least once in every Year, and such Meeting shall be on the first Monday in December, unless they shall by Law appoint a different Day.

1. **"The Congress shall assemble at least once in every Year"**- The Constitution simply says that the Congress shall meet at least once in every year. It does not say for how long. Imagine an America where Congress worked part time, or met once a year for one week! It was never the intent of the framers to have an overly active and intrusive government. Jefferson said this regarding the size and role of government, "The true theory of our Constitution is surely the wisest & best, that the states are independent as to everything within themselves, & united as to everything respecting foreign nations. Let the general government be reduced to foreign concerns only, and let our affairs be disentangled from those of all other nations, except as to commerce, which the merchants will manage the better, the more they are left free to manage for themselves, and our general government may be reduced to a very simple organization, & a very unexpensive one; **a few plain duties to be performed by a few servants**." (emphasis added)[101]

2. The requirement for meeting once per year also provided the safeguard against indictments 5 and 6 in the Declaration of Independence.

Section. 5.

Each House shall be the Judge of the Elections, Returns and Qualifications of its own Members, and a Majority of each shall constitute a Quorum to do Business; but a smaller Number may adjourn from day to day, and may be authorized to compel the Attendance of absent Members, in such Manner, and under such Penalties as each House may provide.

Each House may determine the Rules of its Proceedings, punish its Members for disorderly Behaviour, and, with the Concurrence of two thirds, expel a Member.

Each House shall keep a Journal of its Proceedings, and from time to time publish the same, excepting such Parts as may in their Judgment require Secrecy; and the Yeas and Nays of the Members of either House on any question shall, at the Desire of one fifth of those Present, be entered on the Journal.

Neither House, during the Session of Congress, shall, without the Consent of the other, adjourn for more than three days, nor to any other Place than that in which the two Houses shall be sitting.

Section. 6.

The Senators and Representatives shall receive a Compensation for their Services, to be ascertained by Law, and paid out of the Treasury of the United States. They shall in all Cases, except Treason, Felony and Breach of the Peace, be privileged from Arrest during their Attendance at the Session of their respective Houses, and in going to and returning from the same; and for any Speech or Debate in either House, they shall not be questioned in any other Place.

1. On January 23, 2012 KY Senator Rand Paul was detained by the Dept. of Homeland Security at the Nashville International Airport for refusing an unconstitutional pat down after having already passed through the agency's x-ray scanner. Senator Paul was en route to Washington DC for Senate business. This act by a federal government agency appears to be a direct violation of Article 1, Section 6, yet our elected representatives do nothing about the abuses directed at themselves and at us.

No Senator or Representative shall, during the Time for which he was elected, be appointed to any civil Office under the Authority of the United States, which shall have been created, or the Emoluments whereof shall have been encreased during such time; and no Person holding any Office under the United States, shall be a Member of either House during his Continuance in Office.

- EMOL'UMENT:

1. The profit arising from office or employment; that which is received as a compensation for services, or which is annexed to the possession of office, as salary, feels and perquisites.

2. Profit; advantage; gains in general. (Webster 1828)

Section. 7.

All Bills for raising Revenue shall originate in the House of Representatives; but the Senate may propose or concur with Amendments as on other Bills.

1. Any law coming out of congress with the purpose of generating revenue for the nation must originate in the House of Representatives because this is the elected body, as Hamilton says, that is closest to the people, who are the "pure, original fountain of all legitimate authority".[107]

Every Bill which shall have passed the House of Representatives and the Senate, shall, before it become a Law, be presented to the President of the United States: If he approve he shall sign it, but if not he shall return it, with his Objections to that House in which it shall have originated, who shall enter the Objections at large on their Journal, and proceed to reconsider it. If after such Reconsideration two thirds of that House shall agree to pass the Bill, it shall be sent, together with the Objections, to the other House, by which it shall likewise be reconsidered, and if approved by two thirds of that House, it shall become a Law. But in all such Cases the Votes of both Houses shall be determined by yeas and Nays, and the Names of the Persons voting for and against the Bill shall be entered on the Journal of each House respectively. If any Bill shall not be returned by the President within ten Days (Sundays excepted) after it shall have been presented to him, the Same shall be a Law, in like Manner as if he had signed it, unless the Congress by their Adjournment prevent its Return, in which Case it shall not be a Law.

Every Order, Resolution, or Vote to which the Concurrence of the Senate and House of Representatives may be necessary (except on a question of Adjournment) shall be presented to the President of the United States; and before the Same shall take Effect, shall be approved by him, or being disapproved by him, shall be repassed by two thirds of the Senate and House of Representatives, according to the Rules and Limitations prescribed in the Case of a Bill.

1. The check and balance system is outlined here where we see that the House and Senate can generate bills but they must be approved by each other. Then they are sent to the President who has the opportunity to veto the legislation. If he vetoes the legislation Congress must muster a 2/3 majority in each house to override the president's veto.

Section. 8.

- This section outlines the enumerated powers of the federal government. These are the powers ceded to the new government by the states and the people. As Madison said, "The powers delegated by the proposed Constitution to the federal government are few and defined. Those which are to remain in the State governments are numerous and indefinite."[103]

(1) The Congress shall have Power To lay and collect Taxes, Duties, Imposts and Excises, to pay the Debts and provide for the common Defence and general Welfare of the United States; but all Duties, Imposts and Excises shall be uniform throughout the United States;

1. Reason for the "power to lay and collect taxes"- The Articles of Confederation, in Article 8, provided for collection of taxes to pay for common defense and the general welfare. But, the congress was at the mercy of the state legislatures for collection of the requested funds. This was an unsustainable arrangement. Therefore, to rectify this deficiency the framers gave the new federal government the general power to tax. Hamilton noted, **"A nation cannot long exist without revenue."**[104] He then identifies the power of taxation as "the most important of the authorities proposed to be conferred upon the Union."[105]

2. Defense for the power to tax- Several of the Federalist Papers address the subjects of taxation and revenue. Federalist 30-36 were written by Alexander Hamilton and cover taxation in detail. While he was an advocate of a strong central government and had aversion for anything calculated to "disarm the government of a single weapon, which in any possible contingency might be usefully employed for the general defense and security"[106], Hamilton makes a compelling case for the necessity of the new government to be able to sustain itself through taxation.

3. Extent of tax power- In Federalist 30 Hamilton points out that money is considered as the vital principle of the body politic and that which sustains its life and enables it to function. Said he, **"A complete power, therefore to procure a regular and adequate supply of revenue, as far as the resources of the community will permit, may be regarded as an indispensable ingredient in every constitution."**[107]

4. Looking to the future- In Federalist 34 Hamilton includes the subject of taxation in a description of the overall Constitution and how it is designed. Recall in the Preamble that the signers stated that this document was for "Posterity". According to Hamilton the framers did not confine their views to their time period. They were looking forward to "remote futurity" because Constitutions are "not to be framed upon a calculation of existing exigencies, but upon a combination of these with the probable exigencies of ages…"[108]

5. Types of tax- In Federalist 35 Hamilton notes that if the power to tax was restricted to particular objects this would produce an oppression of certain industries and create an unequal distribution of taxes among the states and also citizens of the same state. If federal taxation were confined only to duties on imports the government would be tempted to raise these duties excessively. This would promote smuggling, would be oppressive to merchants, and would also lead to inequality of taxation between the manufacturing and non- manufacturing states. These reasons support his justification for a "complete" power to tax. Now, what types of tax are included in this power?

- External- Duties or imposts on imported goods would be considered an external tax, as well as an "indirect" tax. Recall that the colonists had a disdain for any type of "direct" tax but could stomach "indirect" taxes. In Federalist 30 Hamilton indicates that external taxes alone, are not sufficient even to handle the existing debts of the country at that time, much less "the present and future exigencies of the Union"[109]

- Internal- There are two types of internal tax; direct and indirect. The Constitution provides power for both types of taxation.

-Direct taxes include taxes on land and buildings, as well as poll taxes, which is a type of tax on a person (Federalist Papers 21 and 36). These taxes had to be apportioned among the states according to the census (Art 1, Sec 2)

-Indirect taxes include duties and excises on articles of consumption (Federalist 36). These have to be "uniform" throughout the United States. A national sales tax would fall into this category. Why do we need the IRS and their amazingly complex and tyrannical tax code? Answer, we don't.

6. Original Intent of Taxation- The "chief" part of the revenue raised in this country was intended to come from indirect taxes according to Hamilton in Federalist 21. James Madison, in Federalist 45 acknowledges that the new government will have the power of collecting internal and external taxes throughout the states but, "it is probable that this power will not be resorted to, except for supplemental purposes of revenue.."[110] Hamilton also said in Federalist 36 that the federal government did not have to exercise the power of internal taxation if it was found to be inconvenient.

7. What kind of tax system were they trying to build- Essentially they were trying to build a system for revenue generation that mirrored the Constitution itself; one that was sufficiently powerful and effective, as well as simple and limited. In Federalist 35 Hamilton said, "It might be demonstrated that the most productive system of finance will always be the least burdensome."[111] Madison envisioned that "the number of individuals employed under the Constitution of the United States will be much smaller than the number employed under the particular States."[112] Jefferson affirmed this when writing on the theory of the Constitution, as he indicated that the general government would be a simple and inexpensive organization. A government that has limited revenue intake will remain simple and inexpensive. The revenue streams intended for use by the framers would have kept the government simple and inexpensive. Notice that through all of this exploration on Constitutional taxation the subject of an income tax has not come up and will not come up until the 16th Amendment is passed in 1913.

8. Anti-Federalist opposition to the proposed powers of taxation- During the constitutional ratification conventions in the several states there was significant debate on the powers of taxation contained within the proposed Constitution. Both those for, and those against, ratification acknowledged that the Constitution armed the general government with a complete power of taxation. While Madison and Hamilton, in their Federalist writings, indicate a reliance on the virtue of those in power to limit the use of this power, those opposed to this power were not so willing to place it in the hands of fallible men.

The Anti-Federalist essays that were published during the ratification debates were a counter argument to the Federalist Papers, and highlighted the concerns over the extent of power given to the new government, including the powers of taxation.

Patrick Henry, who was possibly the most famous "anti-federalist", identified the power of direct taxation as a "scourge", but was willing to allow it, only in the event that states did not comply with requisitions from Congress.[114]

"John DeWitt" informed his Massachusetts readers on October 27, 1787 that the future Government, "shall have the exclusive power of imposts and the duties on imports and exports, the power of laying excises and other duties, and the additional power of laying internal taxes upon your lands, your goods, your chattels, as well as your persons at their sovereign pleasure."[115] He also noted that the funds would be, "collected by their own officers, armed with a military force, if a civil aid should not prove sufficient."[116]

Samuel Bryan, writing as the "Centinel" also expresses the concern that this power to tax would be spread throughout the country and would be enforced by a standing army.[117]

Twenty-one of the twenty-three dissenting members of the Pennsylvania ratifying convention produced an address that appeared in newspapers on Dec. 17, 1787. They identify that, "the powers of Congress under the new constitution, are complete and unlimited over the *purse* and the *sword,* and are perfectly independent of, and supreme over, the state governments; whose intervention in these great points is entirely destroyed. By virtue of their power of taxation, Congress may command the whole, or any part of the property of the people."[118] The Pennsylvania dissenters also noted in their address that, "The power of direct taxation will further apply to every individual, as congress may tax land, cattle, trades, occupations, etc. in any amount, and every object of internal taxation is of that nature, that however oppressive, the people will have but this alternative, except to pay the tax, or let their property be taken, for all resistance will be in vain. The standing army and select militia would enforce the collection."[119]

The anti-federalist writer "Brutus" authored a series of essays that were addressed to "the Citizens of the State of New York". It is believed that Brutus was actually Robert Yates, who had been a delegate to the constitutional convention. In his first essay "Brutus" states that the, "authority to lay and collect taxes is the most important of any power that can be granted; it connects with it almost all other powers, or at least will in process of time draw all others after it; it is the great means of protection, security, and defence, in a good government, and the great engine of oppression and tyranny in a bad one."[120]

While the Constitution was ultimately ratified by all thirteen states, the principled stance of those apprehensive of an energetic and powerful government did have an influence in the ratifying conventions. Seven states formally communicated the need for alteration of the wording on taxation or the addition of an amendment limiting the powers of direct taxation. New York's proposed amendment is similar in wording and spirit to the other six and is printed here:

> *"That Congress do not lay direct Taxes but when the Monies arising from the Impost and Excise shall be insufficient for the Public Exigencies, nor then until Congress shall first have made a Requisition upon the States to assess levy and*

pay their respective proportions of such Requisition, agreeably to the Census fixed in the said Constitution, in such way and manner as the Legislatures of the respective States shall judge best..."[121]

History, however, points out that the requests of these seven states, which were a majority at the time, went unanswered, as there was never an amendment to limit the power of taxation given to the new government.

The only change to the original power of taxation has been an augmentation to it, by passage of the 16th Amendment. This amendment removed the barrier that was present in the form of requiring direct taxes to be linked to a census. The concerns of those anti-federalist writers seem to have been largely borne out over time. In our day the Internal Revenue Service is armed with a staff of approx. 100,000 bureaucrats.[122] "John DeWitt", "Brutus" and others had concern that a standing army could be used as a means of enforcing the collection of taxes. As of 2011 the United States had a standing army of approx. 1,459,409 enlisted and officer personnel.[123]

(2) To borrow Money on the credit of the United States;

(3) To regulate Commerce with foreign Nations, and among the several States, and with the Indian Tribes;

1. According to Madison in Federalist 45 there are only a handful of major functions of the new government which include war, peace, negotiation, and foreign commerce.[124]

2. "and among the several States"- This is known as the interstate commerce clause. This clause has been used ever increasingly by the national government to expand regulation and influence over the American people and the economy. For example, the Supreme Court case of Wickard v. Filburn (1942) upheld the Agricultural Adjustment Act of 1938, and held that the national government, under the commerce clause, could regulate the amount of wheat grown on private land that was to be used for private consumption. The purpose of the 1938 Act was to control the volume of wheat moving in interstate and foreign commerce and to control prices.[125] If the national government can control what we grow and eat under the banner of the commerce clause, is there any freedom left?

3. What did the framers think of the commerce clause? In Federalist 22 Hamilton identified why the commerce clause was needed, "In addition to the defects already enumerated in the existing federal system, there are others of not less importance which concur in rendering it altogether unfit for the administration of the affairs of the Union. The want of power to regulate commerce is by all parties allowed to be of the number."[126] He also said, "It is indeed evident, on the most superficial view, that there is no object, either as it respects the interest of trade or finance, that more strongly demands a federal superintendence."[127] What would this federal "superintendence" entail with regard to the states? Madison identifies that there was need to prevent states from burdening each other with duties on goods passing through their borders. He said in Federalist 42, "A very material

object of this power was the relief of the States which import and export through other States from the improper contributions levied on them by the latter. Were these at liberty to regulate the trade between State and State, it must be foreseen that ways would be found out to load the articles of import and export, during the passage through their jurisdiction, with duties which would fall on the makers of the latter and the consumers of the former."[128]

4. Supreme Court Justice and constitutional historian Joseph Story summed up the purpose of the foreign and interstate commerce clause succinctly when he said,

> *"The power, "to regulate foreign commerce," enabled the Government at once to place the whole country upon an equality with foreign nations; to compel them to abandon their narrow and selfish policy towards us; and to protect our own commercial interests against their injurious competitions. The power to regulate commerce "among the several States," in like manner, annihilated the causes of domestic feuds and rivalries. It compelled every State to regard the interest of each, as the interest of all; and thus diffused over all the blessings of a free, active, and rapid exchange of commodities, upon the footing of perfect equality."*[129]

(4) To establish an uniform Rule of Naturalization, and uniform Laws on the subject of Bankruptcies throughout the United States;

1. Prior to the new Constitution naturalization laws were different from state to state and the language of Article 4 of the current confederation is confusing according to Madison in Federalist 42.

- **NATURALIZATION-** The act of investing an alien with the rights and privileges of a native subject or citizen. Naturalization in Great Britain is only by act of parliament. In the United States, it is by act of Congress, vesting certain tribunals with the power. (Webster 1828)

- **BANK'RUPTCY-** The state of being a bankrupt, or insolvent; inability to pay all debts. (Webster 1828)

(5) To coin Money, regulate the Value thereof, and of foreign Coin, and fix the Standard of Weights and Measures;

1. **"To coin money"-** Webster's 1828 definition of the words "coin" and "money" are enlightening as to what the founders and people of early America viewed as money.

COIN- Primarily, the die employed for stamping money. Hence,

1. Money stamped; a piece of metal, as gold, silver, copper, or other metal, converted into money, by impressing on it marks, figures or characters. To make good money, these impressions must be made under the authority of government. That which is stamped without authority is called false or counterfeit coin. Formerly, all coin was made by hammering; but it is now impressed by a machine or mill.

Current coin is coin legally stamped and circulating in trade.

Ancient coins are chiefly those of the Jews, Greeks and Romans, which are kept in cabinets as curiosities.

2. In architecture, a kind of die cut diagonally, after the manner of a flight of a stair case, serving at bottom to support columns in a level, and at top to correct the inclination of an entablature supporting a vault.

3. That which serves for payment.

The loss of present advantage to flesh and blood is repaid in a nobler coin.

COIN, v.t.

1. To stamp a metal, and convert it into money; to mint.

- **MONEY:**

1. Coin; stamped metal; any piece of metal, usually gold, silver or copper, stamped by public authority, and used as the medium of commerce. We sometimes give the name of money to other coined metals, and to any other material which rude nations use a medium of trade. But among modern commercial nations, gold, silver and copper are the only metals used for this purpose. Gold and silver, containing great value in small compass, and being therefore of easy conveyance, and being also durable and little liable to diminution by use, are the most convenient metals for coin or money, which is the representative of commodities of all kinds, of lands, and of every thing that is capable of being transferred in commerce.

2. Bank notes or bills of credit issued by authority, and exchangeable for coin or redeemable, are also called money; as such notes in modern times represent coin, and are used as a substitute for it. If a man pays in hand for goods in bank notes which are current, he is said to pay in ready money.

- The First Secretary of the Treasury, Alexander Hamilton wrote concerning the subject of paper money and the constitution; "The emitting of paper money is wisely prohibited to the State Governments and the spirit of the prohibition ought not to be disregarded by the United States Government."[130]

- In Federalist 44 James Madison writes in detail on the evils of paper money as well as the States' right to coin their own money. Said he, "The loss which America has sustained since the peace, from the pestilent effects of paper money on the necessary confidence between man and man, on the necessary confidence in the public councils, on the industry and morals of the people, and on the character of republican government, constitutes an enormous debt against the States chargeable with this unadvised measure, which must long remain unsatisfied; or rather an accumulation of guilt which can be expiated no otherwise than by a voluntary sacrifice on the altar of justice of the power which has been the instrument of it."[131]

- Thomas Jefferson weighed in on money and said, "[Gold] is the most perfect medium because it will preserve its own level; because having intrinsic and universal value, it can never die in our hands... [Paper money] is liable to be abused, has been, is, and forever will be abused, in every country in which it is permitted."[132]

- Daniel Webster said, "Of all the contrivances for cheating the laboring classes of mankind, none has been found more effectual than that which deludes them with paper money."[133]

- As we can see from these quotations the founders recognized the ills of paper money. They had lived through inflation and saw the damage it inflicts. There are some among us today who recognize the evils of paper money and have fought to do something about it. Congressman Ron Paul has been an ardent advocate for a renewal of the gold standard and an elimination of the Federal Reserve for 30 years. The quotes here were taken from his booklet, *Gold, Peace, and Prosperity-The Birth of a New Currency.* He has written many other books on the subject s of economics, sound money, and the gold standard. His work, *End the Fed,* was a New York Times Bestseller. You and I are living through the evils of a fiat currency and endless inflation caused by an out of control government that prints to satisfy its global empire, wars, and welfare programs. A return to sound constitutional money such as that redeemable in gold or silver would put us on the path to prosperity.

2. **"fix the Standard of Weights and Measures"**- This should be a basic function of government as it will provide a uniform and standard practice throughout the country. A mandate for standard weights and measures goes back to the time of the Israelites:

> "You are to have honest balances, honest weights, an honest dry measure, and an honest liquid measure; I am Yahweh your God, who brought you out of the land of Egypt." Lev 19:36 HCSB

(6) To provide for the Punishment of counterfeiting the Securities and current Coin of the United States;

1. This is one of only three crimes that the federal government is given the power to punish by the Constitution. The others being treason and piracy. Can anyone explain why we have a DEA, FBI, ATF, DHS, Marshal Service, ICE, etc.? Recall that Madison told us in Federalist 45 that it was within the authority of the states to maintain "internal order".[134] Civilian law enforcement was not intended to be a function of the federal government. According to a report by the Heritage Foundation in 2010 there were approx. 4,500 crimes listed in the federal code!![135]

(7) To establish Post Offices and post Roads;

(8) To promote the Progress of Science and useful Arts, by securing for limited Times to Authors and Inventors the exclusive Right to their respective Writings and Discoveries;

(9) To constitute Tribunals inferior to the supreme Court;

(10) To define and punish Piracies and Felonies committed on the high Seas, and Offences against the Law of Nations;

1. **Laws of nations-** the rules that regulate the mutual intercourse of nations or states. These rules depend on natural law, or the principles of justice which spring from the social state; or they are founded on customs, compacts, treaties, leagues and agreements between independent communities.

By the law of nations, we are to understand that code of public instruction, which defines the rights and prescribes the duties of nations, in their intercourse with each other. (Webster 1828)

(11) To declare War, grant Letters of Marque and Reprisal, and make Rules concerning Captures on Land and Water;

1. **"To declare War"**- This power was given to Congress, not the Executive. Interestingly, in the Constitutional system the decision for declaring war is placed in a large body of elected representatives, rather than one man or a small group of men. This adheres to biblical teachings on declaring war:

- Proverbs 20:18- Finalize plans with counsel, and wage war with sound guidance. (HCSB)

- Proverbs 24:5-6 A wise warrior is better than a strong one, and a man of knowledge than one of strength; for you should wage war with sound guidance — victory comes with many counselors. (HCSB)

- Madison discussed war powers in Federalist 41 and said, "Security against foreign danger is one of the primitive objects of civil society. It is an avowed and essential object of the American Union. The powers requisite for attaining it must be effectually confided to the federal councils."[136]

- America has not had a constitutionally declared war since WWII. This should outrage every American because we are involved in numerous conflicts around the world at the expense of precious blood and treasure! If our elected representatives do not uphold their oath to support and defend the Constitution then they do not deserve to be in office. If a congressman, senator, or president sends troops off to fight without a declaration of war from congress they are violating their oath of office!

2. **"grant letters of Marque and Reprisal"**- The Webster's 1913 edition has a substantive definition of the term, *marque*:

A license to pass the limits of a jurisdiction, or boundary of a country, for the purpose of making reprisals.

Letters of marque, **Letters of marque and reprisal**, a license or extraordinary commission granted by a government to a private person to fit out a privateer or armed ship to cruise at sea and make prize of the enemy's ships and merchandise. The ship so commissioned is sometimes called a *letter of marque*.

- Interestingly this constitutional tool was revived by Congressman Ron Paul when he proposed legislation authorizing the President to issue Letters of Marque and Reprisal to respond to the September 11th attack instead of an unconstitutional military engagement.*

(12) To raise and support Armies, but no Appropriation of Money to that Use shall be for a longer Term than two Years;

1. Madison cites the two year limit on military appropriations in Federalist 41, as being a precaution against the dangers presented from standing armies.[137]

(13) To provide and maintain a Navy;

1. Said Madison in Federalist 41, "It must, indeed, be numbered among the greatest blessings of America that as her Union will be the only source of her maritime strength, so this will be a principle source of her security against danger from abroad. In this respect our situation bears another likeness to the insular advantage of Great Britain. The batteries most capable of repelling foreign enterprises on our safety are happily such as can never be turned by a perfidious government against our liberties."[138]

2. A navy was looked upon as the main component of our national defense. Our troubles would come from the sea as we were not under imminent threat from land invasion at the time. While leery of a standing army, the founders were in favor of a strong navy because, as Madison indicates, those batteries would not be used against our liberties because they were stationed in the water.

(14) To make Rules for the Government and Regulation of the land and naval Forces;

(15) To provide for calling forth the Militia to execute the Laws of the Union, suppress Insurrections and repel Invasions;

1. Recall that prior to independence the colonies had been subjected to standing armies among them for 10 years. The 11th indictment in the Declaration of Independence identifies this as a grievance against the king. Cognizant of the dangers of having standing armies the framers of the Constitution built a military system that would provide for the national defense and not impede on the liberties of the American people.

2. **MILI'TIA-** The body of soldiers in a state enrolled for discipline, but not engaged in actual service except in emergencies; as distinguished from regular troops, whose sole occupation is war or military service. The militia of a country are the able bodied men organized into companies, regiments and brigades, with officers of all grades, and required by law to attend military exercises on certain days only, but at other times left to pursue their usual occupations. (Webster 1828)

3. From Webster's definition above we see that a militia is not a formal standing army in full time service. A militia is comprised of able bodied men from the states. A true volunteer force! This was the founders' infantry and fighting force. One that could be called upon at a moment's notice, through power given to Congress, but one that was under the leadership of officers appointed by the states (see next enumerated power). The framers built a system of separation of powers into

the military, which would work toward protecting the liberties of Americans and preventing tyranny or military coup and dictatorship. A volunteer force such as this is not built for military adventurism and, as John Quincy Adams put it, "would surely not go abroad in search of monsters to destroy."[139]

(16) To provide for organizing, arming, and disciplining, the Militia, and for governing such Part of them as may be employed in the Service of the United States, reserving to the States respectively, the Appointment of the Officers, and the Authority of training the Militia according to the discipline prescribed by Congress;

1. According to Hamilton, in Federalist 29 it was crucial for the national government to have authority over the regulation of the militia, which would construct the system of discipline and organization. Otherwise you may have 13 different armies trying to coordinate on the field of battle. Chaos and disorganization could ensue. Hamilton also pointed out that a well-trained citizen militia is a check against standing armies and a check in favor of the defense of liberties. Said he,

> "It will be possible to have an excellent body of well-trained militia ready to take the field whenever the defense of the State shall require it. This will not only lessen the call for military establishments, but if circumstances should at any time oblige the government to form an army of any magnitude that army can never be formidable to the liberties of the people while there is a large body of citizens, little if at all inferior to them in discipline and the use of arms, who stand ready to defend their own rights and those of their fellow citizens. This appears to me the only substitute that can be devised for a standing army, and the best possible security against it, if it should exist."[140]

(17) To exercise exclusive Legislation in all Cases whatsoever, over such District (not exceeding ten Miles square) as may, by Cession of particular States, and the Acceptance of Congress, become the Seat of the Government of the United States, and to exercise like Authority over all Places purchased by the Consent of the Legislature of the State in which the Same shall be, for the Erection of Forts, Magazines, Arsenals, dock-Yards, and other needful Buildings;--And

1. **"To exercise exclusive Legislation in all Cases whatsoever"**- Congress has exclusive power to make and enforce law in the geographical area of Washington DC and on federally owned property. Here are the definitions from Webster:

- **EXCLU'SIVE-** Having the power of preventing entrance; as exclusive bars.

1. Debarring from participation; possessed and enjoyed to the exclusion of others; as an exclusive privilege.

- **LEGISLA'TION-** The act of passing a law or laws; the enacting of laws. (Webster 1828)

2. While Congress does have exclusive legislative authority over the district, a local municipal government is established based on elections by the residents of the district, however the local government could be abolished at any time by Congress. Madison discusses this in Federalist 43.

(18) To make all Laws which shall be necessary and proper for carrying into Execution the foregoing Powers, and all other Powers vested by this Constitution in the Government of the United States, or in any Department or Officer thereof.

1. Known as the necessary and proper clause or elastic clause. In Federalist 33 Hamilton reports that this clause was referred to as the "sweeping clause" in their day. He believed that, "the danger which most threatens our political welfare is that the State governments will finally sap the foundations of the Union" and those at the convention "might therefore think it necessary, in so cardinal a point, to leave nothing to construction."[141] The federal government had to have supremacy in certain enumerated areas, otherwise the new government would be no better or beneficial than the government that existed under the Articles of Confederation.

2. Any laws passed by Congress outside of the "foregoing Powers" would be unconstitutional. Art. 6, Section 2 affirms that the Laws made "in Pursuance of" the Constitution will be the Supreme Law of the Land. Hamilton continued in Federalist 33, " If the federal government should overpass the just bounds of its authority and make a tyrannical use of its powers, the people, whose creature it is, must appeal to the standard they have formed, and take such measures to redress the injury done to the Constitution as the exigency may suggest and prudence justify."[142]

Section 9.

- Whereas Section 8 defined what the federal government can do by way of specific enumerated or delegated powers, Section 9 enumerates specific things that the federal government cannot do.

(1) The Migration or Importation of such Persons as any of the States now existing shall think proper to admit, shall not be prohibited by the Congress prior to the Year one thousand eight hundred and eight, but a Tax or duty may be imposed on such Importation, not exceeding ten dollars for each Person.

1. The words slave and slavery are not found in the Constitution, however this clause deals with the issue. A contentious topic, for obvious reasons, the subject of slavery was debated at the convention. George Mason, a Virginia delegate, planter, and owner of slaves, was an abolitionist and said, "I hold it essential in every point that the general government should have power to prevent the increase of slavery."[143] John Dickinson, another anti-slavery man, "considered it as inadmissible on every principle of honor and safety that the importation of slaves should be authorized to the states by the Constitution. The true question was whether the national happiness would be promoted or impeded by the importation,

and this question ought to be left to the national government, not to the states particularly interested."[144]

2. According to Professor Richard Beeman, it was Georgia and South Carolina who were insistent that no legislation interfering with the slave trade be enacted for twenty years.[145] John Rutledge, of South Carolina, indicated at the convention that the true question was "whether the Southern states shall or shall not be parties to the Union."[146]

3. If slavery was left under the control of the states individually it could continue perpetually in states such as Georgia or South Carolina, and could possibly extend to new states that came into the Union. This section of the Constitution, while written as a prohibition on government authority, actually places another enumerated power in the hands of the federal government. Authority for regulation would fall under federal jurisdiction but it would not be able to restrict the practice until 1808.

4. In Federalist 42 Madison defends the Constitution in this area and poses that "It ought to be considered as a great point gained in favor of humanity that a period of twenty years may terminate forever, within these States, a traffic which has so long and so loudly upbraided the barbarism of modern policy; that within that period it will receive a considerable discouragement from the federal government and may be totally abolished, by a concurrence of the few states which continue the unnatural traffic in the prohibitory example which has been given by so great a majority of the Union."[147]

(2) The Privilege of the Writ of Habeas Corpus shall not be suspended, unless when in Cases of Rebellion or Invasion the public Safety may require it.

1. Habeas Corpus: [Latin "you should have the body"] A writ employed to bring a person before a court, most frequently to ensure that the party's imprisonment is not illegal. (Black's Law Dictionary 1996 Pocket Ed.)

2. Hamilton, while writing on this subject in Federalist 84, recites a quote from Blackstone and his Commentaries, "To bereave a man of life or by violence to confiscate his estate, without accusation or trial, would be so gross and notorious an act of despotism as must at once convey the alarm of tyranny throughout the whole nation; but confinement of the person, by secretly hurrying him to jail, where his sufferings are unknown or forgotten, is a less public, a less striking, and therefore a more dangerous engine of arbitrary government." Blackstone had also referred to the habeas corpus act (1679) as "the bulwark of the British Constitution."[148]

2. Habeas Corpus is an unalienable and essential right of all men, especially, as Blackstone points out, the forgotten man.

3. On Dec 31, 2011 President Barack Obama signed the 2012 National Defense Authorization Act. This is a military funding bill that makes for a great constitutional case study, as it shows how the Constitution has been destroyed by the current national government. This is a military funding bill but unfortunately, like most bills

in Washington DC, it has numerous other items attached that become law as well. The NDAA bill is actually 565 pages long. Very scary when you consider that the original Constitution is four pages in length! Contained within this NDAA bill is a provision (section 1021*) that abolishes the writ of habeas corpus for American citizens, who can now be arrested on American soil by military troops (violation of posse comitatus) and be detained without charge or trial. And this is based on an Authorization for Use of Military Force that was passed after the 9/11 attacks, not on a congressionally declared war, as required by the Constitution. As Blackstone indicated, this is indeed a "dangerous engine of arbitrary government."

I urge you to research how your congressional representatives voted on this legislation. It is a good measure of how they view the Constitution, their oath to the Constitution, and Liberty in general.

(3) No Bill of Attainder or ex post facto Law shall be passed.

- **ATTA'INDER:**

1. Literally a staining, corruption, or rendering impure; a corruption of blood. Hence,

2. The judgment of death, or sentence of a competent tribunal upon a person convicted of treason or felony, which judgment attaints, taints or corrupts his blood, so that he can no longer inherit lands. The consequences of this judgment are, forfeiture of lands, tenements and hereditaments, loss of reputation, and disqualification to be a witness in any court of law. A statute of Parliament attainting a criminal, is called an act of attainder.

Upon the thorough demonstration of which guilt by legal attainder, the feudal covenant is broken. -Blackstone

Note. By the constitution of the United States, no crime words an attainder. (Webster 1828)

- **ex post facto law -** A law passed after an action in order to retroactively change the legal treatment of the action to the disadvantage of the actor. (Black's Law Dictionary)

(4) No Capitation, or other direct, Tax shall be laid, unless in Proportion to the Census or enumeration herein before directed to be taken.

1. **"No Capitation"** - A tax, or imposition upon each head or person; a poll-tax. Sometimes written Capitation-tax. (Webster 1828)

- Hamilton discussed poll taxes in federalist 36. He said:

"As to poll taxes, I, without scruple, confess my disapprobation of them; and though they have prevailed from an early period in these States (he is referring to New England) which have uniformly been the most tenacious of their rights, I should lament to see them introduced into practice under the national government."[149]

2. **"or other direct, Tax"-** According to Hamilton, direct taxes would include taxes on land and buildings, as well as, capitation taxes or poll taxes. In Federalist 21 Hamilton discusses direct taxes and the method of collection, "Those of the direct kind, which principally relate to land and buildings, may admit of a rule of apportionment. Either the value of land, or the number of the people, may serve as a standard."[150]

3. While the federal government was given the power of taxation in broad terms (internal and external, direct and indirect), Art 1, Sec 8, Clause 1 required indirect taxes to be "uniform" throughout the States and now in Art 1, Sec 9 taxes of the direct kind are being tied to the census or enumeration.

4. The first direct tax was assessed by Congress in July 1798, during the administration of President John Adams. The money, two million dollars, was needed for a military buildup due to the looming potential for war with France. This federal direct tax was to be levied on land, dwellings, and slaves.[151] It was a tax as Hamilton had described in Federalist 21, with each state being assessed a portion of the two million dollars. The state would then be responsible for collecting its portion through valuation of land and property as described in the statute passed by Congress. Once the two million dollars was collected by the federal government the tax would be complete. The founders' original intent for taxation was very different than what we are subjected to today by the national government, which directly taxes the individual on a continuous basis (income, social security, Medicare). A limited government with limited authority and power will have a limited appetite for revenue. A government that knows no spending boundary will have a limitless appetite.

(5) No Tax or Duty shall be laid on Articles exported from any State.

(6) No Preference shall be given by any Regulation of Commerce or Revenue to the Ports of one State over those of another; nor shall Vessels bound to, or from, one State, be obliged to enter, clear, or pay Duties in another.

(7) No Money shall be drawn from the Treasury, but in Consequence of Appropriations made by Law; and a regular Statement and Account of the Receipts and Expenditures of all public Money shall be published from time to time.

(8) No Title of Nobility shall be granted by the United States: And no Person holding any Office of Profit or Trust under them, shall, without the Consent of the Congress, accept of any present, Emolument, Office, or Title, of any kind whatever, from any King, Prince, or foreign State.

1. **"No Title of Nobility shall be granted by the United States"-** In Federalist 84 Hamilton describes this as the cornerstone of republican government, "for so long as they are excluded there can never be serious danger that the government will be any other than that of the people."[152]

Section 10.

- This section identifies the restrictions on state power. They are few indeed! Madison's identification of the magnitude of state sovereignty and power is worth repeating here; in Federalist 45 he said, "The powers delegated by the proposed Constitution to the federal government are few and defined. Those which are to remain in the State governments are numerous and indefinite." Madison spends much of Federalist 44 dealing with this section of the Constitution.

(1) No State shall enter into any Treaty, Alliance, or Confederation; grant Letters of Marque and Reprisal; coin Money; emit Bills of Credit; make any Thing but gold and silver Coin a Tender in Payment of Debts; pass any Bill of Attainder, ex post facto Law, or Law impairing the Obligation of Contracts, or grant any Title of Nobility.

1. **No State shall "coin money"**- Under the Articles of Confederation the States had power to coin money. Madison notes that in taking this power from the States the framers have improved upon the old system. He said further, "Whilst the alloy and value depended on the general authority, a right of coinage in the particular States could have no other effect than to multiply expensive mints and diversify the forms and weights of the circulating pieces."

2. **No State shall "emit Bills of Credit; make any Thing but gold and silver Coin a Tender in Payment of Debts"**- Inflation had ravaged the colonies due to expansion of the money supply in the states, which all printed their own paper. See Article 1, Section 8, Clause 5

(2) No State shall, without the Consent of the Congress, lay any Imposts or Duties on Imports or Exports, except what may be absolutely necessary for executing it's inspection Laws: and the net Produce of all Duties and Imposts, laid by any State on Imports or Exports, shall be for the Use of the Treasury of the United States; and all such Laws shall be subject to the Revision and Controul of the Congress.

(3) No State shall, without the Consent of Congress, lay any Duty of Tonnage, keep Troops, or Ships of War in time of Peace, enter into any Agreement or Compact with another State, or with a foreign Power, or engage in War, unless actually invaded, or in such imminent Danger as will not admit of delay.

Article II

Section 1

(1) The executive Power shall be vested in a President of the United States of America. He shall hold his Office during the Term of four Years, and, together with the Vice President, chosen for the same Term, be elected, as follows:

(2) Each State shall appoint, in such Manner as the Legislature thereof may direct, a Number of Electors, equal to the whole Number of Senators and Representatives to which the State may be entitled in the Congress: but no Senator or Representative, or Person holding an Office of Trust or Profit under the United States, shall be appointed an Elector.

1. **ELECT'OR-** One who elects, or one who has the right of choice; a person who has, by law or constitution, the right of voting for an officer. In free governments, the people or such of them as possess certain qualifications of age, character and property, are the electors of their representatives, &c., in parliament, assembly, or other legislative body. In the United States, certain persons are appointed or chosen to be electors of the president or chief magistrate. In Germany, certain princes were formerly electors of the emperor, and elector was one of their titles, as the elector of Saxony. (Webster 1828)

2. The original intent of the Constitutional framers was not for a popular election of the president by the people at large, but rather by an "electoral college", comprised of men (at that time) chosen to be electors, according to the manner of each state legislature. Madison identifies this method of electing the president as another guarantee of States' rights and sovereignty, which is consistent with a republican form of government. In Federalist 45 Madison states;

> "The State governments may be regarded as constituent and essential parts of the federal government; whilst the latter is nowise essential to the operation or organization of the former. Without the intervention of the State legislatures, the President of the United States cannot be elected at all. They must in all cases have a great share in his appointment, and will, perhaps in most cases, of themselves determine it. The Senate will be elected absolutely and exclusively by the State legislatures. Even the House of Representatives, though drawn immediately from the people, will be chosen very much under the influence of that class of men whose influence over the people obtains for themselves an election into the State legislatures. Thus, each of the principal branches of the federal government will owe its existence more or less to the favor of the State governments, and must consequently feel a dependence, which is much more likely to beget a disposition too obsequious than too overbearing towards them."

3. John Jay, in Federalist 64, discusses at length, why the framers intended for the President to be elected by an assembly of electors, rather than a direct popular vote;

> "As the select assemblies for choosing the President, as well as the State legislatures who appoint the senators, will in general be composed of the most enlightened and respectable citizens, there is reason to presume that their attention and their votes will be directed to those men only who have become the most **distinguished by their abilities and virtue**, and in whom the people perceive just grounds for confidence."[154]

- Jay then described the relationship between the citizen and the elector. He said that the electors will be men "whom the people have had time to form a judgment, and with respect to whom they will not be liable to be deceived by those brilliant appearances of genius and patriotism which, like transient meteors, sometimes mislead as well as dazzle."[155]

4. Professor Beeman points out that the election of 1800 basically turned the electoral college system, as designed, by the framers, on its head. This was due to the organization of political parties, which at that time consisted of Federalists, who supported John Adams, and Republicans, who supported Thomas Jefferson. Now electors were pledging to support a candidate based on his party affiliation.[156]

(3) The Electors shall meet in their respective States, and vote by Ballot for two Persons, of whom one at least shall not be an Inhabitant of the same State with themselves. And they shall make a List of all the Persons voted for, and of the Number of Votes for each; which List they shall sign and certify, and transmit sealed to the Seat of the Government of the United States, directed to the President of the Senate. The President of the Senate shall, in the Presence of the Senate and House of Representatives, open all the Certificates, and the Votes shall then be counted. The Person having the greatest Number of Votes shall be the President, if such Number be a Majority of the whole Number of Electors appointed; and if there be more than one who have such Majority, and have an equal Number of Votes, then the House of Representatives shall immediately chuse by Ballot one of them for President; and if no Person have a Majority, then from the five highest on the List the said House shall in like Manner chuse the President. But in chusing the President, the Votes shall be taken by States, the Representation from each State having one Vote; A quorum for this purpose shall consist of a Member or Members from two thirds of the States, and a Majority of all the States shall be necessary to a Choice. In every Case, after the Choice of the President, the Person having the greatest Number of Votes of the Electors shall be the Vice President. But if there should remain two or more who have equal Votes, the Senate shall chuse from them by Ballot the Vice President.

(4) The Congress may determine the Time of chusing the Electors, and the Day on which they shall give their Votes; which Day shall be the same throughout the United States.

(5) No Person except a natural born Citizen, or a Citizen of the United States, at the time of the Adoption of this Constitution, shall be eligible to the Office of President; neither shall any Person be eligible to that Office who shall not have attained to the Age of thirty five Years, and been fourteen Years a Resident within the United States.

1. **"No Person except a natural born Citizen"**- Representative John Bingham was the primary author of the 14th Amendment and had this to say concerning the term *natural born citizen*;

"All from other lands, who by the terms of your laws and a compliance with their provisions become naturalized, are adopted citizens of the United States; all other persons born within the Republic, of parents owing allegiance to no other sovereignty, are natural born citizens. Gentlemen can find no exception to this statement touching natural-born citizens except what is said in the Constitution relating to Indians."[157]

- Bingham also said, "Every human being born within the jurisdiction of the United States of parents not owing allegiance to any foreign sovereignty is, in the language of your Constitution itself, a natural born citizen."[158]

- Swiss jurist Emmerich de Vattel, in his 1758 work, *The Law of Nations or the Principles of Natural Law,* defined natural born citizen as such, "The citizens are the members of the civil society; bound to this society by certain duties, and subject to its authority, they equally participate in its advantages. The natives, or natural-born citizens, are those born in the country, of parents who are citizens. As the society cannot exist and perpetuate itself otherwise than by the children of the citizens, those children naturally follow the condition of their fathers, and succeed to all their rights. The society is supposed to desire this, in consequence of what it owes to its own preservation; and it is presumed, as a matter of course, that each citizen, on entering into society, reserves to his children the right of becoming members of it. The country of the fathers is therefore that of the children; and these become true citizens merely by their tacit consent. We shall soon see whether, on their coming to the years of discretion, they may renounce their right, and what they owe to the society in which they were born. I say, that, in order to be of the country, it is necessary that a person be born of a father who is a citizen; for, if he is born there of a foreigner, it will be only the place of his birth, and not his country."[159]

- Vattel's work was highly influential on the American founders during the struggle for independence and the formation of our system of government. *The Law of Nations* appears to have first made its way to America in 1775 when Charles Dumas sent Benjamin Franklin three copies from Europe. Franklin responded to Dumas, "It came to us in good season, when the circumstances of a rising State make it necessary frequently to consult the Law of Nations."[160] Albert de Lapradelle states in the Introduction to the 1916 edition of Law of Nations, "In the United States the authority of Vattel is at least as great as in England. From the day when, thanks to the parcel sent by Dumas to Franklin, Vattel made his entrance into American libraries, he was followed as the most competent, the wisest, and the safest guide, in all the discussions of Congress, in all the trials in court, and in diplomatic correspondence, especially that concerned with questions of legality."[161] If Vattel's work was substantive enough for the founders to establish a system of government upon, shouldn't his work be a trusted guide for us today, especially when it comes to the important matter of electing presidents?

2. The current president, Barack Hussein Obama, was reportedly born in Hawaii in 1961 to an American mother, while his father was reported to be a Kenyan national named Barack Obama Sr. This man was elected president of the United States by a majority of those who voted and it appears that he is constitutionally ineligible to be president because he does not meet the qualifications of a natural born citizen. Interestingly, there is a rising star in the Republican Party who may have presidential aspirations. Marco Rubio was elected to the US Senate in 2010. While he is eligible to be a Senator it seems that he does not fit the eligibility requirements of the Constitution to be President. Rubio's parents were Cuban citizens at the time of his birth, which means he does not fit the definition of a natural born citizen.[162]

(6) In Case of the Removal of the President from Office, or of his Death, Resignation, or Inability to discharge the Powers and Duties of the said Office, the Same shall devolve on the Vice President, and the Congress may by Law provide for the Case of Removal, Death, Resignation or Inability, both of the President and Vice President, declaring what Officer shall then act as President, and such Officer shall act accordingly, until the Disability be removed, or a President shall be elected.

(7) The President shall, at stated Times, receive for his Services, a Compensation, which shall neither be increased nor diminished during the Period for which he shall have been elected, and he shall not receive within that Period any other Emolument from the United States, or any of them.

(8) Before he enter on the Execution of his Office, he shall take the following Oath or Affirmation:--"I do solemnly swear (or affirm) that I will faithfully execute the Office of President of the United States, and will to the best of my Ability, preserve, protect and defend the Constitution of the United States."

1. On April 30, 1789 George Washington took the oath of office and added the words, "So help me God" at the end.[163]

Section 2

(1) The President shall be Commander in Chief of the Army and Navy of the United States, and of the Militia of the several States, when called into the actual Service of the United States; he may require the Opinion, in writing, of the principal Officer in each of the executive Departments, upon any Subject relating to the Duties of their respective Offices, and he shall have Power to grant Reprieves and Pardons for Offences against the United States, except in Cases of Impeachment.

1. Under the principle of separation of powers we see that the Congress has the authority to declare war, while it is the President who is given the authority to manage it once declared. Hamilton explains why there is need for a single Commander-in-Chief in Federalist 74;

> "Of all the cares and concerns of government, the direction of war most peculiarly demands those qualities which distinguish the exercise of power by a single hand. The direction of war implies the direction of the common strength; and the power of directing and employing the common strength forms a usual and essential part in the definition of the executive authority."[164]

(2) He shall have Power, by and with the Advice and Consent of the Senate, to make Treaties, provided two thirds of the Senators present concur; and he shall nominate, and by and with the Advice and Consent of the Senate, shall appoint Ambassadors, other public Ministers and Consuls, Judges of the supreme Court, and all other Officers of the United States, whose Appointments are not herein otherwise provided for, and which shall be established by Law: but the Congress may by Law vest the Appointment of such inferior Officers, as they think proper, in the President alone, in the Courts of Law, or in the Heads of Departments.

(3) The President shall have Power to fill up all Vacancies that may happen during the Recess of the Senate, by granting Commissions which shall expire at the End of their next Session.

Section 3

He shall from time to time give to the Congress Information of the State of the Union, and recommend to their Consideration such Measures as he shall judge necessary and expedient; he may, on extraordinary Occasions, convene both Houses, or either of them, and in Case of Disagreement between them, with Respect to the Time of Adjournment, he may adjourn them to such Time as he shall think proper; he shall receive Ambassadors and other public Ministers; he shall take Care that the Laws be faithfully executed, and shall Commission all the Officers of the United States.

Section 4

The President, Vice President and all civil Officers of the United States, shall be removed from Office on Impeachment for, and Conviction of, Treason, Bribery, or other high Crimes and Misdemeanors.

1. Not only can the President and Vice President be impeached, but civil Officers of the United States can as well. This would apparently apply to high ranking officials within the government, such as cabinet members.

Article III

- Alexander Hamilton discusses the judiciary, its authority, and its design at length in Federalist Papers' 78-83. Interestingly, he states that "the judiciary is beyond comparison the weakest of the three departments of power" and that "the judiciary, from the nature of its functions, will always be the least dangerous to the political rights of the Constitution."[165] In summarizing the extent of authority of the federal judiciary Hamilton states, "It may truly be said to have neither FORCE nor WILL but merely judgment."[166] This view of the strength, or possibly more appropriately, of its weakness, certainly seems a contradiction to the federal judiciary as we know it today. The cries of judicial activism and of legislating from the bench are heard from coast to coast.

-It is also interesting to note that Article III does not identify how many Supreme Court justices are to be on the bench.

Section 1

(1) The judicial Power of the United States shall be vested in one supreme Court, and in such inferior Courts as the Congress may from time to time ordain and establish. The Judges, both of the supreme and inferior Courts, shall hold their Offices during good Behaviour, and

shall, at stated Times, receive for their Services a Compensation, which shall not be diminished during their Continuance in Office.

1. **"shall hold their Offices during good Behaviour"**- Hamilton addresses the subject of judicial tenure in Federalist 78. He states that permanency in office contributes to the firmness and independence of the judiciary and may be "justly regarded as an indispensable ingredient in its constitution, and, in a great measure, as the citadel of the public justice and the public security."[167] Hamilton also notes that holding office during "good Behaviour" is conformable to the constitutions of several states.

- Hamilton also maintains that judges who hold their offices by temporary commission could not be expected to maintain an "inflexible and uniform adherence to the rights of the Constitution, and of individuals", which are perceived to be indispensable in courts of justice.[168]

2. **"receive for their Services a Compensation, which shall not be diminished during their Continuance in Office"**- In Federalist 79 Hamilton states, "we can never hope to see realized in practice the complete separation of the judicial from the legislative power, in any system which leaves the former dependent for pecuniary resources on the occasional grants of the latter."[169] A judge who is sure in his livelihood "may be sure of the ground upon which he stands, and can never be deterred from his duty by the apprehension of being placed in a less eligible situation."[170]

3. In Federalist 79 Hamilton also indicates that the possibility of being impeached for malconduct should serve to maintain their independence and good behavior. Only one Supreme Court Justice has ever been impeached. Samuel Chase, a signer of the Declaration of Independence, was impeached in 1804, but at his trial in 1805 he was acquitted by the Senate and continued to serve on the court until his death. The judicial legislation of today begs the question, why have there been no impeachments of Supreme Court Justices in modern times?

Section. 2.

(1) The judicial Power shall extend to all Cases, in Law and Equity, arising under this Constitution, the Laws of the United States, and Treaties made, or which shall be made, under their Authority;--to all Cases affecting Ambassadors, other public Ministers and Consuls;--to all Cases of admiralty and maritime Jurisdiction;--to Controversies to which the United States shall be a Party;--to Controversies between two or more States;-- between a State and Citizens of another State,--between Citizens of different States,--between Citizens of the same State claiming Lands under Grants of different States, and between a State, or the Citizens thereof, and foreign States, Citizens or Subjects.

1. According to Hamilton, in Federalist 80, this clause "constitutes the entire mass of the judicial authority of the Union."[171]

2. This clause identifies eleven areas of federal jurisdiction. Two of these were eliminated by passage of the 11th Amendment (1. between a State and Citizens of another State, 2. between a State, or the Citizens thereof, and foreign States, Citizens or Subjects)

3. There are three types of legal venue identified in this clause: law (statute or civil), equity (chancery), and admiralty.

-EQ'UITY:

1. Justice; right. In practice, equity is the impartial distribution of justice, or the doing that to another which the laws of God and man, and of reason, give him a right to claim. It is the treating of a person according to justice and reason.

The Lord shall judge the people with equity. Ps.98.

With righteousness shall he judge the poor, and reprove with equity. Is.11.

2. Justice; impartiality; a just regard to right or claim; as, we must, in equity, allow this claim.

3. In law, an equitable claim. "I consider the wife's equity to be too well settled to be shaken."

4. In jurisprudence, the correction or qualification of law, when too severe or defective; or the extension of the words of the law to cases not expressed, yet coming within the reason of the law. Hence a court of equity or chancery, is a court which corrects the operation of the literal text of the law, and supplies its defects, by reasonable construction, and by rules of proceeding and deciding, which are not admissible in a court of law. Equity then is the law of reason, exercised by the chancellor or judge, giving remedy in cases to which the courts of law are not competent. (Webster 1828)

-AD'MIRALTY- In Great Britain, the office of Lord High Admiral. This office is discharged by one person, or by Commissioners, called Lords of the Admiralty; usually seven in number.

The admiralty court, or court of admiralty, is the supreme court for the trial of maritime causes, held before the Lord High Admiral, or Lords of the admiralty.

In general, a court of admiralty is a court for the trial of causes arising on the high seas, as prize causes and the like. In the United States, there is no admiralty court, distinct from others; but the district courts, established in the several states by Congress, are invested with admiralty powers. (Webster 1828)

(2) In all Cases affecting Ambassadors, other public Ministers and Consuls, and those in which a State shall be Party, the supreme Court shall have original Jurisdiction. In all the other Cases before mentioned, the supreme Court shall have appellate Jurisdiction, both as to Law and Fact, with such Exceptions, and under such Regulations as the Congress shall make.

1. Hamilton addresses this clause in Federalist 81. The Supreme Court's original jurisdiction is limited to two classes of cases and Hamilton describes these two cases as "of a nature rarely to occur."

(3) The Trial of all Crimes, except in Cases of Impeachment, shall be by Jury; and such Trial shall be held in the State where the said Crimes shall have been committed; but when not committed within any State, the Trial shall be at such Place or Places as the Congress may by Law have directed.

Section. 3.

(1) Treason against the United States, shall consist only in levying War against them, or in adhering to their Enemies, giving them Aid and Comfort. No Person shall be convicted of Treason unless on the Testimony of two Witnesses to the same overt Act, or on Confession in open Court.

1. Treason is the only crime that is defined by the framers within the body of the Constitution.

(2) The Congress shall have Power to declare the Punishment of Treason, but no Attainder of Treason shall work Corruption of Blood, or Forfeiture except during the Life of the Person attainted.

1. No **"Attainder of Treason"** will extend beyond the life of the person convicted for treason. This means essentially that the son cannot be punished for the sins of the father.

- ATTA'INDER:

1. Literally a staining, corruption, or rendering impure; a corruption of blood. Hence,

2. The judgment of death, or sentence of a competent tribunal upon a person convicted of treason or felony, which judgment attaints, taints or corrupts his blood, so that he can no longer inherit lands. The consequences of this judgment are, forfeiture of lands, tenements and hereditaments, loss of reputation, and disqualification to be a witness in any court of law. A statute of Parliament attainting a criminal, is called an act of attainder.

Upon the thorough demonstration of which guilt by legal attainder, the feudal covenant is broken.

3. The act of attainting.

An act was made for the attainder of several persons.

Note. By the constitution of the United States, no crime words an attainder. (Webster 1828)

- **CORRUPTION-** In law, taint; impurity of blood, in consequence of an act of attainder of treason or felony, by which a person is disabled to inherit lands from an ancestor, nor can retain those in his possession, nor transmit them by descent to his heirs.

Corruption of blood can be removed only by act of parliament. (Webster 1828)

Article IV

Section 1

Full Faith and Credit shall be given in each State to the public Acts, Records, and judicial Proceedings of every other State. And the Congress may by general Laws prescribe the Manner in which such Acts, Records and Proceedings shall be proved, and the Effect thereof.

Section 2

(1) The Citizens of each State shall be entitled to all Privileges and Immunities of Citizens in the several States.

(2) A Person charged in any State with Treason, Felony, or other Crime, who shall flee from Justice, and be found in another State, shall on Demand of the executive Authority of the State from which he fled, be delivered up, to be removed to the State having Jurisdiction of the Crime.

- This clause is establishing procedures for extradition of suspects from one state to another.

(3) No Person held to Service or Labour in one State, under the Laws thereof, escaping into another, shall, in Consequence of any Law or Regulation therein, be discharged from such Service or Labour, but shall be delivered up on Claim of the Party to whom such Service or Labour may be due.

Section 3

(1) New States may be admitted by the Congress into this Union; but no new State shall be formed or erected within the Jurisdiction of any other State; nor any State be formed by the Junction of two or more States, or Parts of States, without the Consent of the Legislatures of the States concerned as well as of the Congress.

(2) The Congress shall have Power to dispose of and make all needful Rules and Regulations respecting the Territory or other Property belonging to the United States; and nothing in this Constitution shall be so construed as to Prejudice any Claims of the United States, or of any particular State.

Section 4

The United States shall guarantee to every State in this Union a Republican Form of Government, and shall protect each of them against Invasion; and on Application of the Legislature, or of the Executive (when the Legislature cannot be convened), against domestic Violence.

1. **"The United States shall guarantee to every State in this Union a Republican Form of Government"**- We have discussed the terms *republic* and *republican* at other points in this study. Here in Art. 4, Sec. 4 we see that the framers are establishing for posterity that each STATE in this UNION will be GUARANTEED a REPUBLICAN form of government. This assertion contains a fundamental principle that needs to be observed and appreciated. The states are being referred to as a Union of United States (plural), which indicates that they are still sovereign bodies retaining powers not delegated to the federal government. They have not morphed into one contiguous nation state, like many today would like to believe. If the borders, language, culture, and sovereignty of the states were being thrown away for a single central nation state there would be no need for the framers to guarantee a Republican form of government to the individual states. We should look again at how James Madison defined a republic in Federalist 39:

> *" we may define a republic to be, or at least may bestow that name on, a government which derives all its powers directly or indirectly from the great body of the people, and is administered by persons holding their offices during pleasure for a limited period, or during good behavior. It is essential to such a government that it be derived from the great body of the society, not from an inconsiderable proportion or a favored class of it; otherwise a handful of tyrannical nobles, exercising their oppressions by a delegation of their powers, might aspire to the rank of republicans and claim for their government the honorable title of republic. It is sufficient for such a government that the persons administering it be appointed, either directly or indirectly, by the people; and that they hold their appointments by either of the tenures just*

specified; otherwise every government in the United States, as well as every other popular government that has been or can be well organized or well executed, would be degraded from the republican character."[172]

- Madison also identified why we must have a republican form of government:

"The first question that offers itself is whether the general form and aspect of the government be strictly republican. It is evident that no other form would be reconcilable with the genius of the people of America; with the fundamental principles of the Revolution; or with that honorable determination which animates every votary of freedom to rest all our political experiments on the capacity of mankind for self-government. If the plan of the convention, therefore, be found to depart from the republican character, its advocates must abandon it as no longer defensible."[173]

- In our day the term R.I.N.O. (Republican in name only) has been used to describe so-called phony conservatives that masquerade as members of the Republican Party. It sure looks as if these initials could also be used to describe what is masquerading as a government in Washington today, "Republic In Name Only". You and I need to change this and we can only accomplish it through expanding our knowledge of first principles and true American history. If we compared most people calling themselves republicans today to Thomas Jefferson they too would be RINO's.

2. **"and shall protect each of them against Invasion"**- Here again, we see the states being referred to as individual bodies by use of the word, each. The states, through the Constitution, are uniting together, and in this clause are mandating mutual protection.

Article V

The Congress, whenever two thirds of both Houses shall deem it necessary, shall propose Amendments to this Constitution, or, on the Application of the Legislatures of two thirds of the several States, shall call a Convention for proposing Amendments, which, in either Case, shall be valid to all Intents and Purposes, as Part of this Constitution, when ratified by the Legislatures of three fourths of the several States, or by Conventions in three fourths thereof, as the one or the other Mode of Ratification may be proposed by the Congress; Provided that no Amendment which may be made prior to the Year One thousand eight hundred and eight shall in any Manner affect the first and fourth Clauses in the Ninth Section of the first Article; and that no State, without its Consent, shall be deprived of its equal Suffrage in the Senate.

1. Proposed amendments can originate from Congress by a vote of two thirds of both houses, or they can originate from the States through a convention process

upon the Application of the legislatures of two thirds of the states. Ratification requires approval by three fourths of the state legislatures or conventions. One has to wonder how the 16th and 17th Amendments were ever passed! One has to wonder why there isn't an outcry to repeal these amendments throughout America!

Article VI

(1) All Debts contracted and Engagements entered into, before the Adoption of this Constitution, shall be as valid against the United States under this Constitution, as under the Confederation.

1. Joseph Andrews tells us in his Guide to Teaching the Constitution that a war debt of some $79 million dollars was owed to France and Holland as well as to the states and some citizens.[174] Madison points out in Federalist 43 that moral obligations, such as paying one's debts, have a tendency to disappear when governments change or come into existence. He states that this clause, "can only be considered a declaratory proposition; and may have been inserted, among other reasons, for the satisfaction of the foreign creditors of the United States, who cannot be strangers to the pretended doctrine that a change in the political form of civil society has the magical effect of dissolving its moral obligations."[175] As a new nation emerging on the scene it was in the best interests of the United States to honor existing debt obligations.

(2) This Constitution, and the Laws of the United States which shall be made in Pursuance thereof; and all Treaties made, or which shall be made, under the Authority of the United States, shall be the supreme Law of the Land; and the Judges in every State shall be bound thereby, any Thing in the Constitution or Laws of any State to the Contrary notwithstanding.

1. This is referred to as the Supremacy Clause

2. In Federalist 33 Hamilton indicates that the Supremacy Clause, along with the Necessary and Proper Clause (Art. 1, Sec. 8, last clause), "have been the source of much virulent invective and petulant declamation against the proposed Constitution."[176] As he challenges the detractors he defines the clause and establishes its boundaries;

> *"But it is said that the laws of the Union are to be the supreme law of the land. What inference can be drawn from this, or what would they amount to, if they were not to be supreme? It is evident they would amount to nothing. A LAW, by the very meaning of the term, includes supremacy. It is a rule which those to whom it is prescribed are bound to observe. This results from every political association. If individuals enter into a state of society the laws of that society must be the supreme regulator of their conduct. If a number of political societies enter into a larger political society, the laws which the latter may enact, pursuant to the powers intrusted to it by its constitution, must necessarily be supreme over those societies and the individuals of whom they are composed.*

It would otherwise be a mere treaty, dependent on the good faith of the parties, and not a government, which is only another word for POLITICAL POWER AND SUPREMACY.[177]

3. The Supremacy Clause is used regularly in our day to expand national reach into areas where there was no original delegated authority. The key to the Supremacy Clause is "made in Pursuance thereof". Laws made by Congress must be made in pursuance of the Constitution, which means that the laws made by Congress must be contained to within the limited sphere of power delegated to the national body. If laws crafted in Washington DC are outside the confines of the Constitution are they valid under the Supremacy Clause? If the framers and founding fathers were alive today I believe they would tell us no and I believe that rings true in their writings that are referenced in this work.

(3) The Senators and Representatives before mentioned, and the Members of the several State Legislatures, and all executive and judicial Officers, both of the United States and of the several States, shall be bound by Oath or Affirmation, to support this Constitution; but no religious Test shall ever be required as a Qualification to any Office or public Trust under the United States.

1. Madison asks why this clause is necessary in Federalist 44 and then answers his own question:

"It has been asked why it was thought necessary that the State magistracy should be bound to support the federal Constitution, and unnecessary that a like oath should be imposed on the officers of the United states in favor of the State constitutions."

'Several reasons might be assigned for the distinction. I content myself with one, which is obvious and conclusive. The members of the federal government will have no agency in carrying the State constitutions into effect. The members and officers of the State governments, on the contrary, will have an essential agency in giving effect to the federal Constitution. The election of the President and Senate will depend, in all cases, on the legislatures of the several States."[178]

Article VII

(1) The Ratification of the Conventions of nine States, shall be sufficient for the Establishment of this Constitution between the States so ratifying the Same.

1. In Federalist 39 Madison makes it clear that this Constitution is being ratified by the States, not individual people. "Each State, in ratifying the Constitution, is considered as a sovereign body independent of all others, and only to be bound by its own voluntary act. In this relation then, the new Constitution will, if established, be a *federal* and not a *national* constitution."[179]

2. In Federalist 40 Madison points out candidly that it would be absurd to subject the fate of twelve States "to the perverseness and corruption of a thirteenth." The framers had experience with the requirement of unanimous approval, as this is what was required for amending the Articles of Confederation. It did not work.

(2) The Word, "the," being interlined between the seventh and eighth Lines of the first Page, the Word "Thirty" being partly written on an Erazure in the fifteenth Line of the first Page, The Words "is tried" being interlined between the thirty second and thirty third Lines of the first Page and the Word "the" being interlined between the forty third and forty fourth Lines of the second Page.

Attest William Jackson Secretary

(3) Done in Convention by the Unanimous Consent of the States present the Seventeenth Day of September in the Year of our Lord one thousand seven hundred and Eighty seven and of the Independence of the United States of America the Twelfth In witness whereof We have hereunto subscribed our Names,

1. **"Unanimous Consent of the States present"** - As has been indicated previously Rhode Island did not participate in the Convention. So, while the vote was "unanimous", it was not "unanimously" consented to by all of the States on September 17, 1787.

2. **"Seventeenth Day of September in the Year of our Lord one thousand seven hundred and Eighty seven"**- This is another instance where God is mentioned in the Constitution. The men signing the document are saying that they are signing on this date in the year of "our" Lord. They are formally and officially affixing their signature to a document that will be esteemed by prosperity and they are referring to the Lord as "our" Lord. They are saying that He is their Lord. Are we left to assume that the framers carefully considered each and every word of this document except for those at the end?

G°. Washington
President *and deputy from Virginia*

Delaware
Geo: Read
Gunning Bedford jun
John Dickinson
Richard Bassett
Jaco: Broom

Maryland
James McHenry
Dan of St Thos. Jenifer
Danl. Carroll

Virginia
John Blair
James Madison Jr.

North Carolina
Wm. Blount
Richd. Dobbs Spaight
Hu Williamson

South Carolina
J. Rutledge
Charles Cotesworth Pinckney
Charles Pinckney
Pierce Butler

Georgia
William Few
Abr Baldwin

New Hampshire
John Langdon
Nicholas Gilman

Massachusetts
Nathaniel Gorham
Rufus King

Connecticut
Wm. Saml. Johnson
Roger Sherman

New York
Alexander Hamilton

New Jersey
Wil: Livingston
David Brearley
Wm. Paterson
Jona: Dayton

Pennsylvania
B Franklin
Thomas Mifflin
Robt. Morris
Geo. Clymer
Thos. FitzSimons
Jared Ingersoll
James Wilson
Gouv Morris

Bill of Rights

The Bill of Rights listed below is the original set of amendments that were proposed to the States by Congress on September 28, 1789. Seven states specifically identified a need for amendments to the Constitution and/or an addition of a bill of rights (Mass, SC, NH, VA, NY, NC, RI) in their ratification conventions and supporting documents that were sent back to Congress. On December 15, 1791 the States ratified articles 3-12 from the list below. We know these as our Bill of Rights.

Congress of the United States
begun and held at the City of New-York, on
Wednesday the fourth of March, one thousand seven hundred and eighty nine.

THE Conventions of a number of the States, having at the time of their adopting the Constitution, expressed a desire, in order to prevent misconstruction or abuse of its powers, that further declaratory and restrictive clauses should be added: And as extending the ground of public confidence in the Government, will best ensure the beneficent ends of its institution.

RESOLVED by the Senate and House of Representatives of the United States of America, in Congress assembled, two thirds of both Houses concurring, that the following Articles be proposed to the Legislatures of the several States, as Amendments to the Constitution of the United States, all, or any of which Articles, when ratified by three fourths of the said Legislatures, to be valid to all intents and purposes, as part of the said Constitution; viz.

ARTICLES in addition to, and Amendment of the Constitution of the United States of America, proposed by Congress, and ratified by the Legislatures of the several States, pursuant to the fifth Article of the original Constitution.

Article the first... After the first enumeration required by the first article of the Constitution, there shall be one Representative for every thirty thousand, until the number shall amount to one hundred, after which the proportion shall be so regulated by Congress, that there shall be not less than one hundred Representatives, nor less than one Representative for every forty thousand persons, until the number of Representatives shall amount to two hundred; after which the proportion shall be so regulated by Congress, that there shall not be less than two hundred Representatives, nor more than one Representative for every fifty thousand persons.

Article the second... No law, varying the compensation for the services of the Senators and Representatives, shall take effect, until an election of Representatives shall have intervened.

- This amendment was resurrected and ratified on May 7, 1992 as the 27th and most recent amendment to the Constitution.

1st ~~Article the third~~...

Congress shall make no law respecting an establishment of religion, or prohibiting the free exercise thereof; or abridging the freedom of speech, or of the press; or the right of the people peaceably to assemble, and to petition the Government for a redress of grievances.

1. There are five basic rights identified in this amendment; free exercise of religion, freedom of speech, press, assembly, and petition.

2. This amendment is directed specifically at the United States Congress.As we have learned any authority not specifically delegated to the new government would fall under the realm of the states and the people (Madison- Federalist 45). Constitutionally, matters of legislation dealing with these rights are left to the jurisdiction of the states.

3. **"Congress shall make no law respecting an establishment of religion, or prohibiting the free exercise thereof"**- This statement says what it means and means what it says. Congress has no authority to intervene, regulate, or impede religion and the "free exercise thereof".The framers were building a republic where there would be no national church as there was in England.

Now may be a good time to venture into the arena of religion in America. First we will explore what the founders thought of religion. Some quotes will shed light on their views:

George Washington identified the importance of religion and morality in his Farewell Address* in 1796:

> *"Of all the dispositions and habits which lead to political prosperity, religion and morality are indispensable supports. In vain would that man claim the tribute of patriotism, who should labor to subvert these great pillars of human happiness - these firmest props of the duties of men and citizens. The mere politician, equally with the pious man, ought to respect and to cherish them. A volume could not trace all their connections with private and public felicity. Let it simply be asked, Where is the security for property, for reputation, for life, if the sense of religious obligation desert the oaths which are the instruments of investigation in courts of justice? And let us with caution indulge the supposition that morality can be maintained without religion. Whatever may be conceded to the influence of refined education on minds of peculiar structure, reason and experience both forbid us to expect that national morality can prevail in exclusion of religious principles."*[180]

John Adams, like Washington, identified the principles and what type of people the Constitution was built for:

> *"We have no government armed with power capable of contending with human passions unbridled by morality and religion. Avarice, ambition, revenge, or gallantry, would break the strongest cords of our Constitution as a whale goes through a net. Our Constitution was made only for a moral and religious people. It is wholly inadequate to the government of any other."*[181]

What kind of religion were they talking about? John Quincy Adams, a child of the revolution, said:

> *"The highest, the transcendent glory of the American Revolution was this—it connected, in one indissoluble bond, the principles of civil government with the precepts of Christianity."*[182]

We see above that our first and second presidents were equating morality with religion. Samuel Adams added another character trait. In a letter to James Warren on February 12, 1779 Adams said:

> *"A general dissolution of principles and manners will more surely overthrow the liberties of America than the whole force of the common enemy. While the people are virtuous they cannot be subdued; but when they lose their virtue they will be ready to surrender their liberties to the first external or internal invader... If virtue and knowledge are diffused among the people, they will never be enslaved. This will be their great security."*[183]

When discussing a model public school system for Pennsylvania Dr. Benjamin Rush, who was a signer of the Declaration of Independence and true patriot, said:

> *"I proceed in the next place, to enquire, what mode of education we shall adopt so as to secure to the state all the advantages that are to be derived from the proper instruction of youth; and here I beg leave to remark, that the only foundation for a useful education in a republic is to be laid in Religion. Without this there can be no virtue, and without virtue there can be no liberty, and liberty is the object and life of all republican governments."*[184]

The Confederate Congress exemplified a belief that religion and education go hand in hand. In the Northwest Ordinance of 1787 the Congress encouraged the furtherance of religion through education. Section 14, Article 3 of that document says:

> *Religion, morality, and knowledge being necessary to good government and the happiness of mankind, schools and the means of education shall forever be encouraged.*

The founders believed in liberty, and from these quotes we see that they understood that you had to have virtue to have liberty. And to have virtue and morality you needed religion. We also see that they believed in Bible teaching within schools. The founders mentioned here are placing an emphasis on religion, virtue, and morality as character traits that should mark all Americans.

So what did early America look like? Were the precepts of virtue, morality, religion, Biblical education, etc. evident? Thankfully a French magistrate by the name of Alexis de Tocqueville also had a desire to see what made America great. He came over and spent nine months here during 1831 and 1832. Tocqueville traveled across America interviewing a wide cross section of Americans. His notes were subsequently produced as a four volume work called *Democracy In America*. Some of his observations:

-There is no country in the whole world in which the Christian religion retains a greater influence over the souls of men than in America; and there can be no greater proof of its utility, and of its conformity to human nature, than that its influence is most powerfully felt over the most enlightened and free nation of the earth.[185]

-In the United States religion exercises but little influence upon the laws and upon the details of public opinion, but it directs the manners of the community, and by regulating domestic life it regulates the State.[186]

-Religion in America takes no direct part in the government of society, but it must nevertheless be regarded as the foremost of the political institutions of that country; for if it does not impart a taste for freedom, it facilitates the use of free institutions. Indeed, it is in this same point of view that the inhabitants of the United States themselves look upon religious belief. I do not know whether all the Americans have a sincere faith in their religion, for who can search the human heart? but I am certain that they hold it to be indispensable to the maintenance of republican institutions. This opinion is not peculiar to a class of citizens or to a party, but it belongs to the whole nation, and to every rank of society.[187]

-Despotism may govern without faith, but liberty cannot.[188]

-Upon my arrival in the United States, the religious aspect of the country was the first thing that struck my attention; and the longer I stayed there the more did I perceive the great political consequences resulting from this state of things, to which I was unaccustomed. In France I had almost always seen the spirit of religion and the spirit of freedom pursuing courses diametrically opposed to each other; but in America I found that they were intimately united, and that they reigned in common over the same country.[189]

Tocqueville was curious about these findings and sought out clergy from "all the different sects". He found that, "*they mainly attributed the peaceful dominion of religion in their country to the separation of Church and State. I did not meet with a single individual, of the clergy or of the laity, who was not of the same opinion on this point.*"[190]

The America of 1831 exhibited the morality, virtue, and religion that our founders said was necessary for survival of the Republic. As demonstrated above the founders believed an education that included religion was necessary and practical and our early Congress "encouraged" it. So, what did Tocqueville observe with regard to education in America in 1831?

"In New England every citizen receives the elementary notions of human knowledge; he is moreover taught the doctrines and the evidences of his religion, the history of his country, and the leading features of its Constitution. In the States of Connecticut and Massachusetts it is extremely rare to find a man imperfectly acquainted with all these things, and a person wholly ignorant of them is a sort of phenomenon.[191]

Is it not obvious that the founders held biblical worldviews and that those qualities of religion were the source and guard of liberty? In 1831 we see that the system was working and religion was "indispensable" to the maintenance of the Republic. The only mention of "separation of church and state" in those days came from the clergy, who did not want the government interfering or usurping their arena. While religion took no direct part in the government according to Tocqueville it was "the foremost of the political institutions" of our country.

So how did America erode from being, as Tocqueville described, "the most enlightened and free nation of the earth" where religion was deemed essential to the Republic, and even encouraged by government, to today where religion, and Christianity, in particular has been thrown to the curb in the name of secular humanism and separation of church and state?

The original intent of the First Amendment was to prohibit the federal government from making any laws respecting an establishment of religion or the free exercise thereof. The founders felt that this subject was left under the control of the states. Proof of this can be found in Thomas Jefferson's 2nd inaugural address* where he said,

"In matters of religion, I have considered that its free exercise is placed by the Constitution independent of the powers of the general government. I have therefore undertaken on no occasion to prescribe the religious exercises suited to it; but have left them, as the Constitution found them, under the direction and discipline of state or church authorities acknowledged by the several religious societies."[192]

Supreme Court Justice Joseph Story echoed this truth in his work, Commentaries on the Constitution, when he said, "the whole power over the subject of religion is left exclusively to the state governments, to be acted upon according to their own sense of justice, and the state constitutions."[193]

James Madison was even more precise when he said, "There is not a shadow of right in the general (federal) government to intermeddle with religion. Its least interference with it would be a most flagrant usurpation."[194]

Was our federal government "separated" from religion in the formative years of our nation? The answer is a definitive, NO! From 1800 through the Civil War church services were held in the U.S. Capitol building, and the speaker's podium was used as the pulpit.[195] As president, Jefferson approved a treaty in 1803 that provided annual monetary support for a Catholic priest to the Kaskaskia Indians, out of the federal treasury.[196] Thomas Jefferson also chaired the school board for the District of Columbia, while president. He authored the first plan of education adopted by the city, which included Watt's Hymnal and the Bible as textbooks to teach reading.[197]

These are just a few of the numerous examples of our government condoning and supporting religion during the founding era of our nation.

In 1947 a US Supreme Court Case, Everson v. Board of Education, butchered the original intent of the founders when they found that the 1st Amendment prohibition on federal government involvement with religion also applied to the states. The court cited the now notorious letter from Thomas Jefferson to the Danbury Baptists in 1802 and the phrase "a wall of separation between Church & State". As we see above, Jefferson clearly held that state authorities did have jurisdiction over religious matters. This erroneous interpretation of Jefferson's statement violated the intent of the 1st Amendment and also violated the sovereignty of the states, who according to Madison, would retain powers that were "numerous and indefinite". It has been downhill ever since, as a string of Supreme Court cases have reiterated this fallacious interpretation of the Constitution. Prayer in school was ruled unconstitutional in 1962 and Bible reading was outlawed in 1963, all under the banner of a false ruling and interpretation of "separation of church and state". How is America doing since religion has been eliminated from the public square and public education?

2nd ~~Article the fourth~~...

A well regulated Militia, being necessary to the security of a free State, the right of the people to keep and bear Arms, shall not be infringed.

- This article should be read as one sentence because you and I, the American people, are the militia. Therefore, our right to keep and bear arms was, and still is, an essential part of our duty as American citizens and as members of our state militias. There are attempts today to try and separate militia from the right to bear arms. If opponents of guns can do this then they can chip away at our God given natural right to self-defense, and say for instance, that you only have a right to own a gun for "sporting" purposes. Well, our founding fathers believed owning a gun was necessary for the defense of our lives and liberties. For the sake of discussion we will break this down in two sections but hopefully through this analysis we will see why this article is one unbreakable sentence and philosophy from the first word to the last word.

1. **"A well regulated Militia, being necessary to the security of a free State"-** Remember Jefferson's indictment in the Declaration of Independence; *"He has kept among us, in times of peace, Standing Armies without the Consent of our legislatures"...* The citizens were tired and weary of British oppression through standing armies and quartering of troops. After securing independence they prohibited standing armies in Article 1, Section 8. If we review clause 12 we see that armies will be funded for no more than two years. Then in clause 15 and 16 the framers established the militia system as America's fighting force. Its control was balanced through separation of powers. Congress was given the authority to make the rules for land forces and the authority to call up the militia (Art 1, sec 8, Clauses 14,15,16), while the states appointed the officers and conducted training (Art 1, Sec 8, Clause 16). The President is Commander-in-Chief of the militia according to Article 2, Section 2, Clause 1.

- What did the “Father of the Constitution” think of militias and standing armies? In his inaugural address of March 4, 1809* James Madison included among his principles, “to keep within the requisite limits a standing military force, always remembering that an armed and trained militia is the firmest bulwark of republics—that without standing armies their liberty can never be in danger, nor with large ones safe”[198]

- Who is the militia comprised of? The Virginia ratification convention drafted a proposed Bill of rights June 27, 1788. Their version of the 2nd Amendment identified who the militia is, “That the people have a right to keep and bear arms; that a well regulated militia, composed of the body of the people trained to arms, is the proper, natural, and safe defence of a free state; that standing armies, in time of peace, are dangerous to liberty, and therefore ought to be avoided, as far as the circumstances and protection of the community will admit; and that, in all cases, the military should be under strict subordination to, and governed by, the civil power.”[199] The people, you and I, were to comprise the militia. Over time we have abdicated our responsibility for self-defense to a standing army and police state. George Mason stated, “Once a standing army is established, in any country, the people lose their liberty.”[200]

2. **“the right of the people to keep and bear Arms, shall not be infringed” –** Samuel Adams identified the right to self-defense as a natural right, “Among the natural rights of the Colonists are these: First, a right to life; Secondly, to liberty; Thirdly, to property; together with the right to support and defend them in the best manner they can.”[201] George Mason said that the means to self-defense has been given to every individual by Divine Providence.[202] You and I, as individuals have a God given, natural right to self defense. This right existed before governments were established. It cannot be taken away from you or me by governments. To do so, would be a moral crime, and an act of tyranny.

- In Federalist 46 James Madison compares the influences of the federal and state governments. He makes, what seem like, prophetic statements that summarize this article and why a militia should be comprised of the people and why the American people possess arms. This is a lengthy quotation but very worthy of our attention:

> *“The only refuge for those left who prophesy the downfall of the State governments is the visionary supposition that the federal government may previously accumulate a military force for the projects of ambition. The reasonings contained in these papers must have been employed to little purpose indeed, if it could be necessary now to disprove the reality of this danger. That the people and the States should, for a sufficient period of time, elect an uninterrupted succession of men ready to betray both; that the traitors should, throughout this period, uniformly and systematically pursue some fixed plan for the extension of the military establishment; that the governments and the people of the States should silently and patiently behold the gathering storm and continue to supply the materials until it should be prepared to burst on their own heads must appear to everyone more like the incoherent dreams of a delirious jealousy, or the misjudged exaggerations of a counterfeit zeal, than like the sober apprehensions of*

genuine patriotism. Extravagant as the supposition is, let it, however, be made. Let a regular army, fully equal to the resources of the country, be formed; and let it be entirely at the devotion of the federal government: still it would not be going too far to say that the State governments with the people on their side would be able to repel the danger. The highest number to which, according to the best computation, a standing army can be carried in any country does not exceed one hundredth part of the whole number of souls; or one twenty-fifth part of the number able to bear arms. This proportion would not yield, in the United States, an army of more than twenty-five or thirty thousand men. To these would be opposed a militia amounting to near half a million of citizens with arms in their hands, officered by men chosen from among themselves, fighting for their common liberties and united and conducted by governments possessing their affections and confidence. It may well be doubted whether a militia thus circumstanced could ever be conquered by such a proportion of regular troops. Those who are best acquainted with the late successful resistance of this country against the British arms will be most inclined to deny the possibility of it. Besides the advantage of being armed, which the Americans possess over the people of almost every other nation, the existence of subordinate governments, to which the people are attached and by which the militia officers are appointed, forms a barrier against the enterprises of ambition, more insurmountable than any which a simple government of any form can admit of...... Let us rather no longer insult them (the American people) with the supposition that they can ever reduce themselves to the necessity of making the experiment by a blind and tame submission to the long train of insidious measures which must precede and produce it."[203]

3. Are we at the precipice of what Madison ponders in the above statement? Has the "military establishment" been constructed? Have the people of the states sat silently and patiently during the gathering storm?

It is also evident from Madison's statement here that the "arms" in question are not to be limited to sporting or hunting varieties, otherwise a militia could not fight against and repel a fully armed standing army. Judge Andrew Napolitano summed up the types of arms that Americans have a right to possess and bear, "The historical reality of the Second Amendment's protection of the right to keep and bear arms is not that it protects the right to shoot deer. It protects the right to shoot tyrants, and it protects the right to shoot at them effectively, thus, with the same instruments they would use upon us."[204]

4. As of 2013 the American people have been sitting idly by while the military establishment that Madison warns about has been completely built by men elected from both parties. We have lost our attachments to our State governments because of things like the 17th Amendment and federal handouts to states and individuals. The last thing we have left is our unalienable right to bear arms and they have been eroding that for years through unconstitutional regulation and bureaucracy.

3rd ~~Article the fifth~~...

No Soldier shall, in time of peace be quartered in any house, without the consent of the Owner, nor in time of war, but in a manner to be prescribed by law.

1. This grievance was levied in the indictment of the Declaration of Independence and is now being answered in the Constitution.

4th ~~Article the sixth~~...

The right of the people to be secure in their persons, houses, papers, and effects, against unreasonable searches and seizures, shall not be violated, and no Warrants shall issue, but upon probable cause, supported by Oath or affirmation, and particularly describing the place to be searched, and the persons or things to be seized.

1. This amendment is a response to injuries inflicted upon the colonists through the use of "writs of assistance". Parliament had utilized these writs as part of the Navigation Acts and the Townshend Acts. They were designed to reduce smuggling of goods, especially in New England. These writs, however, did not expire, except on death of the king, and they were not specific as to place to be searched or, of things to be seized. James Otis, an early patriot and Son of Liberty, argued against writs of assistance in a famous hearing in 1761, known as the Paxton Case. A young lawyer named John Adams was present during Otis' oration against tyranny and the violation of natural rights. Adams said this about the event, "Then and there was the first scene of the first act of opposition to the arbitrary claims of Great Britain." And, "then and there the child independence was born."[205]

- **Warrant-** To authorize; to give authority or power to do or forbear any thing, by which the person authorized is secured or saved harmless from any loss or damage by the act. A commission warrants an officer to seize an enemy. We are not warranted to resist legitimate government, except in extreme cases. (Webster 1828)

- **Probable Cause-** A reasonable ground to suspect that a person has committed a particular crime or that a place contains specific items connected with a crime; under the Fourth Amendment, probable cause - which amounts to more than a bare suspicion but less than legal evidence - must be shown before an arrest warrant or search warrant may be issued. (Black's Law Dictionary Pocket Edition 1996)

- **Oath-** A solemn affirmation or declaration, made with an appeal to God for the truth of what is affirmed. The appeal to God in an oath, implies that the person imprecates his vengeance and renounces his favor if the declaration is false, or if the declaration is a promise, the person invokes the vengeance of God if he should fail to fulfill it. A false oath is called perjury. (Webster 1828)

- **Affirmation-** A solemn declaration made under the penalties of perjury, by persons who conscientiously decline taking an oath; which affirmation is in law equivalent to testimony given under oath. (Webster 1828)

5th ~~Article the seventh~~...

No person shall be held to answer for a capital, or otherwise infamous crime, unless on a presentment or indictment of a Grand Jury, except in cases arising in the land or naval forces, or in the Militia, when in actual service in time of War or public danger; nor shall any person be subject for the same offence to be twice put in jeopardy of life or limb; nor shall be compelled in any criminal case to be a witness against himself, nor be deprived of life, liberty, or property, without due process of law; nor shall private property be taken for public use, without just compensation.

- This amendment identifies five very important rights that cannot be violated by the federal government, primarily the judicial branch.

1. Right to have a Grand Jury hear a case against you if it concerns a capital or infamous crime. This is a safeguard of liberty that one will not be required to answer for a capital crime unless the Grand Jury issues an indictment.

- **Capital-** Punishable by loss of the head or of life; incurring the forfeiture of life; punishable with death; as, treason and murder are capital offenses or crimes. (Webster 1828)

- **Infamous-** Of ill report, emphatically; having a reputation of the worst kind; publicly branded with odium for vice of guilt; base; scandalous; notoriously vile; used of persons; as an infamous liar; an infamous rake or gambler. (Webster 1828)

- **Presentment-** In the United States, a presentment is an official accusation presented to a tribunal by the grand jury in an indictment; or it is the act of offering an indictment. It is also used for the indictment itself. The grand jury are charged to inquire and due presentment make of all crimes, &c. The use of the word is limited to accusations by grand jurors. (Webster 1828)

- **Indictment-** A written accusation or formal charge of a crime or misdemeanor, preferred by a grand jury under oath to a court. (Webster 1828)

- **Grand Jury-** A body of (often 23) people who are chosen to sit permanently for at least a month- and sometimes a year- and who, in exparte proceedings, decide whether indictments should be issued; if the grand jury decides that evidence is strong enough to hold a suspect for trial, it returns a bill of indictment (a *true bill*) charging the suspect with a specific crime. (Black's Law Dictionary Pocket Edition 1996)

2. Right to not be tried twice for the same offense (also commonly known as double jeopardy)

3. Right to not testify against yourself (commonly referred to as "pleading the fifth")

4. Right to maintain life, liberty, and property by protection of due process.

- **Due Process-** The conduct of legal proceedings according to the rules and principles in the systems of jurisprudence for the protection and enforcement of private rights, including notice and the right to a fair hearing before a tribunal with the power to decide the case. (Black's Law Dictionary Pocket Edition 1996)

5. Right to be compensated for private property taken for public use.

- **Private-** Relating or belonging to an individual, as opposed to the public or the government (Black's Law Dictionary Pocket Edition 1996)

- **Property-** The exclusive right of possessing, enjoying and disposing of a thing; ownership. In the beginning of the world, the Creator gave to man dominion over the earth, over the fish of the sea and the fowls of the air, and over every living thing. This is the foundation of man's property in the earth and in all its productions. Prior occupancy of land and of wild animals gives to the possessor the property of them. The labor of inventing, making or producing any thing constitutes one of the highest and most indefeasible titles to property. Property is also acquired by inheritance, by gift or by purchase. Property is sometimes held in common, yet each man's right to his share in common land or stock is exclusively his own. One man may have the property of the soil, and another the right of use, by prescription or by purchase. (Webster 1828)

- **Public-** Relating or belonging to an entire community, state, or nation. (Black's Law Dictionary Pocket Edition 1996)

- **Use-** The application, employment, or enjoyment of something. (Black's Law Dictionary Pocket Edition 1996)

- **Just-** Equitable; due; merited; as a just recompense or reward. (Webster 1828)

- **Compensation-** That which is given or received as an equivalent for services, debt, want, loss, or suffering; amends; remuneration; recompense. (Webster 1828)

6th ~~Article the eighth~~...

In all criminal prosecutions, the accused shall enjoy the right to a speedy and public trial, by an impartial jury of the State and district wherein the crime shall have been committed, which district shall have been previously ascertained by law, and to be informed of the nature and cause of the accusation; to be confronted with the witnesses against him; to have compulsory process for obtaining witnesses in his favor, and to have the Assistance of Counsel for his defence.

1. This article deals with judicial procedure and rights in the federal court system. If you are prosecuted for a federal crime you have the have the following rights:

a. A speedy AND public trial in front of an impartial jury from the district where the crime allegedly occurred (this is what is referred to as a jury of your peers). A trial that is public is less likely to be maliciously and unfairly prosecuted.

b. To be informed of the charges against you

c. To be confronted with the witnesses against you, and;

d. To have compulsory process for obtaining witnesses in your favor (subpoena power)

e. To be provided with counsel (i.e. public defender)

2. This article also answered the indictments levied in the Declaration of Independence that stated the British were depriving colonists of trial by jury (indictment #18) under the Sugar and Townshend Acts, and that they were transporting colonists across the ocean to be tried for "pretended offences" (indictment #19), which was occurring under the Intolerable Acts.

3. Alexander Hamilton discusses the importance of trial by jury for both civil and criminal cases in Federalist 83: *"I cannot readily discern the inseparable connection between the existence of liberty and the trial by jury in civil cases. Arbitrary impeachments, arbitrary methods of prosecuting pretended offenses, and arbitrary punishments upon arbitrary convictions have ever appeared to me to be the great engines of judicial despotism; and these have all relation to criminal proceedings. The trial by jury in criminal cases, aided by habeas corpus act, seems therefore to be alone concerned in the question. And both of these are provided for in the most ample manner in the plan of the convention."*[206]

In the same essay Hamilton indicates that the "trial by jury must still be a valuable check upon corruption."[207]

7th ~~Article the ninth~~...

In Suits at common law, where the value in controversy shall exceed twenty dollars, the right of trial by jury shall be preserved, and no fact tried by a jury, shall be otherwise re-examined in any Court of the United States, than according to the rules of the common law.

1. In this article we see that the right to a jury trial is maintained for civil suits of a substantial dollar amount, which at that time was $20 dollars. Juries were also cemented as the examiners of fact in a trial. Their findings could not be arbitrarily overturned by another body such as a panel of judges at an appeals court.

8th ~~Article the tenth~~...

Excessive bail shall not be required, nor excessive fines imposed, nor cruel and unusual punishments inflicted.

1. The bail, fine, and punishment should fit the crime or offense. Ask yourself... is a $116 citation for not wearing a seat belt an excessive fine?

9th ~~Article the eleventh~~...

The enumeration in the Constitution, of certain rights, shall not be construed to deny or disparage others retained by the people.

1. While several states called for the addition of a Bill of Rights to the Constitution in their ratification conventions, multiple members of the constitutional convention did not think there was a need for a Bill of Rights because it may limit the vast unalienable rights that the people inherently possess. Alexander Hamilton expounded on this topic in Federalist 84 when he addressed those who were opposing the proposed Constitution because it did not have a specific Bill of Rights:

> *"It has been several times truly remarked that bills of rights are, in their origin, stipulations between kings and their subjects, abridgments of prerogative in favor of privilege, reservations of rights not surrendered to the prince. Such was MAGNA CARTA, obtained by the barons, sword in hand, from King John... It is evident, therefore, that according to their primitive signification, they have no application to constitutions, professedly founded upon the power of the people and executed by their immediate representatives and servants. Here, in strictness, the people surrender nothing; and as they retain everything they have no need of particular reservations, "WE, THE PEOPLE of the United States, to secure the blessings of liberty to ourselves and our posterity, do ordain and establish this Constitution for the United States of America." Here is a better recognition of popular rights than volumes of those aphorisms which make the principal figure in several of our State bills of rights and which would sound much better in a treatise of ethics than in a constitution of government."*[208]

Hamilton went on to explain why a Bill of Rights could be dangerous;

> *"I go further and affirm that bills of rights, in the sense and to the extent in which they are contended for, are not only unnecessary in the proposed Constitution but would even be dangerous. They would contain various exceptions to powers which are not granted; and, on this very account, would afford a colorable pretext to claim more than were granted. For why declare that things shall not be done which there is no power to do? Why, for instance, should it be said that the liberty of the press shall not be restrained, when no power is given by which restrictions may be imposed?"*[209]

And finally, Hamilton identified the true genius and power of the Constitution itself and why, in his mind, there was no need for a specific Bill of Rights;

> *"The truth is, after all the declamations we have heard, that the Constitution is itself, in every rational sense, and to every useful purpose, A BILL OF RIGHTS. The several bills of rights in Great Britain form its Constitution, and conversely the constitution of each state is its bill of rights. And the proposed Constitution, if adopted, will be the bill of rights of the Union."*[210]

2. The 9th Amendment answers the concerns of Hamilton and others and attempts to leave no doubt that *WE THE PEOPLE* retain all of our unalienable rights regardless of whether they have been identified or not within the text of the Constitution.

- It is interesting to ponder the effects and consequences of our Bill of Rights and if America would look different today had the Bill of Rights not been added. Surely, the issues of religion and guns have been made controversial when government has stepped in to regulate around the edges of these identified rights, almost as Hamilton suspected.If they had not been included in a Bill of Rights would the government have ever muddied the waters or would the government have stayed out because there was no specific authority delegated to it over those issues in the Constitution?

10th ~~Article the twelfth~~...

The powers not delegated to the United States by the Constitution, nor prohibited by it to the States, are reserved to the States respectively, or to the people.

1. The federal government has no authority to regulate, legislate, or adjudicate anything that is not specifically delegated to it within the body of the Constitution. If something is not specifically prohibited to the States they will retain authority over the matter. This amendment confirms that WE THE PEOPLE of the UNITED STATES, are establishing this government for our own use and benefit and we are giving it very limited powers. Recall the famous words of Madison from Federalist 45;

"The powers delegated by the proposed Constitution to the federal government are few and defined. Those which are to remain in the State governments are numerous and indefinite."

ATTEST,

Frederick Augustus Muhlenberg, Speaker of the House of Representatives

John Adams, Vice-President of the United States, and President of the Senate

John Beckley, Clerk of the House of Representatives.

Sam. A Otis Secretary of the Senate

Amendments 11-27

11th Amendment

The Judicial power of the United States shall not be construed to extend to any suit in law or equity, commenced or prosecuted against one of the United States by Citizens of another State, or by Citizens or Subjects of any Foreign State.

1. This amendment modifies Article III, Sec 2, Clause 1, which originally extended judicial power or jurisdiction to the types of suits listed in the amendment. This amendment took jurisdiction away from the federal judiciary.

2. This amendment was ratified February 7, 1795.

12th Amendment

The Electors shall meet in their respective states and vote by ballot for President and Vice-President, one of whom, at least, shall not be an inhabitant of the same state with themselves; they shall name in their ballots the person voted for as President, and in distinct ballots the person voted for as Vice-President, and they shall make distinct lists of all persons voted for as President, and of all persons voted for as Vice-President, and of the number of votes for each, which lists they shall sign and certify, and transmit sealed to the seat of the government of the United States, directed to the President of the Senate; -- the President of the Senate shall, in the presence of the Senate and House of Representatives, open all the certificates and the votes shall then be counted; -- The person having the greatest number of votes for President, shall be the President, if such number be a majority of the whole number of Electors appointed; and if no person have such majority, then from the persons having the highest numbers not exceeding three on the list of those voted for as President, the House of Representatives shall choose immediately, by ballot, the President. But in choosing the President, the votes shall be taken by states, the representation from each state having one vote; a quorum for this purpose shall consist of a member or members from two-thirds of the states, and a majority of all the states shall be necessary to a choice. And if the House of Representatives shall not choose a President whenever the right of choice shall devolve upon them, before the fourth day of March next following, then the Vice-President shall act as President, as in case of the death or other constitutional disability of the President. The person having the greatest number of votes as Vice-President, shall be

the Vice-President, if such number be a majority of the whole number of Electors appointed, and if no person have a majority, then from the two highest numbers on the list, the Senate shall choose the Vice-President; a quorum for the purpose shall consist of two-thirds of the whole number of Senators, and a majority of the whole number shall be necessary to a choice. But no person constitutionally ineligible to the office of President shall be eligible to that of Vice-President of the United States.

1. This amendment modifies the original mode of electing a President as outlined in Article 2, Section 1. Originally, the Electors would each vote for two candidates and after tallying all votes the person with the most votes would be President, while the person with the next highest vote total would be Vice-President. Now, Electors will identify specifically when they vote who is their choice for President and who is their choice for Vice-President.

2. This amendment was brought about by the political party system that developed early in our nation's history. In the election of 1796 John Adams, a "federalist", was elected President, while Thomas Jefferson, a "republican" was elected Vice-President. While these two men had worked together and been friends for many years the beginnings of party faction had made it difficult for the executive branch to be operated with a President and Vice-President of opposing parties.

3. This amendment was ratified on June 15, 1804.

13th Amendment

Section 1. Neither slavery nor involuntary servitude, except as a punishment for crime whereof the party shall have been duly convicted, shall exist within the United States, or any place subject to their jurisdiction.

Section 2. Congress shall have power to enforce this article by appropriate legislation.

This amendment was ratified on December 6, 1865 and put an end to slavery in the United States of America.

14th Amendment

Section 1 All persons born or naturalized in the United States, and subject to the jurisdiction thereof, are citizens of the United States and of the State wherein they reside. No State shall make or enforce any law which shall abridge the privileges or immunities of citizens of the United States; nor shall any State deprive any person of life, liberty, or property, without due process of law; nor deny to any person within its jurisdiction the equal protection of the laws.

1. This amendment, much like the subsequent 16th and 17th amendments, significantly altered our constitutional system from its original design by expanding the power of the national government and reducing state sovereignty. Remember Madison's words from Federalist #45, "The powers delegated by the proposed Constitution to the federal government are few and defined. Those which are to remain in the State governments are numerous and indefinite." Originally, the Bill of Rights was an acknowledgement of our rights at the federal level and restricted the federal government from infringing on them. The 14th Amendment makes the federal Bill of Rights binding on the states through the "incorporation doctrine". Since the early 20th century this amendment has been used increasingly by the Supreme Court to expand federal reach and has been cited in cases such as Gitlow v. New York (1925), Brown v. Topeka Board of Education (1954), Gideon v. Wainwright (1963), Miranda v. Arizona (1966), and Roe v. Wade (1973).

Section 2. Representatives shall be apportioned among the several States according to their respective numbers, counting the whole number of persons in each State, excluding Indians not taxed. But when the right to vote at any election for the choice of electors for President and Vice-President of the United States, Representatives in Congress, the Executive and Judicial officers of a State, or the members of the Legislature thereof, is denied to any of the male inhabitants of such State, being twenty-one years of age, and citizens of the United States, or in any way abridged, except for participation in rebellion, or other crime, the basis of representation therein shall be reduced in the proportion which the number of such male citizens shall bear to the whole number of male citizens twenty-one years of age in such State.

1. This section modifies Article 1, Section 2, Clause 3 of the Constitution by doing away with the 3/5 Compromise for purposes of apportionment of representatives. All men 21 years and up have a right to vote and the States cannot infringe without penalty.

Section 3. No person shall be a Senator or Representative in Congress, or elector of President and Vice-President, or hold any office, civil or military, under the United States, or under any State, who, having previously taken an oath, as a member of Congress, or as an officer of the United States, or as a member of any State legislature, or as an executive or judicial officer of any State, to support the Constitution of the United States, shall have engaged in insurrection or rebellion against the same, or given aid or comfort to the enemies thereof. But Congress may by a vote of two-thirds of each House, remove such disability.

1. This section will effectively keep former confederate military and government officers out of federal positions unless the House of Representatives conducts case by case inquiries and is able to garner a 2/3 vote.

Section 4. The validity of the public debt of the United States, authorized by law, including debts incurred for payment of pensions and bounties for services in suppressing insurrection or rebellion, shall not be questioned. But neither the United States nor any State shall assume or pay any debt or obligation incurred in aid of insurrection or rebellion against the United States, or any claim for the loss or emancipation of any slave; but all such debts, obligations and claims shall be held illegal and void.

1. Debts incurred by the southern States are an issue and are written off by the federal government who is not willing to pick up the tab.

Section 5. The Congress shall have the power to enforce, by appropriate legislation, the provisions of this article.

1. This amendment was ratified on July 9, 1868

15th Amendment

Section 1. The right of citizens of the United States to vote shall not be denied or abridged by the United States or by any State on account of race, color, or previous condition of servitude—

Section 2. The Congress shall have the power to enforce this article by appropriate legislation.

1. This amendment affirms what was indicated in the 14th Amendment, that all males over 21 have a right to vote regardless of skin color. Women still are not allowed to vote in the United States but their day is coming.

2. This amendment was ratified on February 3, 1870.

16th Amendment

The Congress shall have power to lay and collect taxes on incomes, from whatever source derived, without apportionment among the several States, and without regard to any census or enumeration.

1. This amendment completely went against the founders' philosophy with regard to unalienable rights, natural law, and taxation. Recall that the colonists loathed direct taxes (see notes in Section II on Rumblings and the Stamp Act). The Constitution, in Article 1, Section 8, gave Congress the power to tax, and this included levying direct taxes. We also see, however, in Article 1, Section 2 and Article 1, Section 9 that any direct tax would have to be levied in proportion to the census for each of the States. Direct taxes were not individualized under the original Constitutional model, in other words, you would not pay a different tax rate than your neighbor at the federal level. The necessary amount of tax would be requisitioned from the States and then it was up to them to collect how they saw fit.

2. This amendment obliterates the Constitutional protections of Article 1 Sections 2 and 9 and goes against the founders views on taxes, see notes on Article 1 Sections 2, 8, and 9. While the power of taxation was "complete" under the original constitutional framework, the census and apportionment requirements served as a bulwark against oppressive taxation. It is the opinion of this writer that the 16th and 17th Amendments have done more damage to the United States than any foreign invader could dream of doing. Nonetheless, this amendment is the law of the land. If this tragedy is to be rectified it must be done through the constitutional amendment process. If we heaped an income tax upon ourselves we surely can throw it off if the American people are armed with knowledge, concern, and courage.

3. It is also worthy of note that one of the planks of Karl Marx' Communist Manifesto is a heavy progressive or graduated income tax.

3. This amendment was ratified February 3, 1913.

17th Amendment

The Senate of the United States shall be composed of two Senators from each State, elected by the people thereof, for six years; and each Senator shall have one vote. The electors in each State shall have the qualifications requisite for electors of the most numerous branch of the State legislatures.

When vacancies happen in the representation of any State in the Senate, the executive authority of such State shall issue writs of election to fill such vacancies: *Provided*, That the legislature of any State may empower the executive thereof to make temporary appointments until the people fill the vacancies by election as the legislature may direct.

This amendment shall not be so construed as to affect the election or term of any Senator chosen before it becomes valid as part of the Constitution.

1. This amendment destroyed our federal system of government. According to Webster's 1828 Dictionary the definition of federal is:

> Consisting in a compact between parties, particularly and chiefly between states or nations; founded on alliance by contract or mutual agreement; as a federal government, such as that of the United States.

2. The Constitution was created by the People but was ratified by the States. State sovereignty was an integral portion of the mutual agreement that led to the creation of the federal government. The 17th Amendment removed the States' ability to check the usurpation of power by the federal government. Today we are seeing the consequences of this amendment, along with the other terrible events of 1913, namely, passage of the 16th Amendment and passage of the Federal Reserve Act. If we are to restore our Constitutional system of government and restore the

American republic the 17th Amendment must be repealed. Please see Article 1, Section 3 for additional details about this subject.

3. This amendment was ratified April 8, 1913.

18th Amendment

Section 1. After one year from the ratification of this article the manufacture, sale, or transportation of intoxicating liquors within, the importation thereof into, or the exportation thereof from the United States and all territory subject to the jurisdiction thereof for beverage purposes is hereby prohibited.

Section 2. The Congress and the several States shall have concurrent power to enforce this article by appropriate legislation.

Section 3. This article shall be inoperative unless it shall have been ratified as an amendment to the Constitution by the legislatures of the several States, as provided in the Constitution, within seven years from the date of the submission hereof to the States by the Congress.

1. As one reads through the Constitution it will be observed that the document identifies what government can and can't do; not what people can and can't do. This amendment eroded the founders belief in the principle of self-government and went outside the original intent of the Constitution in an attempt to regulate behavior, or shall we say, legislate morality.

2. This amendment was ratified January 16, 1919.

19th Amendment

The right of citizens of the United States to vote shall not be denied or abridged by the United States or by any State on account of sex.

Congress shall have power to enforce this article by appropriate legislation.

1. Originally, voter qualifications were determined by the States according to Article 1, Section 4 of the Constitution. Several states had already granted women the right to vote prior to this amendment.

2. Susan B. Anthony and Elizabeth Cady Stanton drafted the 19th Amendment. California Senator Aaron Sargent first introduced the amendment in January 1878. The amendment was rejected several times and finally passed both houses in 1919 and was then sent to the states where Tennessee was the final state to approve the amendment and cross the necessary three-fourths threshold.

3. This amendment was ratified August 18, 1920

20th Amendment

Section 1. The terms of the President and the Vice President shall end at noon on the 20th day of January, and the terms of Senators and Representatives at noon on the 3d day of January, of the years in which such terms would have ended if this article had not been ratified; and the terms of their successors shall then begin.

- This amendment alters the 12th Amendment pertaining to the inauguration date for President. Historically, up until this point the date for the President to take office was March 4th. Now it will be January 20th.

Section 2. The Congress shall assemble at least once in every year, and such meeting shall begin at noon on the 3d day of January, unless they shall by law appoint a different day.

- This section alters Article 1, Section 4, Clause 2 of the Constitution. Originally, Congress was to meet at least once per year with the opening meeting to be on the first Monday in December. Sections 1 and 2 of this amendment drew the commencement dates for Congress and President closer together, thereby reducing the lame duck period from three months to three weeks.

Section 3. If, at the time fixed for the beginning of the term of the President, the President elect shall have died, the Vice President elect shall become President. If a President shall not have been chosen before the time fixed for the beginning of his term, or if the President elect shall have failed to qualify, then the Vice President elect shall act as President until a President shall have qualified; and the Congress may by law provide for the case wherein neither a President elect nor a Vice President shall have qualified, declaring who shall then act as President, or the manner in which one who is to act shall be selected, and such person shall act accordingly until a President or Vice President shall have qualified.

- Section 3 of this amendment does some housekeeping with regard to continuity of government in the event that there is a snag in the qualification of President and Vice-President prior to inauguration, and also identifies that the Vice President elect will become President if the President elect has died.

Section 4. The Congress may by law provide for the case of the death of any of the persons from whom the House of Representatives may choose a President whenever the right of choice shall have devolved upon them, and for the case of the death of any of the persons from whom the Senate may choose a Vice President whenever the right of choice shall have devolved upon them.

Section 5. Sections 1 and 2 shall take effect on the 15th day of October following the ratification of this article.

Section 6. This article shall be inoperative unless it shall have been ratified as an amendment to the Constitution by the legislatures of three-fourths of the several States within seven years from the date of its submission.

- This amendment was ratified January 23, 1933.

21st Amendment

Section 1. The eighteenth article of amendment to the Constitution of the United States is hereby repealed.

Section 2. The transportation or importation into any State, Territory, or Possession of the United States for delivery or use therein of intoxicating liquors, in violation of the laws thereof, is hereby prohibited.

Section 3. This article shall be inoperative unless it shall have been ratified as an amendment to the Constitution by conventions in the several States, as provided in the Constitution, within seven years from the date of the submission hereof to the States by the Congress.

1. To date, this is the only time an amendment to the Constitution has been repealed. The 21st has set a precedent though, so there may be hope that the 16th and 17 Amendments can be repealed someday.

2. Interestingly, section 3 of this amendment calls for ratification to be done by state conventions, not the state legislatures.

3. This amendment was ratified December 5, 1933.

22nd Amendment

Section 1. No person shall be elected to the office of the President more than twice, and no person who has held the office of President, or acted as President, for more than two years of a term to which some other person was elected President shall be elected to the office of President more than once. But this Article shall not apply to any person holding the office of President when this Article was proposed by Congress, and shall not prevent any person who may be holding the office of President, or acting as President, during the term within which this Article becomes operative from holding the office of President or acting as President during the remainder of such term.

Section 2. This article shall be inoperative unless it shall have been ratified as an amendment to the Constitution by the legislatures of three-fourths of the several States within seven years from the date of its submission to the States by the Congress.

1. This amendment was passed in response to Franklin D. Roosevelt being elected to four terms as President, serving from 1933 until his death in 1945. Prior to Roosevelt all other Presidents had followed the precedent set by George Washington and had limited themselves to two terms in office. Until passage of the 22nd amendment there was no mandatory term limit mentioned in the Constitution. In fact, Alexander Hamilton provided a detailed argument against term limits for the chief Executive in Federalist 72.

2. This amendment was ratified February 27, 1951.

23rd Amendment

Section 1. The District constituting the seat of Government of the United States shall appoint in such manner as Congress may direct:

A number of electors of President and Vice President equal to the whole number of Senators and Representatives in Congress to which the District would be entitled if it were a State, but in no event more than the least populous State; they shall be in addition to those appointed by the States, but they shall be considered, for the purposes of the election of President and Vice President, to be electors appointed by a State; and they shall meet in the District and perform such duties as provided by the twelfth article of amendment.

Section 2. The Congress shall have power to enforce this article by appropriate legislation.

1. This amendment allows for the residents of Washington DC to participate in presidential elections by appointing electors. The electors cannot be more numerous than the amount allowed for the least populous State. Currently there are three electoral votes for Washington DC. Other than presidential electors, people living within the "seat of Government" do not have any elected representation at the federal level. The "seat of Government" is not a State and is therefore not constitutionally eligible to elect representatives.

2. This amendment was ratified March 29, 1961.

24th Amendment

Section 1. The right of citizens of the United States to vote in any primary or other election for President or Vice President, for electors for President or Vice President, or for Senator or Representative in Congress, shall not be denied or abridged by the United States or any State by reason of failure to pay poll tax or other tax.

Section 2. The Congress shall have power to enforce this article by appropriate legislation.

1. As discussed in the notes on Article 1, Section 9, Clause 4 a poll tax is a direct tax on an individual and is also known as a capitation. The Constitution is being amended here to declare that in national elections the right to vote cannot be denied because of a poll tax or "any other tax".

2. This amendment was ratified January 23, 1964.

25th Amendment

Section 1. In case of the removal of the President from office or of his death or resignation, the Vice President shall become President.

Section 2. Whenever there is a vacancy in the office of the Vice President, the President shall nominate a Vice President who shall take office upon confirmation by a majority vote of both Houses of Congress.

Section 3. Whenever the President transmits to the President pro tempore of the Senate and the Speaker of the House of Representatives his written declaration that he is unable to discharge the powers and duties of his office, and until he transmits to them a written declaration to the contrary, such powers and duties shall be discharged by the Vice President as Acting President.

Section 4. Whenever the Vice President and a majority of either the principal officers of the executive departments or of such other body as Congress may by law provide, transmit to the President pro tempore of the Senate and the Speaker of the House of Representatives their written declaration that the President is unable to discharge the powers and duties of his office, the Vice President shall immediately assume the powers and duties of the office as Acting President.

Thereafter, when the President transmits to the President pro tempore of the Senate and the Speaker of the House of Representatives his written declaration that no inability exists, he shall resume the powers and duties of his office unless the Vice President and a majority of either the principal officers of the executive department or of such other body as Congress may by law provide, transmit within four days to the President pro tempore of the Senate and the Speaker of the House of Representatives their written declaration that the President is unable to discharge the powers and duties of his office. Thereupon Congress shall decide the issue, assembling within forty-eight hours for that purpose if not in session. If the Congress, within twenty-one days after receipt of the latter written declaration, or, if Congress is not in session, within twenty-one days after Congress is required to assemble, determines by two-thirds vote of both Houses that the President is unable to discharge the powers and duties of his office, the Vice President shall continue to discharge the same as Acting President; otherwise, the President shall resume the powers and duties of his office.

1. This amendment affects Article II, Section 1, Clause 6 and adds additional procedures to be followed in the event that the President is unable to carry out the duties of office. This amendment also rectifies an omission in the original Constitution, namely that there was no framework established for replacement of a Vice President who had vacated his office during the middle of a term.

2. It seems that the language in this amendment does open the door for a potential coup d'état of the government. It is conceivable that a Vice President could usurp the presidency with the aid of the cabinet and key officers and this amendment would make it legal.

3. This amendment was ratified February 10, 1967.

26th Amendment

Section 1. The right of citizens of the United States, who are eighteen years of age or older, to vote shall not be denied or abridged by the United States or by any State on account of age.

Section 2. The Congress shall have power to enforce this article by appropriate legislation.

1. Passed during the time that America was involved in the Vietnam War, this amendment identified a federal right that citizens 18 years of age and older can vote.

2. This amendment was ratified July 1, 1971.

27th Amendment

No law, varying the compensation for the services of the Senators and Representatives, shall take effect, until an election of representatives shall have intervened.

- As indicated in the section on the Bill of Rights, this amendment was originally submitted to the States for approval in 1789. It did not pass and was shelved for 200 years. With incumbency rates around or above 80% for both houses of Congress there is a good chance of voting for your own pay raise regardless of this amendment.[211]

Conclusion

You and I owe a never ending debt of gratitude to the founding fathers of America. From the Pilgrims that landed at Plymouth in 1620, to the colonists that pledged their lives, fortunes, and sacred honor to secure independence from Great Britain, to the men that gathered in Philadelphia in 1787 to establish a Constitution for Posterity that would secure the "Blessings of Liberty"; they all played an in important role in building and advancing the American experiment.

They gave us a Constitution that had never been tried anywhere in the world. Our form of government is intricate, complicated, and delicate, while also being simple and durable. You may be scratching your head with that statement and think that I am contradicting myself. Think about it, the founders pulled components from governments that had been tried in world history and also utilized political philosophies from many sources to develop this hybrid. Separation of powers, three branches of government, dual sovereignty; this is complicated and intricate. I say that the form of government established for our Republic is also delicate because it requires, as Washington, Adams, and others have said; morality, virtue, and knowledge among the people. If we lose these character traits as a people we can lose the gift that was bestowed on us by the founders. The Constitution is simple, in that, the original document is four pages in length. The Constitution is durable because it has stood for 223 years, during which time it has withered the assault of friend and foe.

It can be argued that today the Constitution is not being followed or adhered to by most of our people as well as our elected representatives. If we would have continued to follow the Constitution in the manner that the founders intended we would not be in the predicament that we are today. What was their intent? Hopefully this book has provided insight into their worldview in the 18th and early 19th centuries. It is evident that the founders of America had a biblical worldview. Whether they were all evangelical Christians is not our concern here. What can be said is that the vast majority of them believed in a Sovereign God who governed in the affairs of men. They believed, as did Blackstone and Locke that rights and law come from God. This worldview led them to hold the belief that, as Franklin said, only a virtuous people were capable of freedom. If God and the Bible didn't matter why would George Washington have said, "let us with caution indulge the supposition that morality can be maintained without religion"? With this worldview they believed that man was answerable to God, not to earthly kings. So, they set about to build a system of limited government where life, liberty, and property were protected, and man could have maximum freedom to pursue his God given potential. Sadly, the national government in Washington D.C. now stamps out creativity and ingenuity through regulation and taxation. If we are to restore the Republic we must ask ourselves, "What would George Washington do?" Now after reading this book you have a basis for being able to understand what George Washington and his compatriots would do when it comes to voting, or holding your elected representative accountable.

I encourage you to pursue virtue and moral excellence. I encourage you to read, study, discuss, teach, and get involved in the civic affairs of your community, state, and country. There is no time left for anyone to sit on the sidelines.

APPENDIX

1. Mayflower Compact -1620
2. Fundamental Orders of Connecticut -1639
3. Declaration of Rights and Grievances -1765
4. Suffolk Resolves -1774
5. Declaration and Resolves of the First Continental Congress -October 14, 1774
6. Give Me Liberty – Patrick Henry - 1775
7. Olive Branch Petition – July 1775
8. Declaration of the Causes and Necessity of Taking Up Arms – July 1775
9. Thomas Jefferson letter to Gideon Granger -Aug. 13, 1800
10. Thomas Jefferson First Inaugural Address - 1801
11. Essay on Property, James Madison - 1792
12. Virginia Declaration of Rights – June 1776
13. Summary View of the Rights of British America in 1774
14. Massachusetts Circular Letter - 1768
15. Address of the Annapolis Convention - 1786
16. Virginia Plan - 1787
17. New Jersey Plan - 1787
18. Ron Paul Congressional Speech 10/10/2001, text HR 3074, text HR 3076
19. NDAA section 1021
20. George Washington Farewell Address - 1796
21. Thomas Jefferson Second Inaugural Address - 1805
22. James Madison First Inaugural - 1809

Appendix 1

Mayflower Compact Nov. 11, 1620

In the name of God, Amen. We, whose names are underwritten, the Loyal Subjects of our dread Sovereign Lord, King James, by the Grace of God, of Great Britain, France, and Ireland, King, Defender of the Faith, &c. Having undertaken for the Glory of God, and Advancement of the Christian Faith, and the Honour of our King and Country, a Voyage to plant the first Colony in the northern Parts of Virginia; Do by these Presents, solemnly and mutually, in the Presence of God and one another, covenant and combine ourselves into a civil Body Politick, for our better Ordering and Preservation, and the Furtherance of the Ends aforesaid: And by Virtue hereof do enact, constitute, and frame, such just and equal Laws, Ordinances, Acts, Constitutions, and Officers, from time to time, as shall be thought most meet and convenient for the general Good of the Colony, unto which we promise all due Submission and Obedience.

In Witness whereof we have hereunto subscribed subscribed our names at Cape-Cod, the eleventh of November, in the Reign of our Sovereign Lord King James of England, France, and Ireland, the eighteenth, and of Scotland, the fifty-fourth, Anno Domini, 1620.[212]

Signers

John Alden	Edward Leister	Thomas Rogers
Isaac Allerton	Edmund Margeson	George Soule
John Allerton	John Craxton	Miles Standish
John Billington	Edward Doten	Edward Tilly
Richard Bitteridge	Francis Eaton	John Tilly
William Bradford	Thomas English	Thomas Tinker
William Brewster	Moses Fletcher	John Turner
Peter Brown	Edward Fuller	Richard Warren
John Carver	Samuel Fuller	William White
James Chilton	Richard Gardiner	Thomas Williams
Richard Clark	Christopher Martin	Edward Winslow
Francis Cooke	William Mullins	Gilbert Winslow
Stephen Hopkins	Digery Priest	John Goodman
John Howland	John Rigdale	

Appendix 2
Fundamental Orders of CT
January 14, 1639

FORASMUCH as it has pleased the Almighty God by the wise disposition of his divine providence so to order and dispose of things that we the Inhabitants and Residents of Windsor, Hartford and Wethersfield are now cohabiting and dwelling in and upon the River of Connectecotte and the lands thereunto adjoining; and well knowing where a people are gathered together the word of God requires that to maintain the peace and union of such a people there should be an orderly and decent Government established according to God, to order and dispose of the affairs of the people at all seasons as occasion shall require; do therefore associate and conjoin ourselves to be as one Public State or Commonwealth; and do, for ourselves and our Successors and such as shall be adjoined to us at any time hereafter, enter into Combination and Confederation together, to maintain and preserve the liberty and purity of the Gospel of our Lord Jesus which we now profess, as also the discipline of the Churches, which according to the truth of the said Gospel is now practiced amongst us; as also in our Civil Affairs to be guided and governed according to such Laws, Rules, Orders and Decrees as shall be made, ordered and decreed, as followeth:-

1. It is Ordered, sentenced and decreed, that there shall be yearly two General Assemblies or Courts, the one the second Thursday in April, the other the second Thursday in September, following; the first shall be called the Court of Election, wherein shall be yearly chosen from time to time so many Magistrates and other public Officers as shall be found requisite: Whereof one to be chosen Governor for the year ensuing and until another be chosen, and no other Magistrate to be chosen for more than one year; provided always there be six chosen besides the Governor; which being chosen and sworn according to an Oath recorded for that purpose shall have the power to administer justice according to the Laws here established, and for want thereof according to the rule of the Word of God; which choice shall be made by all that are admitted freemen and have taken the Oath of Fidelity, and do cohabit within this Jurisdiction, (having been admitted inhabitants by the major part of the Town wherein they live), or the major part of such as shall be then present.

2. It is Ordered, sentenced and decreed, that the Election of the aforesaid Magistrates shall be on this manner: every person present and qualified for choice shall bring in (to the persons deputed to receive them) one single paper with the name of him written in it whom he desires to have Governor, and he that hath the greatest number of papers shall be Governor for that year. And the rest of the Magistrates or public Officers to be chosen in this manner: the Secretary for the time being shall first read the names of all that are to be put to choice and then shall severally nominate them distinctly, and every one that would have the person nominated to be chosen shall bring in one single paper written upon, and he that would not have him chosen shall bring a blank: and every one that hath more written papers than blanks shall be a Magistrate for that year; which papers shall be received and told by one or more that shall be then chosen by the court and sworn to be faithful therein; but in case there should not be six chosen as aforesaid, besides the Governor, out of those which are nominated, then he or they which have the most written papers shall be a Magistrate or Magistrates for the ensuing year, to make up the aforesaid number.

3. It is Ordered, sentenced and decreed, that the Secretary shall not nominate any person, nor shall any person be chosen newly into the Magistracy which was not propounded in some General Court before, to be nominated the next Election; and to that end it shall be lawful for each of the Towns aforesaid by their deputies to nominate any two whom they conceive fit to be put to election; and the Court may add so many more as they judge requisite.

4. It is Ordered, sentenced and decreed, that no person be chosen Governor above once in two years, and that the Governor be always a member of some approved congregation, and formerly of the Magistracy within this Jurisdiction; and that all the Magistrates Freemen of this Commonwealth: and that no Magistrate or other public officer shall execute any part of his or their office before they are severally sworn, which shall be done in the face of the court if they be present, and in case of absence by some deputed for that purpose.

5. It is Ordered, sentenced and decreed, that to the aforesaid Court of Election the several Towns shall send their deputies, and when the Elections are ended they may proceed in any public service as at other Courts. Also the other General Court in September shall be for making of laws, and any other public occasion, which concerns the good of the Commonwealth.

6. It is Ordered, sentenced and decreed, that the Governor shall, either by himself or by the secretary, send out summons to the constables of our Town for the calling of these two standing Courts one month at least before their several times: And also if the Governor and the greatest part of the Magistrates

see cause upon any special occasion to call a General Court, they may give order to the Secretary so to do within fourteen days warning; and if urgent necessity so require, upon a shorter notice, giving sufficient grounds for it to the deputies when they meet, or else be questioned for the same; And if the Governor and major part of Magistrates shall either neglect or refuse to call the two General standing Courts or either of them, as also at other times when the occasions of the Commonwealth require, the Freemen thereof, or the major part of them, shall petition to them so to do: if then it be either denied or neglected the said Freemen or the major part of them shall have the power to give order to the Constables of the several Towns to do the same, and so may meet together, and choose to themselves a Moderator, and may proceed to do any act of power, which any other General Courts may.

7. It is Ordered, sentenced and decreed, that after there are warrants given out for any of the said General Courts, the Constable or Constables of each town shall forthwith give notice distinctly to the inhabitants of the same, in some public assembly or by going or sending from house to house, that at a place and time by him or them limited and set, they meet and assemble themselves together to elect and choose certain deputies to be at the General Court then following to agitate the affairs of the Commonwealth; which said deputies shall be chosen by all that are admitted Inhabitants in the several Towns and have taken the oath of fidelity; provided that none be chosen a Deputy for any General Court which is not a Freeman of this Commonwealth.

The aforesaid deputies shall be chosen in manner following: every person that is present and qualified as before expressed, shall bring the names of such, written in several papers, as they desire to have chosen for that employment, and these three or four, more or less, being the number agreed on to be chosen for that time, that have the greatest number of papers written for them shall be deputies for that Court; whose names shall be endorsed on the back side of the warrant and returned into the Court, with the constable or constables hand unto the same.

8. It is Ordered, sentenced and decreed, that Windsor, Hartford and Wethersfield shall have power, each Town, to send four of their Freemen as deputies to every General Court; and whatsoever other Towns shall be hereafter added to this Jurisdiction, they shall send so many deputies as the Court shall judge meet, a reasonable proportion to the number of Freemen that are in the said Towns being to be attended therein; which deputies shall have the power of the whole Town to give their votes and allowance to all such laws and orders as may be for the public good, and unto which the said Towns are to be bound.

9. It is Ordered, sentenced and decreed, that the deputies thus chosen shall have power and liberty to appoint a time and a place of meeting together before any

General Court to advise and consult of all such things as may concern the good of the public, as also to examine their own Elections, whether according to the order, and if they or the greatest part of them find any election to be illegal they may seclude such for present from their meeting, and return the same and their reasons to the Court; and if it prove true, the Court may fine the party or parties so intruding and the Town, if they see cause, and give out a warrant to go to a new election in a legal way, either in part or in whole. Also the said deputies shall have power to fine any that shall be disorderly at their meetings, or for not coming in due time or place according to appointment; and they may return the said fines into the Court if it be refused to be paid, and the Treasurer to take notice of it, and to estreat or levy the same as he does other fines.

10. It is Ordered, sentenced and decreed, that every General Court, except such as through neglect of the Governor and the greatest part of the Magistrates the Freemen themselves do call, shall consist of the Governor, or someone chosen to moderate the Court, and four other Magistrates at least, with the major part of the deputies of the several Towns legally chosen; and in case the Freemen, or major part of them, through neglect or refusal of the Governor and major part of the Magistrates, shall call a Court, it shall consist of the major part of Freemen that are present or their deputies, with a Moderator chosen by them: In which said General Courts shall consist the supreme power of the Commonwealth, and they only shall have power to make laws or repeal them, to grant levies, to admit of Freemen, dispose of lands undisposed of, to several Towns or persons, and also shall have power to call either court or Magistrate or any other person whatsoever into question for any misdemeanor, and may for just causes displace or deal otherwise according to the nature of the offense; and also may deal in any other matter that concerns the good of this Commonwealth, except election of Magistrates, which shall be done by the whole body of Freemen. In which Court the Governor or Moderator shall have power to order the court to give liberty of speech, and silence unseasonable and disorderly speaking, to put all things to vote, and in case the vote be equal to have the casting voice. But none of these Courts shall be adjourned or dissolved without the consent of the major part of the Court.

11. It is Ordered, sentenced and decreed, that when any General Court upon the occasions of the Commonwealth have agreed upon any sum or sums of money to be levied upon the several Towns within this Jurisdiction, that a committee be chosen to set out and appoint what shall be the proportion of every Town to pay of the said levy, provided the committees be made up of an equal number out of each Town.

14th January, 1638, [N.S., 24th January, 1639] the 11 Orders above said are voted.[213]

Appendix 3

Declaration of Rights and Grievances

October 1765

The members of this Congress, sincerely devoted, with the warmest sentiments of affection and duty to his Majesty's person and government, inviolably attached to the present happy establishment of the Protestant succession and with minds deeply impressed by a sense of the present and impending misfortunes of the British Colonies on this continent; having considered as maturely as time will permit, the circumstances of the said colonies, esteem it our indispensable duty to make the following declarations of our humble opinion, respecting the most essential rights and liberties of the colonists, and of the grievances under which they labour, by reason of several late Acts of Parliament.

I. That his Majesty's subjects in these colonies owe the same allegiance to the Crown of Great Britain, that is owing from his subjects born within the realm, and all due subordination to that august body, the Parliament of Great Britain.

II. That his Majesty's liege subjects in these colonies are intitled to all the inherent rights and liberties of his natural born subjects, within the kingdom of Great Britain.

III. That it is inseparably essential to the freedom of a people, and the undoubted right of Englishmen, that no Taxes be imposed on them but with their own consent, given personally, or by their representatives.

IV. That the people of these colonies are not, and, from their local circumstances cannot be, represented in the House of Commons in Great Britain.

V. That the only representatives of the people of these colonies are persons chosen therein by themselves, and that no taxes ever have been, or can be constitutionally imposed on them, but by their respective legislatures.

VI. That all supplies to the Crown being free gifts of the people, it is unreasonable and inconsistent with the principles and spirit of the British Constitution, for the people of Great Britain to grant to his Majesty the property of the colonists.

VII. That trial by jury is the inherent and invaluable right of every British subject in these colonies.

VIII. That — [the Stamp Act] ... by imposing taxes on the in habitants of these colonies, and the said Act, and several other Acts, by extending the jurisdiction of the courts of admiralty beyond its ancient limits, have a manifest tendency to subvert the rights and liberties of the colonists.

IX. That the duties imposed by several late Acts of Parliament, from the peculiar circumstances of these colonies, will be extremely burthensome and grievous; and from the scarcity of specie, the payment of them absolutely unpracticable.

X. That as the profits of the trade of these colonies ultimately centre in Great Britain, to pay for the manufactures which they are obliged to take from thence, they eventually contribute very largely to all supplies granted there to the Crown.

XI. That the restrictions imposed by several late Acts of Parliament on the trade of these colonies, will render them unable to purchase the manufactures of Great Britain.

XII. That the increase, prosperity, and happiness of these colonies, depend on the full and free enjoyments of their rights and liberties, and an intercourse with Great Britain mutually affectionate and advantageous.

XIII. That it is the right of the British subjects in these colonies to petition the King, or either House of Parliament.

Lastly, That it is the indispensable duty of these colonies, to the best of sovereigns, to the Mother Country, and to themselves, to endeavour by a loyal and dutiful address to his Majesty and humble applications to both Houses of Parliament, to procure the repeal of the Act for granting and applying certain stamp duties, of all clauses of any other Acts of Parliament, Whereby the jurisdiction of the admiralty is extended as aforesaid, and of the other late Acts for the restriction of American Commerce.[214]

Appendix 4

Suffolk Resolves 1774

Joseph Warren

At a Meeting of the Delegates of every Town & District in the County of Suffolk, on Tuesday the Sixth of September, at the House of Mr. Richard Woodward of Deadham, and by Adjournment at the House of Mr. Daniel Vose of Milton, on Friday the Ninth instant, Joseph Palmer, Esq; being chosen Moderator, and William Thompson, Esq; Clerk, a Committee was chosen to bring in a Report to the Convention, and the following being several Times read and put Paragraph by Paragraph, was UNANIMOUSLY voted, viz.

WHEREAS the Power, but not the Justice; the Vengeance, but not the Wisdom of Great-Britain, which of old persecuted, scourged and exiled our fugitive Parents from their native Shores, now pursues us their guiltless Children with unrelenting Severity - And whereas this then savage and uncultivated Desert was purchased by the Toil and Treasure or acquired by the Valor and Blood of those our venerable Progenitors, who bequeathed to us the dear-bought Inheritance, who consigned it to our Care and Protection; the most sacred Obligations are upon us to transmit the glorious Purchase, unfettered by Power, unclogged with Shackles, to our innocent and beloved Offspring. On the Fortitude- on the Wisdom and on the Exertions of this important Day, is suspended the Fate of this New World; and of unborn Millions.-- If a boundless Extent of Continent, swarming with Millions, will tamely submit to live move and have their Being at the arbitrary Will of a licentious Minister, they basely yield to voluntary Slavery, and future Generations shall load their Memories with incessant Execrations.--On the other Hand, if we arrest the Hand which would ransack our Pockets, if we disarm the Parricide who points the Dagger to our Bosoms, if we nobly defeat that fatal Edict which proclaims a Power to frame Laws for us in all Cases whatsoever, thereby entailing the endless and numberless Curses of Slavery upon Us, our Heirs and their Heirs forever; if we successfully resist that unparalleled Usurpation of unconstitutional Power, whereby our Capital is robbed of the Means of Life, whereby the Streets of Boston are thronged with military Executioners, whereby our Coasts are lined, and Harbours crowded with Ships of War, whereby the Charter of the Colony, that sacred Barrier against the Encroachments of Tyranny, is mutilated, and in effect annihilated; whereby a murderous Law is framed to shelter Villains from the Hands of Justice; whereby that unalienable and inestimable Inheritance, which we derived from Nature, the Constitution of Britain, which was covenanted to us in the charter of the Province, is totally wrecked, annulled, and vacated; Posterity will acknowledge that Virtue which preserved them free and happy; and while we enjoy the Rewards and Blessings of the Faithful, the Torrent of Panegyrick will roll our Reputations to that latest Period, when the Streams of Time shall be absorbed in the Abyss of Eternity.

Therefore, WE HAVE RESOLVED, AND DO RESOLVE,

1. That whereas his Majesty George the Third is the rightful Successor to the Throne of Great-Britain, and justly entitled to the Allegiance of the British Realm, and agreeable to Compact, of the English Colonies in America,-- Therefore we the Heirs and Successors of the first Planters of this Colony, do cheerfully acknowledge the said George the Third to be our rightful Sovereign, and that said Covenant is the Tenure and Claim on which are founded our Allegiance and Submission.

2. That it is an indispensable Duty which we owe to God, our Country, Ourselves and Posterity, by all lawful Ways and Means in our Power to maintain, defend and preserve those civil and religious Rights and Liberties, for which many of our Fathers fought – bled -- and died; and to hand them down entire to future Generations.

3. That the late Acts of the British Parliament for blocking up the Harbour of Boston, and for altering the established Form of Government in this Colony; and for screening the most flagitious Violators of the Laws of the Province from a legal Trial, are gross Infractions of those Rights to which we are justly entitled by the Laws of Nature, the British Constitution, and the Charter of the Province.

4. That no Obedience is due from this Province to either or any Part of the Acts above-mentioned; but that they be rejected as the Attempts of a wicked Administration to enslave America.

5. That so long as the Justices of our Superior Court of Judicature, Court of Assize, and General Goal Delivery, and Inferior Courts of Common Pleas in this County are appointed, or hold their Places by any other Tenure than that which the Charter and the Laws of the Province direct; they must be considered as under undue Influence, and are therefore unconstitutional Officers, and as such no Regard ought to be paid to them by the people of this county.

6. That if the Justices of the Superior Court of Judicature, Court of Assize, &c. Justices of the Court of Common Pleas, or of the General Sessions

of the Peace, shall sit and act during their present disqualified State, this County will support and bear harmless all Sheriffs and their Deputies, Constables, Jurors and other Officers, who shall refuse to carry into Execution the Orders of said Courts; And as far as possible, to prevent the Inconveniencies that must attend the Suspension of the Courts of Justice, we do earnestly recommend it to all Creditors to exercise all reasonable and generous Forbearance to their Debtors, and to all Debtors to discharge their just Debts with all possible Speed, and if any Disputes concerning debts or trespasses should arise, which cannot be settled by the Parties, we recommend it to them to submit all such Causes to Arbitration; and if the Parties or either of them shall refuse so to do, they ought to be considered as co-operating with the Enemies of this Country.

7. That it be recommended to the Collectors of Taxes, Constables and all other Officers who have public Monies in their Hands, to retain the same, and not to make any Payment thereof to the Province or County treasurers, until the Civil Government of the Province is placed upon a constitutional Foundation, or until it shall otherwise be ordered by the proposed Provincial Congress.

8. That the Persons who have accepted seats at the Council Board, by Virtue of a Mandamus from the King, in Conformity to the late Act of the British parliament, entitled, "An act for the regulating the Government of the Massachusetts-Bay," have acted in direct Violation of the Duty they owe to their Country, and have thereby given great and just Offence to this People. Therefore, Resolved, That this County do recommend it to all Persons who have so highly offended by accepting said Departments and have not already publicly resigned their Seats at the Council Board, to make public Resignations of their Places at said Board, on or before the TWENTIETH DAY of this Instant September; and that all Persons refusing so to do shall from and after said Day be considered by this County as obstinate and incorrigible Enemies to this Colony.

9. That the Fortifications begun and now carrying on upon Boston Neck are justly alarming to this County, and gives us Reason to apprehend some hostile Intention against that Town, more especially as the Commander in Chief has in a very extraordinary Manner, removed the Powder from the Magazine at Charlestown, and has also forbidden the Keeper of the Magazine at Boston to deliver out to the Owners the Powder which they had lodged in said Magazine.

10. That the late Act of Parliament for establishing the Roman Catholic Religion, and the French Laws in that extensive Country now called

Canada, is dangerous in an extreme Degree to the Protestant Religion, and to the civil Rights and Liberties of all America; and therefore as Men and Protestant Christians we are indispensably obliged to take all proper Measures for our Security.

11. That whereas our Enemies have flattered themselves that they shall make an easy Prey of this numerous, brave and hardy People, from an Apprehension that they are unacquainted with military Discipline, We therefore for the Honour, Defence and Security of this County and Province advise, as it has been recommended to take away all Commissions from the Officers of the Militia, that those who now hold Commissions or such other Persons be elected in each Town as Officers in the Militia as shall be judged of sufficient Capacity for that Purpose, and who have evidenced themselves the inflexible Friends to the Rights of the People, and that the Inhabitants of those Towns and Districts who are qualified do use their utmost Diligence to acquaint themselves with the Art of War as soon as possible and do for that purpose appear under Arms at least once every week.

12. That during the present hostile Appearances on the Part of Great-Britain, notwithstanding the many Insults and Oppressions which we most sensibly resent; yet nevertheless from our Affection to his Majesty which we have at all Times evidenced; we are determined to act merely upon the Defensive, so long as such Conduct may be vindicated by Reason and the Principles of Self-preservation, but no longer.

13. That as we understand it has been in Contemplation to apprehend sundry Persons of this County who have rendered themselves conspicuous in contending for the violated Rights and Liberties of their Countrymen, we do recommend that, should such an audacious Measure be put in practice, to seize and keep in safe Custody every Servant of the present tyrannical and unconstitutional Government throughout the County and Province, until the Persons so apprehended be liberated from the Hands of our Adversaries, and restored safe and uninjured to their respective Friends and Families.

14. That until our Rights are fully restored to us, we will to the utmost of our Power (and we recommend the same to the other Counties) withhold all commercial Intercourse with Great-Britain Ireland and the West-Indies, and abstain from the Consumption of British Merchandize and Manufactures, and especially of East-India Teas and Piece Goods, with such Additions, Alterations and Exceptions only, as the Grand Congress of the Colonies may agree to.

15. That under our present Circumstances it is incumbent on us to encourage Arts and Manufactures amongst us by all Means in our Power, and that

Joseph Palmer, Esq; of Braintree, Mr. Ebenezer Dorr of Roxbury, Mr. James Boies and Mr. Edward Preston of Milton, and Mr. Nathaniel Guild of Walpole, be and are hereby appointed a Committee to consider of the best Ways and Means to promote and establish the same, and to report to this Convention as soon as may be.

16. That the Exigencies of our public Affairs demand that a provincial Congress be called to consult such Measures as may be adopted and vigorously executed by the whole People; and we do recommend it to the several Towns in this County, to chuse Members for such a Provincial Congress, to be holden at Concord on the second Tuesday of October next ensuing.

17. That this County confiding in the Wisdom and Integrity of the Continental Congress now sitting at Philadelphia, pay all due Respect and Submission to such Measures as may be recommended by them to the Colonies, for the Restoration and Establishment of our just Rights, civil and religious, and for renewing that Harmony and Union between Great-Britain and the Colonies so earnestly wished for by all good Men.

18. Whereas the universal Uneasiness which prevails among all Orders of Men, arising from the wicked and oppressive Measures of the present Administration, may influence some unthinking Persons to commit Outrage upon private Property: We would heartily recommend to all Persons of this Community, not to engage in any Routs, Riots or licentious Attacks upon the Properties of any Person whatsoever, as being subversive of all Order and Government; but, by a steady, manly, uniform and persevering Opposition, to convince our Enemies that in a Contest so important, in a Cause so solemn, our Conduct shall be such as to merit the Approbation of the Wise, and the Admiration of the brave and free of every Age and of every Country.

19. That should our Enemies, by any sudden Manoeuvres, render it necessary for us to ask the Aid and Assistance of our Brethren in the Country, some one of the Committee of Correspondence, or a Selectman of such Town, or the Town adjoining, where such Hostilities shall commence, or shall be expected to commence, shall dispatch Couriers with written Messages to the Selectmen or Committees of Correspondence of the several Towns in the Vicinity, with a written Account of such Matter, who shall dispatch others to Committees or Selectmen more remote, 'till proper and sufficient Assistance be obtained; and that the Expense of said Couriers be defrayed by the County, until it shall be otherwise ordered by the Provincial Congress.

Attest. WILLIAM THOMPSON. Clerk[215]

Appendix 5

Declaration and Resolves of the First Continental Congress

OCTOBER 14, 1774

Whereas, since the close of the last war, the British parliament, claiming a power, of right, to bind the people of America by statutes in all cases whatsoever, hath, in some acts, expressly imposed taxes on them, and in others, under various pretences, but in fact for the purpose of raising a revenue, hath imposed rates and duties payable in these colonies, established a board of commissioners, with unconstitutional powers, and extended the jurisdiction of courts of admiralty, not only for collecting the said duties, but for the trial of causes merely arising within the body of a county.

And whereas, in consequence of other statutes, judges, who before held only estates at will in their offices, have been made dependant on the crown alone for their salaries, and standing armies kept in times of peace: And whereas it has lately been resolved in parliament, that by force of a statute, made in the thirty-fifth year of the reign of King Henry the Eighth, colonists may be transported to England, and tried there upon accusations for treasons and misprisions, or concealments of treasons committed in the colonies, and by a late statute, such trials have been directed in cases therein mentioned:

And whereas, in the last session of parliament, three statutes were made; one entitled, "An act to discontinue, in such manner and for such time as are therein mentioned, the landing and discharging, lading, or shipping of goods, wares and merchandise, at the town, and within the harbour of Boston, in the province of Massachusetts-Bay in New England;" another entitled, "An act for the better regulating the government of the province of Massachusetts-Bay in New England;" and another entitled, "An act for the impartial administration of justice, in the cases of persons questioned for any act done by them in the execution of the law, or for the suppression of riots and tumults, in the province of the Massachusetts-Bay in New England;" and another statute was then made, "for making more effectual provision for the government of the province of Quebec, etc." All which statutes are impolitic, unjust, and cruel, as well as unconstitutional, and most dangerous and destructive of American rights:

And whereas, assemblies have been frequently dissolved, contrary to the rights of the people, when they attempted to deliberate on grievances; and their dutiful, humble, loyal, and reasonable petitions to the crown for redress, have been repeatedly treated with contempt, by his Majesty's ministers of state:

The good people of the several colonies of New-Hampshire, Massachusetts-Bay, Rhode Island and Providence Plantations, Connecticut, New-York, New-Jersey, Pennsylvania, Newcastle, Kent, and Sussex on Delaware, Maryland, Virginia, North- Carolina and South-Carolina, justly alarmed at these arbitrary proceedings of parliament and administration, have severally elected, constituted, and appointed deputies to meet, and sit in general Congress, in the city of Philadelphia, in order to obtain such establishment, as that their religion, laws, and liberties, may not be subverted: Whereupon the deputies so appointed being now assembled, in a full and free representation of these colonies, taking into their most serious consideration, the best means of attaining the ends aforesaid, do, in the first place, as Englishmen, their ancestors in like cases have usually done, for asserting and vindicating their rights and liberties, DECLARE,

That the inhabitants of the English colonies in North-America, by the immutable laws of nature, the principles of the English constitution, and the several charters or compacts, have the following RIGHTS:

Resolved, N.C.D. 1. That they are entitled to life, liberty and property: and they have never ceded to any foreign power whatever, a right to dispose of either without their consent.

Resolved, N.C.D. 2. That our ancestors, who first settled these colonies, were at the time of their emigration from the mother country, entitled to all the rights, liberties, and immunities of free and natural- born subjects, within the realm of England.

Resolved, N.C.D. 3. That by such emigration they by no means forfeited, surrendered, or lost any of those rights, but that they were, and their descendants now are, entitled to the exercise and enjoyment of all such of them, as their local and other circumstances enable them to exercise and enjoy.

Resolved, 4. That the foundation of English liberty, and of all free government, is a right in the people to participate in their legislative council: and as the English colonists are not represented, and from their local and other circumstances, cannot properly be represented in the British parliament, they are entitled to a free and exclusive power of legislation in their several provincial legislatures, where their right of representation can alone be preserved, in all cases of taxation and internal polity, subject only to the negative of their sovereign, in such manner as has been heretofore used and accustomed: But, from the necessity of the case, and a regard to the mutual interest of both countries, we cheerfully consent to the operation of such acts of the British parliament, as are bona fide, restrained to the regulation of our external commerce, for the purpose of securing the commercial advantages of the whole empire to the mother country, and the commercial benefits of its respective members; excluding every idea of taxation internal or external, for raising a revenue on the subjects, in America, without their consent.

Resolved, N.C.D. 5. That the respective colonies are entitled to the common law of England, and more especially to the great and inestimable privilege of being tried by their peers of the vicinage, according to the course of that law.

Resolved, N.C.D. 6. That they are entitled to the benefit of such of the English statutes, as existed at the time of their colonization; and which they have, by experience, respectively found to be applicable to their several local and other circumstances.

Resolved, N.C.D. 7. That these, his majesty's colonies, are likewise entitled to all the immunities and privileges granted and confirmed to them by royal charters, or secured by their several codes of provincial laws.

Resolved, N.C.D. 8. That they have a right peaceably to assemble, consider of their grievances, and petition the king; and that all prosecutions, prohibitory proclamations, and commitments for the same, are illegal.

Resolved, N.C.D. 9. That the keeping a standing army in these colonies, in times of peace, without the consent of the legislature of that colony, in which such army is kept, is against law.

Resolved, N.C.D. 10. It is indispensably necessary to good government, and rendered essential by the English constitution, that the constituent branches of the legislature be independent of each other; that, therefore, the exercise of legislative power in several colonies, by a council appointed, during pleasure, by the crown, is unconstitutional, dangerous and destructive to the freedom of American legislation.

All and each of which the aforesaid deputies, in behalf of themselves, and their constituents, do claim, demand, and insist on, as their indubitable rights and liberties; which cannot be legally taken from them, altered or abridged by any power whatever, without their own consent, by their representatives in their several provincial legislatures.

In the course of our inquiry, we find many infringements and violations of the foregoing rights, which, from an ardent desire, that harmony and mutual intercourse of affection and interest may be restored, we pass over for the present, and proceed to state such acts and measures as have been adopted since the last war, which demonstrate a system formed to enslave America.

Resolved, N.C.D. That the following acts of parliament are infringements and violations of the rights of the colonists; and that the repeal of them is essentially necessary, in order to restore harmony between Great Britain and the American colonies, viz.

The several acts of 4 Geo. III. ch. 15, and ch. 34.-5 Geo. III. ch.25.-6 Geo. III ch. 52.-7 Geo.III. ch. 41 and ch. 46.-8 Geo. III. ch. 22. which impose duties for the purpose of raising a revenue in America, extend the power of the admiralty courts beyond their ancient limits, deprive the American subject of trial by jury, authorise the judges certificate to indemnify the prosecutor from damages, that he might otherwise be liable to, requiring oppressive security from a claimant of ships and goods seized, before he shall be allowed to defend his property, and are subversive of American rights.

Also 12 Geo. III. ch. 24, intituled, "An act for the better securing his majesty's dockyards, magazines, ships, ammunition, and stores," which declares a new offence in America, and deprives the American subject of a constitutional trial by jury of the vicinage, by authorising the trial of any person, charged with the committing any offence described in the said act, out of the realm, to be indicted and tried for the same in any shire or county within the realm.

Also the three acts passed in the last session of parliament, for stopping the port and blocking up the harbour of Boston, for altering the charter and government of Massachusetts-Bay, and that which is entitled, "An act for the better administration of justice, etc."

Also the act passed in the same session for establishing the Roman Catholic religion, in the province of Quebec, abolishing the equitable system of English laws, and erecting a tyranny there, to the great danger (from so total a dissimilarity of religion, law and government) of the neighboring British colonies, by the assistance of whose blood and treasure the said country was conquered from France.

Also the act passed in the same session, for the better providing suitable quarters for officers and soldiers in his majesty's service, in North-America.

Also, that the keeping a standing army in several of these colonies, in time of peace, without the consent of the legislature of that colony, in which such army is kept, is against law.

To these grievous acts and measures, Americans cannot submit, but in hopes their fellow subjects in Great Britain will, on a revision of them, restore us to that state, in which both countries found happiness and prosperity, we have for the present, only resolved to pursue the following peaceable measures: 1. To enter into a non-importation, non-consumption, and non-exportation agreement or association. 2. To prepare an address to the people of Great-Britain, and a memorial to the inhabitants of British America: and 3. To prepare a loyal address to his majesty, agreeable to resolutions already entered into.[216]

Appendix 6

Give Me Liberty or Give Me Death

Patrick Henry at St. John's Church, Richmond, VA

March 23, 1775

No man, Mr. President, thinks more highly than I do of the patriotism, as well as the abilities, of the very honorable gentlemen who have just addressed the House. But different men often see the same subject in different lights; and, therefore, I hope it will not be thought disrespectful to those gentlemen if, entertaining, as I do, opinions of a character very opposite to theirs, I should speak forth my sentiments freely, and without reserve. This is no time for ceremony. The question before the house is one of awful moment to this country. For my own part, I consider it as nothing less than a question of freedom or slavery. And in proportion to the magnitude of the subject ought to be the freedom of the debate. It is only in this way that we can hope to arrive at truth, and fulfil the great responsibility which we hold to God and our country. Should I keep back my opinions at such a time, through fear of giving offence, I should consider myself as guilty of treason towards my country, and of an act of disloyalty towards the majesty of Heaven, which I revere above all earthly kings.

Mr. President, it is natural to man to indulge in the illusions of Hope. We are apt to shut our eyes against a painful truth, and listen to the song of that siren till she transforms us into beasts. Is this the part of wise men, engaged in a great and arduous struggle for liberty? Are we disposed to be of the number of those who, having eyes, see not, and having ears, hear not, the things which so nearly concern their temporal salvation? For my part, whatever anguish of spirit it may cost, I am willing to know the whole truth; to know the worst, and to provide for it.

I have but one lamp by which my feet are guided, and that is the lamp of experience. I know of no way of judging of the future but by the past. And, judging by the past, I wish to know what there has been in the conduct of the British ministry, for the last ten years, to justify those hopes with which gentlemen have been pleased to solace themselves and the House. Is it that insidious smile with which our petition has been lately received? Trust it not, sir; it will prove a snare to your feet. Suffer not yourselves to be betrayed with a kiss. Ask yourselves how this gracious reception of our petition comports with those warlike preparations which cover our waters and darken our land. Are fleets and armies necessary to a work of love and reconciliation? Have we shown ourselves so unwilling to be reconciled, that force must be called in to win back our love? Let us not deceive ourselves, sir. These are the implements of war and subjugation, — the last arguments to which kings resort.

I ask gentlemen, sir, what means this martial array, if its purpose be not to force us to submission? Can gentlemen assign any other possible motive for it? Has Great Britain any enemy in this quarter of the world, to call for all this accumulation of navies and armies? No, sir, she has none. They are meant for us: they can be meant for no other. They are sent over to bind and rivet upon us those chains which the British ministry have been so long forging.

And what have we to oppose to them? Shall we try argument? Sir, we have been trying that for the last ten years. Have we anything new to offer upon the subject? Nothing. We have held the subject up in every light of which it is capable; but it has been all in vain. Shall we resort to entreaty, and humble supplication? What terms shall we find which have not been already exhausted?

Let us not, I beseech you, sir, deceive ourselves longer. Sir, we have done everything that could be done to avert the storm which is now coming on. We have petitioned; we have remonstrated; we have supplicated; we have prostrated ourselves before the throne, and have implored its interposition to arrest the tyrannical hands of the ministry and Parliament. Our petitions have been slighted; our remonstrances have produced additional violence and insult; our supplications have been disregarded; and we have been spurned with contempt from the foot of the throne.

In vain, after these things, may we indulge the fond hope of peace and reconciliation. There is no longer any room for hope. If we wish to be free; if we mean to preserve inviolate those inestimable privileges for which we have been so long contending; if we mean not basely to abandon the noble struggle in which we have been so long engaged, and which we have pledged ourselves never to abandon until the glorious object of our contest shall be obtained, — we must fight! I repeat it, sir, — we must fight! An appeal to arms, and to the God of hosts, is all that is left us.'

They tell us, sir, that we are weak, — unable to cope with so formidable an adversary. But when shall we be stronger? Will it be the next week, or the next year? Will it be when we are totally disarmed, and when a British guard shall be stationed in every house? Shall we gather strength by irresolution and inaction? Shall we acquire the means of effectual resistance by lying supinely on our backs, and hugging the delusive phantom of Hope, until our enemies shall have bound us hand and foot?

Sir, we are not weak, if we make a proper use of those means which the God of nature hath placed in our power. Three millions of people armed in the holy cause of liberty, and in such a country as that which we possess, are invincible by any force which our enemy can send against us.

Besides, sir, we shall not fight our battles alone. There is a just God who presides over the destinies of nations, and who will raise up friends to fight our battles for us. The battle, sir, is not to the strong alone: it is to the vigilant, the active, the brave. Besides, sir, we have no election. If we were base enough to desire it, it is now too late to retire from the contest. There is no retreat but in submission and slavery. Our chains are forged. Their clanking may be heard on the plains of Boston. The war is inevitable. And let it come! I repeat it, sir, let it come!

It is in vain, sir, to extenuate the matter. Gentle men may cry peace, peace, but there is no peace. The war is actually begun. The next gale that sweeps from the north will bring to our ears the clash of resounding arms. Our brethren are already in the field. Why stand we here idle? What is it that gentlemen wish? What would they have? Is life so dear, or peace so sweet, as to be purchased at the price of chains and slavery? Forbid it, Almighty God! I know not what course others may take, but as for me, give me liberty, or give me death![217]

Appendix 7

Olive Branch Petition

July 8, 1775

To the king's most excellent Majesty:

Most Gracious Sovereign,

We, your Majesty's faithful subjects of the colonies of new Hampshire, Massachusetts bay, Rhode island and Providence Plantations, Connecticut, New York, New Jersey, Pennsylvania, the counties of New Castle, Kent, and Sussex, on Delaware, Maryland, Virginia, North Carolina, and South Carolina, in behalf of ourselves, and the inhabitants of these colonies, who have deputed us to represent them in general Congress, entreat your Majesty's gracious attention to this our humble petition.

The union between our Mother country and these colonies, and the energy of mild and just government, produced benefits so remarkably important, and afforded such an assurance of their permanency and increase, that the wonder and envy of other Nations were excited, while they beheld Great Britain rising to a power the most extraordinary the world had ever known.

Her rivals, observing that there was no probability of this happy connexion being broken by civil dissensions, and apprehending its future effects, if left any longer undisturbed, resolved to prevent her receiving such continual and formidable accessions of wealth and strength, by checking the growth of these settlements from which they were to be derived.

In the prosecution of this attempt, events so unfavourable to the design took place, that every friend to the interests of Great Britain and these colonies, entertained pleasing and reasonable expectations of seeing an additional force and exertion immediately given to the operations of the union hitherto experienced, by an enlargement of the dominions of the Crown, and the removal of ancient and warlike enemies to a greater distance.

At the conclusion, therefore, of the late war, the most glorious and advantageous that ever had been carried on by British arms, your loyal colonists having contributed to its success, by such repeated and strenuous exertions, as frequently procured them the distinguished approbation of your Majesty, of the late king, and of parliament, doubted not but that they should be permitted, with the rest of the empire, to share in the blessings of peace, and the emoluments of victory and conquest. While these recent and honorable acknowledgments of their merits remained on record in the journals and acts of that august legislature, the Parliament, undefaced by the imputation or even the suspicion of any offence, they were alarmed by a new system of statutes and regulations adopted for the administration of the colonies, that filled their minds with the most painful fears and jealousies; and, to their inexpressible astonishment, perceived the dangers of a foreign quarrel quickly succeeded by domestic dangers, in their judgment, of a more dreadful kind.

Nor were their anxieties alleviated by any tendency in this system to promote the welfare of the Mother country. For tho' its effects were more immediately felt by them, yet its influence appeared to be injurious to the commerce and prosperity of Great Britain.

We shall decline the ungrateful task of describing the irksome variety of artifices, practiced by many of your Majesty's Ministers, the delusive pretences, fruitless terrors, and unavailing severities, that have, from time to time, been dealt out by them, in their attempts to execute this impolitic plan, or of tracing, thro' a series of years past, the progress of the unhappy differences between Great Britain and these colonies, which have flowed from this fatal source.

Your Majesty's Ministers, persevering in their measures, and proceeding to open hostilities for enforcing them, have compelled us to arm in our own defence, and have engaged us in a controversy so peculiarly abhorrent to the affections of your still faithful colonists, that when we consider whom we must oppose in this contest, and if it continues, what may be the consequences, our own particular misfortunes are accounted by us only as parts of our distress.

Knowing to what violent resentments and incurable animosities, civil discords are apt to exasperate and inflame the contending parties, we think ourselves required by indispensable obligations to Almighty God, to your Majesty, to our fellow subjects, and to ourselves, immediately to use all the means in our power, not incompatible with our safety, for stopping the further effusion of blood, and for averting the impending calamities that threaten the British Empire.

Thus called upon to address your Majesty on affairs of such moment to America, and probably to all your dominions, we are earnestly desirous of performing this office, with the utmost deference for your Majesty; and we therefore pray, that your royal magnanimity and benevolence may make the most favourable construction of our expressions on so uncommon an occasion. Could we represent in their full force, the sentiments that agitate the minds of us your dutiful subjects, we are persuaded your Majesty would ascribe any seeming deviation from reverence in our language, and even in our conduct, not to any reprehensible intention, but to the impossibility of reconciling the usual appearances of respect, with a just attention to our own preservation against those artful and cruel enemies, who abuse your royal confidence and authority, for the purpose of effecting our destruction.

Attached to your Majesty's person, family, and government, with all devotion that principle and affection can inspire, connected with Great Britain by the strongest ties that can unite societies, and deploring every event that tends in any degree to weaken them, we solemnly assure your Majesty, that we not only most ardently desire the former harmony between her and these colonies may be restored, but that a concord may be established between them upon so firm a basis as to perpetuate its blessings, uninterrupted by any future dissentions, to succeeding generations in both countries, and to transmit your Majesty's Name to posterity, adorned with that signal and lasting glory, that has attended the memory of those illustrious personages, whose virtues and abilities have extricated states from dangerous convulsions, and, by securing happiness to others, have erected the most noble and durable monuments to their own fame.

We beg leave further to assure your Majesty, that notwithstanding the sufferings of your loyal colonists, during the course of the present controversy, our breasts retain too tender a regard for the kingdom from which we derive our origin, to request such a reconciliation as might in any manner be inconsistent with her dignity or her welfare. These, related as we are to her, honor and duty, as well as inclination, induce us to support and advance; and the apprehensions that now oppress our hearts with unspeakable grief, being once removed, your Majesty will find your faithful subjects on this continent ready and willing at all times, as they ever have been, with their lives and fortunes, to assert and maintain the rights and interests of your Majesty, and of our Mother country.

We, therefore, beseech your Majesty, that your royal authority and influence may be graciously interposed to procure us relief from our afflicting fears and jealousies, occasioned by the system before mentioned, and to settle peace through every part of your dominions, with all humility submitting to your Majesty's wise consideration whether it may not be expedient for facilitating those important purposes, that your Majesty be pleased to direct some mode, by which the united applications of your faithful colonists to the throne, in pursuance of their common councils, may be improved into a happy and permanent reconciliation; and that, in the mean time, measures may be taken for preventing the further destruction of the lives of your Majesty's subjects; and that such statutes as more immediately distress any of your Majesty's colonies may be repealed.

For by such arrangements as your Majesty's wisdom can form, for collecting the united sense of your American people, we are convinced your Majesty would receive such satisfactory proofs of the disposition of the colonists towards their sovereign and parent state, that the wished for opportunity would soon be restored to them, of evincing the sincerity of their professions, by every testimony of devotion becoming the most dutiful subjects, and the most affectionate colonists.

That your Majesty may enjoy a long and prosperous reign, and that your descendants may govern your dominions with honor to themselves and happiness to their subjects, is our sincere and fervent prayer.[218]

Appendix 8

Declaration of the Causes and Necessities of Taking up Arms

July 6, 1775

If it was possible for men, who exercise their reason to believe, that the divine Author of our existence intended a part of the human race to hold an absolute property in, and an unbounded power over others, marked out by his infinite goodness and wisdom, as the objects of a legal domination never rightfully resistible, however severe and oppressive, the inhabitants of these colonies might at least require from the parliament of Great-Britain some evidence, that this dreadful authority over them, has been granted to that body. But a reverence for our great Creator, principles of humanity, and the dictates of common sense, must convince all those who reflect upon the subject, that government was instituted to promote the welfare of mankind, and ought to be administered for the attainment of that end. The legislature of Great-Britain, however, stimulated by an inordinate passion for a power not only unjustifiable, but which they know to be peculiarly reprobated by the very constitution of that kingdom, and desparate of success in any mode of contest, where regard should be had to truth, law, or right, have at length, deserting those, attempted to effect their cruel and impolitic purpose of enslaving these colonies by violence, and have thereby rendered it necessary for us to close with their last appeal from reason to arms. -- Yet, however blinded that assembly may be, by their intemperate rage for unlimited domination, so to slight justice and the opinion of mankind, we esteem ourselves bound by obligations of respect to the rest of the world, to make known the justice of our cause.

Our forefathers, inhabitants of the island of Great-Britain, left their native land, to seek on these shores a residence for civil and religious freedom. At the expense of their blood, at the hazard of their fortunes, without the least charge to the country from which they removed, by unceasing labour, and an unconquerable spirit, they effected settlements in the distant and inhospitable wilds of America, then filled with numerous and warlike barbarians.—Societies or governments, vested with perfect legislatures, were formed under charters from the crown, and an harmonious intercourse was established between the colonies and the kingdom from which they derived their origin. The mutual benefits of this union became in a short time so extraordinary, as to excite astonishment. It is universally confessed, that the amazing increase of the wealth, strength, and navigation of the realm, arose from this source; and the minister, who so wisely and successfully directed the measures of Great-Britain in the late war, publicly declared, that these colonies enabled her to triumph over her enemies.—Towards the conclusion of that war, it pleased our sovereign to make a change in his counsels.—From that fatal movement, the affairs of the British empire began to fall into confusion, and gradually sliding from the summit of glorious prosperity, to which they had been advanced by the virtues and abilities of one man, are at length distracted by the convulsions, that now shake it to its deepest foundations.—The new ministry finding the brave foes of Britain, though frequently defeated, yet still contending, took up the unfortunate idea of granting them a hasty peace, and then subduing her faithful friends.

These devoted colonies were judged to be in such a state, as to present victories without bloodshed, and all the easy emoluments of statuteable plunder.—The uninterrupted tenor of their peaceable and respectful behaviour from the beginning of colonization, their dutiful, zealous, and useful services during the war, though so recently and amply acknowledged in the most honourable manner by his majesty, by the late king, and by parliament, could not save them from the meditated innovations.—Parliament was influenced to adopt the pernicious project, and assuming a new power over them, have in the course of eleven years, given such decisive specimens of the spirit and consequences attending this power, as to leave no doubt concerning the effects of acquiescence under it. They have undertaken to give and grant our money without our consent, though we have ever exercised an exclusive right to dispose of our own property; statutes have been passed for extending the jurisdiction of courts of admiralty and vice-admiralty beyond their ancient limits; for depriving us of the accustomed and inestimable privilege of trial by jury, in cases affecting both life and property; for suspending the legislature of one of the colonies; for interdicting all commerce to the capital of another; and for altering fundamentally the form of government established by charter, and secured by acts of its own legislature solemnly confirmed by the crown; for exempting the *"murderers"* of colonists from legal trial, and in effect, from punishment; for erecting in a neighbouring province, acquired by the joint arms of Great-Britain and America, a despotism dangerous to our very existence; and for quartering soldiers upon the colonists in time of profound peace. It has also been resolved in parliament, that colonists charged with committing certain offences, shall be transported to England to be tried.

But why should we enumerate our injuries in detail? By one statute it is declared, that parliament can *"of right make laws to bind us in all cases whatsoever."* What is to defend us against so enormous, so unlimited a power? Not a single man of those who assume it, is chosen by us; or is subject to our control or influence; but, on the contrary, they are all of them exempt from the operation of such laws, and an American revenue, if not diverted from the ostensible purposes for which it is raised, would actually lighten their own burdens in proportion, as they increase ours. We saw the misery to which such despotism would reduce us. We for ten years incessantly and ineffectually besieged the throne as supplicants; we reasoned, we remonstrated with parliament, in the most mild and decent language.

Administration sensible that we should regard these oppressive measures as freemen ought to do, sent over fleets and armies to enforce them. The indignation of the Americans was roused, it is true; but it was the indignation of a virtuous, loyal, and affectionate people. A Congress of delegates from the United Colonies was assembled at Philadelphia, on the fifth day of last September. We resolved again to offer an humble and dutiful petition to the King, and also addressed our fellow-subjects of Great-Britain. We have pursued every temperate, every respectful measure: we have even proceeded to break off our commercial intercourse with our fellow-subjects, as the last peaceable admonition, that our attachment to no nation upon earth should supplant our attachment to liberty.—This, we flattered ourselves, was the ultimate step of the controversy: but subsequent events have shewn, how vain was this hope of finding moderation in our enemies.

Several threatening expressions against the colonies were inserted in his majesty's speech; our petition, tho' we were told it was a decent one, and that his majesty had been pleased to receive it graciously, and to promise laying it before his parliament, was huddled into both houses among a bundle of American papers, and there neglected. The lords and commons in their address, in the month of February, said, that *"a rebellion at that time actually existed within the province of Massachusetts-Bay; and that those concerned in it, had been countenanced and encouraged by unlawful combinations and engagements, entered into by his majesty's subjects in several of the other colonies; and therefore they besought his majesty, that he would take the most effectual measures to inforce due obedience to the laws and authority of the supreme legislature."*—Soon after, the commercial intercourse of whole colonies, with foreign countries, and with each other, was cut off by an act of parliament; by another several of them were intirely prohibited from the fisheries in the seas near their coasts, on which they always depended for their sustenance; and large reinforcements of ships and troops were immediately sent over to general Gage.

Fruitless were all the entreaties, arguments, and eloquence of an illustrious band of the most distinguished peers, and commoners, who nobly and strenuously asserted the justice of our cause, to stay, or even to mitigate the heedless fury with which these accumulated and unexampled outrages were hurried on.— Equally fruitless was the interference of the city of London, of Bristol, and many other respectable towns in our favor. Parliament adopted an insidious manoeuvre calculated to divide us, to establish a perpetual auction of taxations where colony should bid against colony, all of them uninformed what ransom would redeem their lives; and thus to extort from us, at the point of the bayonet, the unknown sums that should be sufficient to gratify, if possible to gratify, ministerial rapacity, with the miserable indulgence left to us of raising, in our own mode, the prescribed tribute. What terms more rigid and humiliating could have been dictated by remorseless victors to conquered enemies? In our circumstances to accept them, would be to deserve them.

Soon after the intelligence of these proceedings arrived on this continent, general Gage, who in the course of the last year had taken possession of the town of Boston, in the province of Massachusetts-Bay, and still occupied it as a garrison, on the 19th day of April, sent out from that place a large detachment of his army, who made an unprovoked assault on the inhabitants of the said province, at the town of Lexington, as appears by the affidavits of a great number of persons, some of whom were officers and soldiers of that detachment, murdered eight of the inhabitants, and wounded many others. From thence the troops proceeded in warlike array to the town of Concord, where they set upon another party of the inhabitants of the same province, killing several and wounding more, until compelled to retreat by the country people suddenly assembled to repel this cruel aggression. Hostilities, thus commenced by the British troops, have been since prosecuted by them without regard to faith or reputation.—The inhabitants of Boston being confined within that town by the general their governor, and having, in order to procure their dismission, entered into a treaty with him, it was stipulated that the said inhabitants having deposited their arms with their own magistrates, should have liberty to depart, taking with them their other effects. They accordingly delivered up their arms, but in open violation of honour, in defiance of the obligation of treaties, which even savage nations esteemed sacred, the governor ordered the arms deposited as aforesaid, that they might be preserved for their owners, to be seized by a body of soldiers;

detained the greatest part of the inhabitants in the town, and compelled the few who were permitted to retire, to leave their most valuable effects behind.

By this perfidy wives are separated from their husbands, children from their parents, the aged and the sick from their relations and friends, who wish to attend and comfort them; and those who have been used to live in plenty and even elegance, are reduced to deplorable distress.

The general, further emulating his ministerial masters, by a proclamation bearing date on the 12th day of June, after venting the grossest falsehoods and calumnies against the good people of these colonies, proceeds to *"declare them all, either by name or description, to be rebels and traitors, to supersede the course of the common law, and instead thereof to publish and order the use and exercise of the law martial."*—His troops have butchered our countrymen, have wantonly burnt Charlestown, besides a considerable number of houses in other places; our ships and vessels are seized; the necessary supplies of provisions are intercepted, and he is exerting his utmost power to spread destruction and devastation around him.

We have received certain intelligence, that general Carleton, the governor of Canada, is instigating the people of that province and the Indians to fall upon us; and we have but too much reason to apprehend, that schemes have been formed to excite domestic enemies against us. In brief, a part of these colonies now feel, and all of them are sure of feeling, as far as the vengeance of administration can inflict them, the complicated calamities of fire, sword and famine. We are reduced to the alternative of chusing an unconditional submission to the tyranny of irritated ministers, or resistance by force.—The latter is our choice.—We have counted the cost of this contest, and find nothing so dreadful as voluntary slavery.—Honour, justice, and humanity, forbid us tamely to surrender that freedom which we received from our gallant ancestors, and which our innocent posterity have a right to receive from us. We cannot endure the infamy and guilt of resigning succeeding generations to that wretchedness which inevitably awaits them, if we basely entail hereditary bondage upon them.

Our cause is just. Our union is perfect. Our internal resources are great, and, if necessary, foreign assistance is undoubtedly attainable.—We gratefully acknowledge, as signal instances of the Divine favour towards us, that his Providence would not permit us to be called into this severe controversy, until we were grown up to our present strength, had been previously exercised in warlike operation, and possessed of the means of defending ourselves. With hearts fortified with these animating reflections, we most solemnly, before God and the world, declare, that, exerting the utmost energy of those powers, which our beneficent Creator hath graciously bestowed upon us, the arms we have been compelled by our enemies to assume, we will, in defiance of every hazard, with unabating firmness and perseverence, employ for the preservation of our liberties; being with one mind resolved to die freemen rather than to live slaves.

Lest this declaration should disquiet the minds of our friends and fellow-subjects in any part of the empire, we assure them that we mean not to dissolve that union which has so long and so happily subsisted between us, and which we sincerely wish to see restored.—Necessity has not yet driven us into that desperate measure, or induced us to excite any other nation to war against them.—We have not raised armies with ambitious designs of separating from Great-Britain, and establishing independent states. We fight not for glory or for conquest. We exhibit to mankind the remarkable spectacle of a people attacked by unprovoked enemies, without any imputation or even suspicion of offence. They boast of their privileges and civilization, and yet proffer no milder conditions than servitude or death.

In our own native land, in defence of the freedom that is our birthright, and which we ever enjoyed till the late violation of it—for the protection of our property, acquired solely by the honest industry of our fore-fathers and ourselves, against violence actually offered, we have taken up arms. We shall lay them down when hostilities shall cease on the part of the aggressors, and all danger of their being renewed shall be removed, and not before.

With an humble confidence in the mercies of the supreme and impartial Judge and Ruler of the Universe, we most devoutly implore his divine goodness to protect us happily through this great conflict, to dispose our adversaries to reconciliation on reasonable terms, and thereby to relieve the empire from the calamities of civil war.[219]

Appendix 9

Thomas Jefferson letter to Gideon Granger

August 13, 1800

DEAR SIR,

-- I received with great pleasure your favor of June 4, and am much comforted by the appearance of a change of opinion in your state; for tho' we may obtain, & I believe shall obtain, a majority in the legislature of the United States, attached to the preservation of the Federal constitution according to it's obvious principles, & those on which it was known to be received; attached equally to the preservation to the states of those rights unquestionably remaining with them; friends to the freedom of religion, freedom of the press, trial by jury & to economical government; opposed to standing armies, paper systems, war, & all connection, other than commerce, with any foreign nation; in short, a majority firm in all those principles which we have espoused and the federalists have opposed uniformly; still, should the whole body of New England continue in opposition to these principles of government, either knowingly or through delusion, our government will be a very uneasy one. It can never be harmonious & solid, while so respectable a portion of its citizens support principles which go directly to a change of the federal constitution, to sink the state governments, consolidate them into one, and to monarchize that. Our country is too large to have all its affairs directed by a single government. Public servants at such a distance, & from under the eye of their constituents, must, from the circumstance of distance, be unable to administer & overlook all the details necessary for the good government of the citizens, and the same circumstance, by rendering detection impossible to their constituents, will invite the public agents to corruption, plunder & waste. And I do verily believe, that if the principle were to prevail, of a common law being in force in the U S, (which principle possesses the general government at once of all the powers of the state governments, and reduces us to a single consolidated government,) it would become the most corrupt government on the earth. You have seen the practises by which the public servants have been able to cover their conduct, or, where that could not be done, delusions by which they have varnished it for the eye of their constituents. What an augmentation of the field for jobbing, speculating, plundering, office-building & office-hunting would be produced by an assumption of all the state powers into the hands of the general government. The true theory of our constitution is surely the wisest & best, that the states are independent as to everything within themselves, & united as to everything respecting foreign nations. Let the general government be reduced to foreign concerns only, and let our affairs be disentangled from those of all other nations, except as to commerce, which the merchants will manage the better, the more they are left free to manage for themselves, and our general government may be reduced to a very simple organization, & a very unexpensive one; a few plain duties to be performed by a few servants. But I repeat, that this simple & economical mode of government can never be secured, if the New England States continue to support the contrary system. I rejoice, therefore, in every appearance of their returning to those principles which I had always imagined to be almost innate in them. In this State, a few persons were deluded by the X. Y. Z. duperies. You saw the effect of it in our last Congressional representatives, chosen under their influence. This experiment on their credulity is now seen into, and our next representation will be as republican as it has heretofore been. On the whole, we hope, that by a part of the Union having held on to the principles of the constitution, time has been given to the states to recover from the temporary frenzy into which they had been decoyed, to rally round the constitution, & to rescue it from the destruction with which it had been threatened even at their own hands. I see copied from the American Magazine two numbers of a paper signed Don Quixotte, most excellently adapted to introduce the real truth to the minds even of the most prejudiced.

I would, with great pleasure, have written the letter you desired in behalf of your friend, but there are existing circumstances which render a letter from me to that magistrate as improper as it would be unavailing. I shall be happy, on some more fortunate occasion, to prove to you my desire of serving your wishes.

I sometime ago received a letter from a Mr. M'Gregory of Derby, in your State; it is written with such a degree of good sense & appearance of candor, as entitles it to an answer. Yet the writer being entirely unknown to me, and the stratagems of the times very multifarious, I have thought it best to avail myself of your friendship, & enclose the answer to you. You will see it's nature. If you find from the character of the person to whom it is addressed, that no improper use would probably be made of it, be so good as to seal & send it. Otherwise suppress it.

How will the vote of your State and R I be as to A. and P.?

I am, with great and sincere esteem, dear Sir, your friend and servant.[220]

Appendix 10

Thomas Jefferson First Inaugural

March 4, 1801

Friends and Fellow-Citizens:

Called upon to undertake the duties of the first executive office of our country, I avail myself of the presence of that portion of my fellow-citizens which is here assembled, to express my grateful thanks for the favor with which they have been pleased to look towards me, to declare a sincere consciousness that the task is above my talents, and that I approach it with those anxious and awful presentiments, which the greatness of the charge, and the weakness of my powers, so justly inspire. A rising nation, spread over a wide and fruitful land, traversing all the seas with the rich productions of their industry, engaged in commerce with nations who feel power and forget right, advancing rapidly to destinies beyond the reach of mortal eye; when I contemplate these transcendent objects, and see the honor, the happiness, and the hopes of this beloved country committed to the issue and the auspices of this day, I shrink from the contemplation, and humble myself before the magnitude of the undertaking. Utterly indeed should I despair, did not the presence of many whom I here see remind me that, in the other high authorities provided by our constitution, I shall find resources of wisdom, of virtue, and of zeal, on which to rely under all difficulties. To you, then, gentlemen, who are charged with the sovereign functions of legislation, and to those associated with you, I look with encouragement for that guidance and support which may enable us to steer with safety the vessel in which we are all embarked, amid the conflicting elements of a troubled world.

During the contest of opinion through which we have passed, the animation of discussion and exertions has sometimes worn an aspect which might impose on strangers unused to think freely, and to speak and to write what they think; but this being now decided by the voice of the nation, announced according to the rules of the constitution, all will of course arrange themselves under the will of the law, and unite in common efforts for the common good. All, too, will bear in mind this sacred principle, that though the will of the majority is in all cases to prevail, that will, to be rightful, must be reasonable; that the minority possess their equal rights, which equal law must protect, and to violate would be oppression. Let us, then, fellow-citizens, unite with one heart and one mind; let us restore to social intercourse that harmony and affection, without which, liberty, and even life itself, are but dreary things. And let us reflect, that, having banished from our land that religious intolerance under which mankind so long bled and suffered, we have yet gained little, if we countenance a political intolerance as despotic, as wicked, and capable of as bitter and bloody persecutions. During the throes and convulsions of the ancient world, during the agonizing spasms of infuriated man, seeking through blood and slaughter his long-lost liberty, it was not wonderful that the agitation of the billows should reach even this distant and peaceful shore; that this should be more felt and feared by some, and less by others; that this should divide opinions as to measures of safety; but every difference of opinion is not a difference of principle. We have called by different names brethren of the same principle. We are all republicans; we are all federalists, if there be any among us who would wish to dissolve this Union, or to change its republican form, let them stand undisturbed as monuments of the safety with which error of opinion may be tolerated, where reason is left free to combat it. I know, indeed, that some honest men fear that a republican government cannot be strong; that this government is not strong enough. But would the honest patriot, in the full tide of successful experiment, abandon a government which has so far kept us free and firm, on the theoretic and visionary fear that this government, the world's best hope, may, by possibility, want energy to preserve itself? I trust not. I believe this, on the contrary, the strongest government on earth. I believe it the only one where every man, at the call of the laws, would fly to the standard of the law, and would meet invasions of the public order as his own personal concern. Sometimes it is said that man cannot be trusted with the government of himself. Can he, then, be trusted with the government of others? Or have we found angels in the form of kings, to govern him? Let history answer this question.

Let us, then, with courage and confidence, pursue our own federal and republican principles, our attachment to our union and representative government. Kindly separated by nature and a wide ocean from the exterminating havoc of one quarter of the globe; too high-minded to endure the degradations of the others; possessing a chosen country, with room enough for our descendants to the thousandth and thousandth generation; entertaining a due sense of our equal right to the use of our own faculties, to the acquisitions of our industry, to honor and confidence from our fellow-citizens, resulting not from birth, but from our actions and their sense of them; enlightened by a benign religion, professed indeed and practised in various forms, yet all of them including honesty, truth, temperance, gratitude, and the love of man, acknowledging and adoring an overruling Providence, which, by all its dispensations, proves that it delights in the happiness of man here, and his greater happiness hereafter; with all these blessings, what more is necessary to make us a happy and prosperous people? Still one thing more, fellow-citizens — a wise and frugal government, which shall restrain men from injuring one another, shall leave them otherwise free to regulate their own pursuits of industry and improvement, and shall not take from the mouth of labor the bread it has earned. This is the sum of good government, and this is necessary to close the circle of our felicities.

About to enter, fellow-citizens, on the exercise of duties which comprehend everything dear and valuable to you, it is proper that you should understand what I deem the essential principles of our government, and consequently those which ought to shape its administration. I will compress them within the narrowest compass they will bear, stating the general principles, but not all its limitations — Equal and exact justice to all men, of whatever state or persuasion, religious or political; peace, commerce, and honest friendship with all nations, entangling alliances with none; the support of the state governments in all their rights, as the most competent administration for our domestic concerns, and the surest bulwarks against anti- republican tendencies; the preservation of the general government in its whole constitutional vigor, as the sheet- anchor of our peace at home and safety abroad; a jealous care of the right of election by the people; a mild and safe corrective of abuses, which are lopped by the sword of revolution, where peaceable remedies are unprovided; absolute acquiescence in the decisions of the majority, the vital principle of republics, from which is no appeal but to force, the vital principle and immediate parent of despotism; a well-disciplined militia, our best reliance in peace, and for the first moments of war, till regulars may relieve them; the supremacy of the civil over the military authority; economy in the public expense, that labor may be lightly burdened; the honest payment of our debts, and sacred preservation of the public faith; encouragement of agriculture, and of commerce as its handmaid; the diffusion of information, and arraignment of all abuses at the bar of public reason; freedom of religion; freedom of the press; and freedom of person, under the protection of the habeas corpus; and trial by juries impartially selected. These principles form the bright constellation which has gone before us, and guided our steps through an age of revolution and reformation. The wisdom of our sages and blood of our heroes have been devoted to their attainment: they should be the creed of our political faith; the text of civil instruction; the touchstone by which to try the services of those we trust; and should we wander from them in moments of error or alarm, let us hasten to retrace our steps, and to regain the road which alone leads to peace, liberty, and safety.

I repair, then, fellow-citizens, to the post you have assigned me. With experience enough in subordinate offices to have seen the difficulties of this, the greatest of all, I have learnt to expect that it will rarely fall to the lot of imperfect man to retire from this station with the reputation and the favor which bring him into it. Without pretensions to that high confidence you reposed in our first and great revolutionary character, whose preeminent services had entitled him to the first place in his country's love, and destined for him the fairest page in the volume of faithful history, I ask so much confidence only as may give firmness and effect to the legal administration of your affairs. I shall often go wrong through defect of judgment. When right, I shall often be thought wrong by those whose positions will not command a view of the whole ground. I ask your indulgence for my own errors, which will never be intentional; and your support against the errors of others, who may condemn what they would not, if seen in all its parts. The approbation implied by your suffrage is a consolation to me for the past; and my future solicitude will be to retain the good opinion of those who have bestowed it in advance, to conciliate that of others by doing them all the good in my power, and to be instrumental to the happiness and freedom of all.

Relying, then, on the patronage of your good-will, I advance with obedience to the work, ready to retire from it whenever you become sensible how much better choice it is in your power to make. And may that infinite Power which rules the destinies of the universe, lead our councils to what is best, and give them a favorable issue for your peace and prosperity.[221]

Appendix 11

Essay on Property – James Madison

March 29, 1792- National Gazette

This term in its particular application means "that dominion which one man claims and exercises over the external things of the world, in exclusion of every other individual."

In its larger and juster meaning, it embraces every thing to which a man may attach a value and have a right; and *which leaves to every one else the like advantage.*

In the former sense, a man's land, or merchandize, or money is called his property.

In the latter sense, a man has a property in his opinions and the free communication of them.

He has a property of peculiar value in his religious opinions, and in the profession and practice dictated by them.

He has a property very dear to him in the safety and liberty of his person.

He has an equal property in the free use of his faculties and free choice of the objects on which to employ them.

In a word, as a man is said to have a right to his property, he may be equally said to have a property in his rights.

Where an excess of power prevails, property of no sort is duly respected. No man is safe in his opinions, his person, his faculties, or his possessions.

Where there is an excess of liberty, the effect is the same, tho' from an opposite cause.

Government is instituted to protect property of every sort; as well that which lies in the various rights of individuals, as that which the term particularly expresses. This being the end of government, that alone is a *just* government, which *impartially* secures to every man, whatever is his *own.*

According to this standard of merit, the praise of affording a just security to property, should be sparingly bestowed on a government which, however scrupulously guarding the possessions of individuals, does not protect them in the enjoyment and communication of their opinions, in which they have an equal, and in the estimation of some, a more valuable property.

More sparingly should this praise be allowed to a government, where a man's religious rights are violated by penalties, or fettered by tests, or taxed by a hierarchy. Conscience is the most sacred of all property; other property depending in part on positive law, the exercise of that, being a natural and unalienable right. To guard a man's house as his castle, to pay public and enforce private debts with the most exact faith, can give no title to invade a man's conscience which is more sacred than his castle, or to withhold from it that debt of protection, for which the public faith is pledged, by the very nature and original conditions of the social pact.

That is not a just government, nor is property secure under it, where the property which a man has in his personal safety and personal liberty, is violated by arbitrary seizures of one class of citizens for the service of the rest. A magistrate issuing his warrants to a press gang, would be in his proper functions in Turkey or Indostan, under appellations proverbial of the most compleat despotism.

That is not a just government, nor is property secure under it, where arbitrary restrictions, exemptions, and monopolies deny to part of its citizens that free use of their faculties, and free choice of their occupations, which not only constitute their property in the general sense of the word; but are the means of acquiring property strictly so called. What must be the spirit of legislation where a manufacturer of linen cloth is forbidden to bury his own child in a linen shroud, in order to favor his neighbor who manufactures woolen cloth; where the manufacturer and wearer of woolen cloth are again forbidden the economical use of buttons of that material, in favor of the manufacturer of buttons of other materials!

A just security to property is not afforded by that government, under which unequal taxes oppress one species of property and reward another species: where arbitrary taxes invade the domestic sanctuaries of the rich, and excessive taxes grind the faces of the poor; where the keenness and competitions of want are deemed an insufficient spur to labor, and taxes are again applied, by an unfeeling policy, as another spur; in violation of that sacred property, which Heaven, in decreeing man to earn his bread by the sweat of his brow, kindly reserved to him, in the small repose that could be spared from the supply of his necessities.

If there be a government then which prides itself in maintaining the inviolability of property; which provides that none shall be taken *directly* even for public use without indemnification to the owner, and yet *directly* violates the property which individuals have in their opinions, their religion, their persons, and their faculties; nay more, which *indirectly* violates their property, in their actual possessions, in the labor that acquires their daily subsistence, and in the hallowed remnant of time which ought to relieve their fatigues and soothe their cares, the influence will have been anticipated, that such a government is not a pattern for the United States.

If the United States mean to obtain or deserve the full praise due to wise and just governments, they will equally respect the rights of property, and the property in rights: they will rival the government that most sacredly guards the former; and by repelling its example in violating the latter, will make themselves a pattern to that and all other governments.[222]

Appendix 12

Virginia Declaration of Rights

June 12, 1776

A DECLARATION OF RIGHTS made by the Representatives of the good people of VIRGINIA, assembled in full and free Convention; which rights do pertain to them and their posterity, as the basis and foundation of Government.

1. That all men are by nature equally free and independent, and have certain inherent rights, of which, when they enter into a state of society, they cannot, by any compact, deprive or divest their posterity; namely, the enjoyment of life and liberty, with the means of acquiring and possessing property, and pursuing and obtaining happiness and safety.

2. That all power is vested in, and consequently derived from, the People; that magistrates are their trustees and servants, and at all times amenable to them.

3. That Government is, or ought to be, instituted for the common benefit, protection, and security of the people, nation, or community; -- of all the various modes and forms of Government that is best which is capable of producing the greatest degree of happiness and safety, and is most effectually secured against the danger of maladministration; -- and that, when any Government shall be found inadequate or contrary to these purposes, a majority of the community hath an indubitable, unalienable, and indefeasible right, to reform, alter, or abolish it, in such manner as shall be judged most conducive to the publick weal.

4. That no man, or set of men, is entitled to exclusive or separate emoluments or privileges from the community, but in consideration of publick services; which, not being descendible, neither ought the offices of Magistrate, Legislator, or Judge, to be hereditary.

5. That the Legislative and Executive powers of the State should be separate and distinct from the Judicative; and, that the members of the two first may be restrained from oppression, by feeling and participating the burdens of the people, they should, at fixed periods, be reduced to a private station, return into that body from which they were originally taken, and the vacancies be supplied by frequent, certain, and regular elections, in which all, or any part, of the former members, to be again eligible, or ineligible, as the laws shall direct.

6. That elections of members to serve as Representatives of the people, in Assembly, ought to be free; and that all men, having sufficient evidence of permanent common interest with, and attachment to, the community, have the right of suffrage, and cannot be taxed or deprived of their property for publick uses without their own consent or that of their Representatives so elected, nor bound by any law to which they have not, in like manner, assembled for the publick good.

7. That all power of suspending laws, or the execution of laws, by any authority, without consent of the Representatives of the people, is injurious to their rights, and ought not to be exercised.

8. That in all capital or criminal prosecutions a man hath a right to demand the cause and nature of his accusation, to be confronted with the accusers and witnesses, to call for evidence in his favour, and to a speedy trial by an impartial jury of his vicinage, without whose unanimous consent he cannot be found guilty, nor can he be compelled to give evidence against himself; that no man be deprived of his liberty except by the law of the land, or the judgment of his peers.

9. That excessive bail ought not to be required, nor excessive fines imposed, nor cruel and unusual punishments inflicted.

10. That general warrants, whereby an officer or messenger may be commanded to search suspected places without evidence of a fact committed, or to seize any person or persons not named, or whose offense is not particularly described and supported by evidence, are grievous and oppressive, and ought not to be granted.

11. That in controversies respecting property, and in suits between man and man, the ancient trial by Jury is preferable to any other, and ought to be held sacred.

12. That the freedom of the Press is one of the great bulwarks of liberty, and can never be restrained but by despotick Governments.

13. That a well-regulated Militia, composed of the body of the people, trained to arms, is the proper, natural, and safe defence of a free State; that Standing Armies, in time of peace, should be avoided as dangerous to liberty; and that, in all cases, the military should be under strict subordination to, and governed by, the civil power.

14. That the people have a right to uniform Government; and, therefore, that no Government separate from, or independent of, the Government of *Virginia,* ought to be erected or established within the limits thereof.

15. That no free Government, or the blessing of liberty, can be preserved to any people but by a firm adherence to justice, moderation, temperance, frugality, and virtue, and by frequent recurrence to fundamental principles.

16. That Religion, or the duty which we owe to our *Creator*, and the manner of discharging it, can be directed only by reason and conviction, not by force or violence; and, therefore, all men are equally entitled to the free exercise of religion, according to the dictates of conscience; and that it is the mutual duty of all to practise Christian forbearance, love, and charity, towards each other.[223]

Appendix 13

Summary View of the Rights of British America

By Thomas Jefferson 1774

RESOLVED, that it be an instruction to the said deputies, when assembled in general congress with the deputies from the other states of British America, to propose to the said congress that an humble and dutiful address be presented to his majesty, begging leave to lay before him, as chief magistrate of the British empire, the united complaints of his majesty's subjects in America; complaints which are excited by many unwarrantable encroachments and usurpations, attempted to be made by the legislature of one part of the empire, upon those rights which God and the laws have given equally and independently to all. To represent to his majesty that these his states have often individually made humble application to his imperial throne to obtain, through its intervention, some redress of their injured rights, to none of which was ever even an answer condescended; humbly to hope that this their joint address, penned in the language of truth, and divested of those expressions of servility which would persuade his majesty that we are asking favours, and not rights, shall obtain from his majesty a more respectful acceptance. And this his majesty will think we have reason to expect when he reflects that he is no more than the chief officer of the people, appointed by the laws, and circumscribed with definite powers, to assist in working the great machine of government, erected for their use, and consequently subject to their superintendance. And in order that these our rights, as well as the invasions of them, may be laid more fully before his majesty, to take a view of them from the origin and first settlement of these countries.

To remind him that our ancestors, before their emigration to America, were the free inhabitants of the British dominions in Europe, and possessed a right which nature has given to all men, of departing from the country in which chance, not choice, has placed them, of going in quest of new habitations, and of there establishing new societies, under such laws and regulations as to them shall seem most likely to promote public happiness. That their Saxon ancestors had, under this universal law, in like manner left their native wilds and woods in the north of Europe, had possessed themselves of the island of Britain, then less charged with inhabitants, and had established there that system of laws which has so long been the glory and protection of that country. Nor was ever any claim of superiority or dependence asserted over them by that mother country from which they had migrated; and were such a claim made, it is believed that his majesty's subjects in Great Britain have too firm a feeling of the rights derived to them from their ancestors, to bow down the sovereignty of their state before such visionary pretensions. And it is thought that no circumstance has occurred to distinguish materially the British from the Saxon emigration. America was conquered, and her settlements made, and firmly established, at the expence of individuals, and not of the British public. Their own blood was spilt in acquiring lands for their settlement, their own fortunes expended in making that settlement effectual; for themselves they fought, for themselves they conquered, and for themselves alone they have right to hold. Not a shilling was ever issued from the public treasures of his majesty, or his ancestors, for their assistance, till of very late times, after the colonies had become established on a firm and permanent footing. That then, indeed, having become valuable to Great Britain for her commercial purposes, his parliament was pleased to lend them assistance against an enemy, who would fain have drawn to herself the benefits of their commerce, to the great aggrandizement of herself, and danger of Great Britain. Such assistance, and in such circumstances, they had often before given to Portugal, and other allied states, with whom they carry on a commercial intercourse; yet these states never supposed, that by calling in her aid, they thereby submitted themselves to her sovereignty. Had such terms been proposed, they would have rejected them with disdain, and trusted for better to the moderation of their enemies, or to a vigorous exertion of their own force. We do not, however, mean to under-rate those aids, which to us were doubtless valuable, on whatever principles granted; but we would shew that they cannot give a title to that authority which the British parliament would arrogate over us, and that they may amply be repaid by our giving to the inhabitants of Great Britain such exclusive privileges in trade as may be advantageous to them, and at the same time not too restrictive to ourselves. That settlements having been thus effected in the wilds of America, the emigrants thought proper to adopt that system of laws under which they had hitherto lived in the mother country, and to continue their union with her by submitting themselves to the same common sovereign, who was thereby made the central link connecting the several parts of the empire thus newly multiplied.

But that not long were they permitted, however far they thought themselves removed from the hand of oppression, to hold undisturbed the rights thus acquired, at the hazard of their lives, and loss of their fortunes. A family of princes was then on the British throne, whose treasonable crimes against their people brought on them afterwards the exertion of those sacred and sovereign rights of punishment reserved in the hands of the people for cases of extreme necessity, and judged by the constitution unsafe to be delegated to any other judicature. While every day brought forth some new and unjustifiable exertion of power over their subjects on that side the water, it was not to be expected that those here, much less able at that time to oppose the designs of despotism, should be exempted from injury.

Accordingly that country, which had been acquired by the lives, the labours, and the fortunes, of individual adventurers, was by these princes, at several times, parted out and distributed among the favourites and followers of their fortunes, and, by an assumed right of the crown alone, were erected into distinct and independent governments; a measure which it is believed his majesty's prudence and understanding would prevent him from imitating at this day, as no exercise of such a power, of dividing and dismembering a country, has ever occurred in his majesty's realm of England, though now of very ancient standing; nor could it be justified or acquiesced under there, or in any other part of his majesty's empire.

That the exercise of a free trade with all parts of the world, possessed by the American colonists, as of natural right, and which no law of their own had taken away or abridged, was next the object of unjust encroachment. Some of the colonies having thought proper to continue the administration of their government in the name and under the authority of his majesty king Charles the first, whom, notwithstanding his late deposition by the commonwealth of England, they continued in the sovereignty of their state; the parliament for the commonwealth took the same in high offence, and assumed upon themselves the power of prohibiting their trade with all other parts of the world, except the island of Great Britain. This arbitrary act, however, they soon recalled, and by solemn treaty, entered into on the 12th day of March, 1651, between the said commonwealth by their commissioners, and the colony of Virginia by their house of burgesses, it was expressly stipulated, by the 8th article of the said treaty, that they should have "free trade as the people of England do enjoy to all places and with all nations, according to the laws of that commonwealth." But that, upon the restoration of his majesty king Charles the second, their rights of free commerce fell once more a victim to arbitrary power; and by several acts of his reign, as well as of some of his successors, the trade of the colonies was laid under such restrictions, as shew what hopes they might form from the justice of a British parliament, were its uncontrouled power admitted over these states. History has informed us that bodies of men, as well as individuals, are susceptible of the spirit of tyranny. A view of these acts of parliament for regulation, as it has been affectedly called, of the American trade, if all other evidence were removed out of the case, would undeniably evince the truth of this observation. Besides the duties they impose on our articles of export and import, they prohibit our going to any markets northward of Cape Finesterre, in the kingdom of Spain, for the sale of commodities which Great Britain will not take from us, and for the purchase of others, with which she cannot supply us, and that for no other than the arbitrary purposes of purchasing for themselves, by a sacrifice of our rights and interests, certain privileges in their commerce with an allied state, who in confidence that their exclusive trade with America will be continued, while the principles and power of the British parliament be the same, have indulged themselves in every exorbitance which their avarice could dictate, or our necessities extort; have raised their commodities, called for in America, to the double and treble of what they sold for before such exclusive privileges were given them, and of what better commodities of the same kind would cost us elsewhere, and at the same time give us much less for what we carry thither than might be had at more convenient ports. That these acts prohibit us from carrying in quest of other purchasers the surplus of our tobaccoes remaining after the consumption of Great Britain is supplied; so that we must leave them with the British merchant for whatever he will please to allow us, to be by him reshipped to foreign markets, where he will reap the benefits of making sale of them for full value. That to heighten still the idea of parliamentary justice, and to shew with what moderation they are like to exercise power, where themselves are to feel no part of its weight, we take leave to mention to his majesty certain other acts of British parliament, by which they would prohibit us from manufacturing for our own use the articles we raise on our own lands with our own labour. By an act passed in the 5th Year of the reign of his late majesty king George the second, an American subject is forbidden to make a hat for himself of the fur which he has taken perhaps on his own soil; an instance of despotism to which no parallel can be produced in the most arbitrary ages of British history. By one other act, passed in the 23d year of the same reign, the iron which we make we are forbidden to manufacture, and heavy as that article is, and necessary in every branch of husbandry, besides commission and insurance, we are to pay freight for it to Great Britain, and freight for it back again, for the purpose of supporting not men, but machines, in the island of Great Britain. In the same spirit of equal and impartial legislation is to be viewed the act of parliament, passed in the 5th year of the same reign, by which American lands are made subject to the demands of British creditors, while their own lands were still continued unanswerable for their debts; from which one of these conclusions must necessarily follow, either that justice is not the same in America as in Britain, or else that the British parliament pay less regard to it here than there. But that we do not point out to his majesty the injustice of these acts, with intent to rest on that principle the cause of their nullity; but to shew that experience confirms the propriety of those political principles which exempt us from the jurisdiction of the British parliament. The true ground on which we declare these acts void is, that the British parliament has no right to exercise authority over us.

That these exercises of usurped power have not been confined to instances alone, in which themselves were interested, but they have also intermeddled with the regulation of the internal affairs of the colonies. The act of the 9th of Anne for establishing a post office in America seems to have had little connection with British convenience, except that of accommodating his majesty's ministers and favourites with the sale of a lucrative and easy office.

That thus have we hastened through the reigns which preceded his majesty's, during which the violations of our right were less alarming, because repeated at more distant intervals than that rapid and bold succession of injuries which is likely to distinguish the present from all other periods of American story. Scarcely have our minds been able to emerge from the astonishment into which one stroke of parliamentary thunder has involved us, before another more heavy, and more alarming, is fallen on us. Single acts of tyranny may be ascribed to the accidental opinion of a day; but a series of oppressions, begun at a distinguished period, and pursued unalterably through every change of ministers, too plainly prove a deliberate and systematical plan of reducing us to slavery.

That the act passed in the 4th year of his majesty's reign, intitled "An act for granting certain duties in the British colonies and plantations in America, &c."

One other act, passed in the 5th year of his reign, intitled "An act for granting and applying certain stamp duties and other duties in the British colonies and plantations in America, &c."

One other act, passed in the 6th year of his reign, intitled "An act for the better securing the dependency of his majesty's dominions in America upon the crown and parliament of Great Britain;" and one other act, passed in the 7th year of his reign, intitled "An act for granting duties on paper, tea, &c." form that connected chain of parliamentary usurpation, which has already been the subject of frequent applications to his majesty, and the houses of lords and commons of Great Britain; and no answers having yet been condescended to any of these, we shall not trouble his majesty with a repetition of the matters they contained.

But that one other act, passed in the same 7th year of the reign, having been a peculiar attempt, must ever require peculiar mention; it is intitled "An act for suspending the legislature of New York." One free and independent legislature hereby takes upon itself to suspend the powers of another, free and independent as itself; thus exhibiting a phenomenon unknown in nature, the creator and creature of its own power. Not only the principles of common sense, but the common feelings of human nature, must be surrendered up before his majesty's subjects here can be persuaded to believe that they hold their political existence at the will of a British parliament. Shall these governments be dissolved, their property annihilated, and their people reduced to a state of nature, at the imperious breath of a body of men, whom they never saw, in whom they never confided, and over whom they have no powers of punishment or removal, let their crimes against the American public be ever so great? Can any one reason be assigned why 160,000 electors in the island of Great Britain should give law to four millions in the states of America, every individual of whom is equal to every individual of them, in virtue, in understanding, and in bodily strength? Were this to be admitted, instead of being a free people, as we have hitherto supposed, and mean to continue ourselves, we should suddenly be found the slaves, not of one, but of 160,000 tyrants, distinguished too from all others by this singular circumstance, that they are removed from the reach of fear, the only restraining motive which may hold the hand of a tyrant.

That by "an act to discontinue in such manner and for such time as are therein mentioned the landing and discharging, lading or shipping, of goods, wares, and merchandize, at the town and within the harbour of Boston, in the province of Massachusetts Bay, in North America," which was passed at the last session of British parliament; a large and populous town, whose trade was their sole subsistence, was deprived of that trade, and involved in utter ruin. Let us for a while suppose the question of right suspended, in order to examine this act on principles of justice: An act of parliament had been passed imposing duties on teas, to be paid in America, against which act the Americans had protested as inauthoritative. The East India company, who till that time had never sent a pound of tea to America on their own account, step forth on that occasion the assertors of parliamentary right, and send hither many ship loads of that obnoxious commodity. The masters of their several vessels, however, on their arrival in America, wisely attended to admonition, and returned with their cargoes. In the province of New England alone the remonstrances of the people were disregarded, and a compliance, after being many days waited for, was flatly refused. Whether in this the master of the vessel was governed by his obstinancy, or his instructions, let those who know, say. There are extraordinary situations which require extraordinary interposition. An exasperated people, who feel that they possess power, are not easily restrained within limits strictly regular. A number of them assembled in the town of Boston, threw the tea into the ocean, and dispersed without doing any other act of violence. If in this they did wrong, they were known and were amenable to the laws of the land, against which it could not be objected that they had ever, in any instance, been obstructed or diverted from their regular course in favour of popular offenders. They should therefore not have been distrusted on this occasion. But that ill fated colony had formerly been bold in their enmities against the house of Stuart, and were now devoted to ruin by that unseen hand which governs the momentous affairs of this great empire. On the partial representations of a few worthless ministerial dependents, whose constant office it has been to keep that government embroiled, and who, by their treacheries, hope to obtain the dignity of the British knighthood, without calling for a party accused, without asking a proof, without attempting a distinction between the guilty and the innocent, the whole of that antient and wealthy town is in a moment reduced from opulence to beggary. Men who had spent their lives in extending the British commerce, who had invested in that place the wealth their honest endeavours had merited, found themselves and their families thrown at once on the world for subsistence by its charities. Not the hundredth part of the inhabitants of that town had been concerned in the act complained of; many of them were in Great Britain and in other parts beyond sea; yet all were involved in one indiscriminate ruin, by a new executive power, unheard of till then, that of a British parliament. A property, of the value of many millions of money, was sacrificed to revenge, not repay, the loss of a few thousands. This is administering justice with a heavy hand indeed! and when is this tempest to be arrested in its course? Two wharfs are to be opened again when his majesty shall think proper. The residue which lined the extensive shores of the bay of Boston are forever interdicted the exercise of commerce. This little exception seems to have been thrown in for no other purpose than that of setting a precedent for investing his majesty with legislative powers. If the pulse of his people shall beat calmly under this experiment, another and another will be tried, till the measure of despotism be filled up. It would be an insult on common sense to pretend that this exception was made in order to restore its commerce to that great town. The trade which cannot be received at two wharfs alone must of necessity be transferred to some other place; to which it will soon be followed by that of the two wharfs. Considered in this light, it would be an insolent and cruel mockery at the annihilation of the town of Boston.

By the act for the suppression of riots and tumults in the town of Boston, passed also in the last session of parliament, a murder committed there is, if the governor pleases, to be tried in the court of King's Bench, in the island of Great Britain, by a jury of Middlesex. The witnesses, too, on receipt of such a sum as the governor shall think it reasonable for them to expend, are to enter into recognizance to appear at the trial. This is, in other words, taxing them to the amount of their recognizance, and that amount may be whatever a governor pleases; for who does his majesty think can be prevailed on to cross the Atlantic for the sole purpose of bearing evidence to a fact? His expences are to be borne, indeed, as they shall be estimated by a governor; but who are to feed the wife and children whom he leaves behind, and who have had no other subsistence but his daily labour? Those epidemical disorders, too, so terrible in a foreign climate, is the cure of them to be estimated among the articles of expence, and their danger to be warded off by the almighty power of parliament? And the wretched criminal, if he happen to have offended on the American side, stripped of his privilege of trial by peers of his vicinage, removed from the place where alone full evidence could be obtained, without money, without counsel, without friends, without exculpatory proof, is tried before judges predetermined to condemn. The cowards who would suffer a countryman to be torn from the bowels of their society, in order to be thus offered a sacrifice to parliamentary tyranny, would merit that everlasting infamy now fixed on the authors of the act! A clause for a similar purpose had been introduced into an act, passed in the 12th year of his majesty's reign, intitled "An act for the better securing and preserving his majesty's dockyards, magazines, ships, ammunition, and stores;" against which, as meriting the same censures, the several colonies have already protested.

That these are the acts of power, assumed by a body of men, foreign to our constitutions, and unacknowledged by our laws, against which we do, on behalf of the inhabitants of British America, enter this our solemn and determined protest; and we do earnestly entreat his majesty, as yet the only mediatory power between the several states of the British empire, to recommend to his parliament of Great Britain the total revocation of these acts, which, however nugatory they be, may yet prove the cause of further discontents and jealousies among us.

That we next proceed to consider the conduct of his majesty, as holding the executive powers of the laws of these states, and mark out his deviations from the line of duty: By the constitution of Great Britain, as well as of the several American states, his majesty possesses the power of refusing to pass into a law any bill which has already passed the other two branches of legislature. His majesty, however, and his ancestors, conscious of the impropriety of opposing their single opinion to the united wisdom of two houses of parliament, while their proceedings were unbiassed by interested principles, for several ages past have modestly declined the exercise of this power in that part of his empire called Great Britain. But by change of circumstances, other principles than those of justice simply have obtained an influence on their determinations; the addition of new states to the British empire has produced an addition of new, and sometimes opposite interests. It is now, therefore, the great office of his majesty, to resume the exercise of his negative power, and to prevent the passage of laws by any one legislature of the empire, which might bear injuriously on the rights and interests of another. Yet this will not excuse the wanton exercise of this power which we have seen his majesty practise on the laws of the American legislatures. For the most trifling reasons, and sometimes for no conceivable reason at all, his majesty has rejected laws of the most salutary tendency. The abolition of domestic slavery is the great object of desire in those colonies, where it was unhappily introduced in their infant state. But previous to the enfranchisement of the slaves we have, it is necessary to exclude all further importations from Africa; yet our repeated attempts to effect this by prohibitions, and by imposing duties which might amount to a prohibition, have been hitherto defeated by his majesty's negative: Thus preferring the immediate advantages of a few African corsairs to the lasting interests of the American states, and to the rights of human nature, deeply wounded by this infamous practice. Nay, the single interposition of an interested individual against a law was scarcely ever known to fail of success, though in the opposite scale were placed the interests of a whole country. That this is so shameful an abuse of a power trusted with his majesty for other purposes, as if not reformed, would call for some legal restrictions.

With equal inattention to the necessities of his people here has his majesty permitted our laws to lie neglected in England for years, neither confirming them by his assent, nor annulling them by his negative; so that such of them as have no suspending clause we hold on the most precarious of all tenures, his majesty's will, and such of them as suspend themselves till his majesty's assent be obtained, we have feared, might be called into existence at some future and distant period, when time, and change of circumstances, shall have rendered them destructive to his people here. And to render this grievance still more oppressive, his majesty by his instructions has laid his governors under such restrictions that they can pass no law of any moment unless it have such suspending clause; so that, however immediate may be the call for legislative interposition, the law cannot be executed till it has twice crossed the Atlantic, by which time the evil may have spent its whole force.

But in what terms, reconcileable to majesty, and at the same time to truth, shall we speak of a late instruction to his majesty's governor of the colony of Virginia, by which he is forbidden to assent to any law for the division of a county, unless the new county will consent to have no representative in assembly? That colony has as yet fixed no boundary to the westward. Their western counties, therefore, are of indefinite extent; some of them are actually seated many hundred miles from their eastern limits. Is it possible, then, that his majesty can have bestowed a single thought on the situation of those people, who, in order to obtain justice for injuries, however great or small, must, by the laws of that colony, attend their county court, at such a distance, with all their witnesses, monthly, till their litigation be determined? Or does his majesty seriously wish, and publish it to the world, that his subjects should give up the glorious right of representation, with all the benefits derived from that, and submit themselves the absolute slaves of his sovereign will? Or is it rather meant to confine the legislative body to their present numbers, that they may be the cheaper bargain whenever they shall become worth a purchase.

One of the articles of impeachment against Tresilian, and the other judges of Westminister Hall, in the reign of Richard the second, for which they suffered death, as traitors to their country, was, that they had advised the king that he might dissolve his parliament at any time; and succeeding kings have adopted the opinion of these unjust judges. Since the establishment, however, of the British constitution, at the glorious revolution, on its free and antient principles, neither his majesty, nor his ancestors, have exercised such a power of dissolution in the island of Great Britain; and when his majesty was petitioned, by the united voice of his people there, to dissolve the present parliament, who had become obnoxious to them, his ministers were heard to declare, in open parliament, that his majesty possessed no such power by the constitution. But how different their language and his practice here! To declare, as their duty required, the known rights of their country, to oppose the usurpations of every foreign judicature, to disregard the imperious mandates of a minister or governor, have been the avowed causes of dissolving houses of representatives in America. But if such powers be really vested in his majesty, can he suppose they are there placed to awe the members from such purposes as these? When the representative body have lost the confidence of their constituents, when they have notoriously made sale of their most valuable rights, when they have assumed to themselves powers which the people never put into their hands, then indeed their continuing in office becomes dangerous to the state, and calls for an exercise of the power of dissolution. Such being the causes for which the representative body should, and should not, be dissolved, will it not appear strange to an unbiased observer, that that of Great Britain was not dissolved, while those of the colonies have repeatedly incurred that sentence?

But your majesty, or your governors, have carried this power beyond every limit known, or provided for, by the laws: After dissolving one house of representatives, they have refused to call another, so that, for a great length of time, the legislature provided by the laws has been out of existence. From the nature of things, every society must at all times possess within itself the sovereign powers of legislation. The feelings of human nature revolt against the supposition of a state so situated as that it may not in any emergency provide against dangers which perhaps threaten immediate ruin. While those bodies are in existence to whom the people have delegated the powers of legislation, they alone possess and may exercise those powers; but when they are dissolved by the lopping off one or more of their branches, the power reverts to the people, who may exercise it to unlimited extent, either assembling together in person, sending deputies, or in any other way they may think proper. We forbear to trace consequences further; the dangers are conspicuous with which this practice is replete.

That we shall at this time also take notice of an error in the nature of our land holdings, which crept in at a very early period of our settlement. The introduction of the feudal tenures into the kingdom of England, though antient, is well enough understood to set this matter in a proper light. In the earlier ages of the Saxon settlement feudal holdings were certainly altogether unknown; and very few, if any, had been introduced at the time of the Norman conquest. Our Saxon ancestors held their lands, as they did their personal property, in absolute dominion, disencumbered with any superior, answering nearly to the nature of those possessions which the feudalists term allodial. William, the Norman, first introduced that system generally. The lands which had belonged to those who fell in the battle of Hastings, and in the subsequent insurrections of his reign, formed a considerable proportion of the lands of the whole kingdom. These he granted out, subject to feudal duties, as did he also those of a great number of his new subjects, who, by persuasions or threats, were induced to surrender them for that purpose. But still much was left in the hands of his Saxon subjects; held of no superior, and not subject to feudal conditions. These, therefore, by express laws, enacted to render uniform the system of military defence, were made liable to the same military duties as if they had been feuds; and the Norman lawyers soon found means to saddle them also with all the other feudal burthens. But still they had not been surrendered to the king, they were not derived from his grant, and therefore they were not holden of him. A general principle, indeed, was introduced, that "all lands in England were held either mediately or immediately of the crown," but this was borrowed from those holdings, which were truly feudal, and only applied to others for the purposes of illustration. Feudal holdings were therefore but exceptions out of the Saxon laws of possession, under which all lands were held in absolute right. These, therefore, still form the basis, or ground-work, of the common law, to prevail wheresoever the exceptions have not taken place. America was not conquered by William the Norman, nor its lands surrendered to him, or any of his successors. Possessions there are undoubtedly of the allodial nature. Our ancestors, however, who migrated hither, were farmers, not lawyers. The fictitious principle that all lands belong originally to the king, they were early persuaded to believe real; and accordingly took grants of their own lands from the crown. And while the crown continued to grant for small sums, and on reasonable rents; there was no inducement to arrest the error, and lay it open to public view. But his majesty has lately taken on him to advance the terms of purchase, and of holding to the double of what they were; by which means the acquisition of lands being rendered difficult, the population of our country is likely to be checked. It is time, therefore, for us to lay this matter before his majesty, and to declare that he has no right to grant lands of himself. From the nature and purpose of civil institutions, all the lands within the limits which any particular society has circumscribed around itself are assumed by that society, and subject to their allotment only. This may be done by themselves, assembled collectively, or by their legislature, to whom they may have delegated sovereign authority; and if they are allotted in neither of these ways, each individual of the society may appropriate to himself such lands as he finds vacant, and occupancy will give him title.

That in order to enforce the arbitrary measures before complained of, his majesty has from time to time sent among us large bodies of armed forces, not made up of the people here, nor raised by the authority of our laws: Did his majesty possess such a right as this, it might swallow up all our other rights whenever he should think proper. But his majesty has no right to land a single armed man on our shores, and those whom he sends here are liable to our laws made for the suppression and punishment of riots, routs, and unlawful assemblies; or are hostile bodies, invading us in defiance of law. When in the course of the late war it became expedient that a body of Hanoverian troops should be brought over for the defence of Great Britain, his majesty's grandfather, our late sovereign, did not pretend to introduce them under any authority he possessed. Such a measure would have given just alarm to his subjects in Great Britain, whose liberties would not be safe if armed men of another country, and of another spirit, might be brought into the realm at any time without the consent of their legislature. He therefore applied to parliament, who passed an act for that purpose, limiting the number to be brought in and the time they were to continue. In like manner is his majesty restrained in every part of the empire. He possesses, indeed, the executive power of the laws in every state; but they are the laws of the particular state which he is to administer within that state, and not those of any one within the limits of another. Every state must judge for itself the number of armed men which they may safely trust among them, of whom they are to consist, and under what restrictions they shall be laid.

To render these proceedings still more criminal against our laws, instead of subjecting the military to the civil powers, his majesty has expressly made the civil subordinate to the military. But can his majesty thus put down all law under his feet? Can he erect a power superior to that which erected himself? He has done it indeed by force; but let him remember that force cannot give right.

That these are our grievances which we have thus laid before his majesty, with that freedom of language and sentiment which becomes a free people claiming their rights, as derived from the laws of nature, and not as the gift of their chief magistrate: Let those flatter who fear; it is not an American art. To give praise which is not due might be well from the venal, but would ill beseem those who are asserting the rights of human nature. They know, and will therefore say, that kings are the servants, not the proprietors of the people. Open your breast, sire, to liberal and expanded thought. Let not the name of George the third be a blot in the page of history. You are surrounded by British counsellors, but remember that they are parties. You have no ministers for American affairs, because you have none taken from among us, nor amenable to the laws on which they are to give you advice. It behoves you, therefore, to think and to act for yourself and your people. The great principles of right and wrong are legible to every reader; to pursue them requires not the aid of many counsellors. The whole art of government consists in the art of being honest. Only aim to do your duty, and mankind will give you credit where you fail. No longer persevere in sacrificing the rights of one part of the empire to the inordinate desires of another; but deal out to all equal and impartial right. Let no act be passed by any one legislature which may infringe on the rights and liberties of another. This is the important post in which fortune has placed you, holding the balance of a great, if a well poised empire. This, sire, is the advice of your great

American council, on the observance of which may perhaps depend your felicity and future fame, and the preservation of that harmony which alone can continue both to Great Britain and America the reciprocal advantages of their connection. It is neither our wish, nor our interest, to separate from her. We are willing, on our part, to sacrifice every thing which reason can ask to the restoration of that tranquility for which all must wish. On their part, let them be ready to establish union and a generous plan. Let them name their terms, but let them be just. Accept of every commercial preference it is in our power to give for such things as we can raise for their use, or they make for ours. But let them not think to exclude us from going to other markets to dispose of those commodities which they cannot use, or to supply those wants which they cannot supply. Still less let it be proposed that our properties within our own territories shall be taxed or regulated by any power on earth but our own. The God who gave us life gave us liberty at the same time; the hand of force may destroy, but cannot disjoin them. This, sire, is our last, our determined resolution; and that you will be pleased to interpose with that efficacy which your earnest endeavours may ensure to procure redress of these our great grievances, to quiet the minds of your subjects in British America, against any apprehensions of future encroachment, to establish fraternal love and harmony through the whole empire, and that these may continue to the latest ages of time, is the fervent prayer of all British America![224]

Appendix 14

Massachusetts Circular Letter 1768

By Samuel Adams and James Otis

SIR,

The House of Representatives of this Province have taken into their serious consideration, the great difficulties that must accrue to themselves and their constituents, by the operation of several acts of Parliament imposing Duties & Taxes on the American colonies.

As it is a subject in which every colony is deeply interested, they have no reason to doubt but your House is duly impressed with its importance, and that such constitutional measures will be come into as are proper. It seems to be necessary, that all possible care should be taken, that the representations of the several assemblies, upon so delicate a point, should harmonize with each other: The House, therefore hope that this letter will be candidly considered in no other light than as expressing a disposition freely to communicate their mind to a sister colony, upon a common concern, in the same manner as they would be glad to receive the sentiments of your or any other House of Assembly on the continent.

The House have humbly represented to the Ministry their own sentiments: That his Majesty's high Court of Parliament is the supreme legislative power over the whole Empire: That in all free States the constitution is fixed; and as the supreme legislative derives its power & authority from the constitution, it cannot overleap the bounds of it, without destroying its own foundation: That the constitution ascertains and limits both sovereignty and allegiance, and therefore his Majesty's American subjects, who acknowledge themselves bound by the ties of allegiance, have an equitable claim, to the full enjoyment of the fundamental rules of the British constitution: That it is in an essential unalterable right, in nature, ingrafted into the British constitution, as a fundamental law, and ever held sacred and irrevocable by the subjects within the realm, that what a man hath honestly acquired is absolutely his own, which he may freely give, but cannot be taken from him without his consent: That the American subjects may therefore, exclusive of any consideration of charter rights, with a decent firmness, adapted to the character of free men and subjects, assert this natural, constitutional right.

It is, moreover, their humble opinion, which they express with the greatest deferrence to the wisdom of the Parliament, that the Acts made there, imposing Duties on the people of this province, with the sole and express purpose of raising a revenue, are infringements of their natural and constitutional rights; because, as they are not represented in the British Parliament, his Majesty's Commons in Britain, by those Acts, grant their property without their consent.

This House further are of opinion, that their constituents, considering their local circumstances, cannot by any possibility be represented in the Parliament; and that it will forever be impracticable, that they should be equally represented there; and consequently not at all; being separated by an ocean of a thousand leagues: That his Majesty's royal predecessors for this reason, were graciously pleased to form a subordinate legislative here, that their subjects might enjoy the unalienable right of a representation; Also, that considering the utter impracticability of their ever being fully and equally represented in Parliament, and the great expence that must unavoidably attend even a partial representation there, this House think that a taxation of their constituents, even without their consent, grievous as it is, would be preferable to any representation that could be admitted for them there.

Upon these principles, and also considering, that were the right in Parliament ever so clear, yet, for obvious reasons, it would be beyond the rules of equity, that their constituents should be taxed, on the manufactures of Great Britain here, in addition to the duties they pay for them in England, and the other advantages arising to Great-Britain from the acts of trade, this House have preferred a humble, dutiful and loyal petition to our most gracious Sovereign, and made such Representations to his Majesty's Ministers, as they apprehended would tend to obtain redress.

They have also submitted to consideration, whether any people can be said to enjoy any degree of freedom, if the Crown, in addition to its undoubted authority of constituting a Governor, should appoint him such a stipend as it shall judge proper, without the consent of the people and at their expence: And whether, while the Judges of the land and other civil officers hold not their commissions during good behaviour, their having salaries appointed for them by the Crown, independent of the people, hath not a tendency to subvert the principles of equity, and endanger the happiness and security of the subject.

In addition to the measures, the House have wrote a letter to their agent, Mr. DeBerdt, the sentiments of which he is directed to lay before the Ministry; wherein they take notice of the hardship of the Act for preventing mutiny and desertion; which requires the Governor and Council to provide enumerated articles for the King's marching troops, and the people to pay the expence: And also the commission of the Gentlemen appointed Commissioners of the Customs to reside in America, which authorizes them to make as many appointment as they think fit, and to pay the appointees what sums they please, for whole mal-conduct they are not accountable: from whence it may happen, that officers of the Crown may be multiplied to such a degree, as to become dangerous to the Liberty of the people, by virtue of a commission which doth not appear to this House to derive any such advantages to trade as many have been led to expect.

These are the sentiments & proceedings of this House: And as they have too much reason to believe that the enemies of the Colonies have represented them to his Majesty's Ministers and the parliament as factious, disloyal, and having a disposition to make themselves independent of the Mother Country, they have taken occasion, in the most humble terms, to assure his Majesty and his Ministers, that with regard to the people of this Province, and, as they doubt not, of all the Colonies, that the charge is unjust.

The House is fully satisfied, that your Assembly is too generous and enlarged in sentiment to believe that this letter proceeds from an ambition of taking the lead, or dictating to the other Assemblies: They freely submit their opinion to the judgment of others; and shall take it kind in your House, to point out to them any thing further that may be thought necessary.

This House cannot conclude, without expressing their firm confidence in the King, our common head and father, that the united and dutiful supplications of his distressed American subjects will meet with his royal and favorable acceptance.[225]

Appendix 15

Address of the Annapolis Convention

September 14, 1786

To the Honorable, the Legislatures of Virginia, Delaware, Pennsylvania, New Jersey, and New York-

The Commissioners from the said States, respectively assembled at Annapolis, humbly beg leave to report.

That, pursuant to their several appointments, they met, at Annapolis in the State of Maryland, on the eleventh day of September Instant, and having proceeded to a Communication of their powers; they found that the States of New York, Pennsylvania, and Virginia, had, in substance, and nearly in the same terms, authorized their respective Commissioners "to meet such Commissioners as were, or might be, appointed by the other States in the Union, at such time and place, as should be agreed upon by the said Commissioners to take into consideration the trade and Commerce of the United States, to considered how far an uniform system in their commercial intercourse and regulations might be necessary to their common interest and permanent harmony, and to report to the several States such an Act, relative to this great object, as when unanimously ratified by them would enable the United States in Congress assembled effectually to provide for the same."

That the State of Delaware, had given similar powers to their Commissioners, with this difference only, that the Act to be framed in virtue of those powers, is required to be reported "to the United States in Congress assembled, to be agreed to by them, and confirmed by the Legislatures of every State."

That the State of New Jersey had enlarged the object of their appointment, empowering their Commissioners, "to consider how far an uniform system in their commercial regulations and *other important matters*, might be necessary to the common interest and permanent harmony of the several States," and to report such an Act on the subject, as when ratified by them "would enable the United States in Congress assembled, effectually to provide for the exigencies of the Union."

That appointments of Commissioners have also been made by the States of New Hampshire, Massachusetts, Rhode Island, and North Carolina, none of whom however have attended; but that no information has been received by your Commissioners, of any appointment having been made by the States of Connecticut, Maryland, South Carolina, or Georgia.

That the express terms of the powers to your Commissioners supposing a deputation from all the States, and having for object the Trade and Commerce of the United States, Your Commissioners did not conceive it advisable to proceed on the business of their mission, under the Circumstance of so partial and defective a representation.

Deeply impressed however with the magnitude and importance of the object confided to them on this occasion, your Commissioners cannot forbear to indulge an expression of their earnest and unanimous wish, that speedy measures may be taken, to effect a general meeting, of the States, in a future Convention, for the same, and such other purposes, as the situation of public affairs, may be found to require.

If in expressing this wish, or in intimating any other sentiment, your Commissioners should seem to exceed the strict bounds of their appointment, they entertain a full confidence, that a conduct, dictated by an anxiety for the welfare, of the United States, will not fail to receive an indulgent construction.

In this persuasion, your Commissioners submit an opinion, that the Idea of extending the powers of their Deputies, to other objects, than those of Commerce, which has been adopted by the State of New Jersey, was an improvement on the original plan, and will deserve to be incorporated into that of a future Convention; they are the more naturally lead to this conclusion, as in the course of their reflections on the subject, they have been induced to think, that the power of regulating trade is of such comprehensive extent and will enter so far into the general System of the Foederal government, that to give it efficacy, and to obviate questions and doubts concerning its precise nature and limits, may require a correspondent adjustment of other parts of the Foederal System.

That there are important defects in the system of the Foederal Government is acknowledged by the Acts of all those States, which have concurred in the present Meeting; That the defects, upon a closer examination, may be found greater and more numerous, than even these acts imply, is at least so far probable, from the embarrassments which characterise the present State of our national affairs, foreign and domestic, as may reasonably be supposed to merit a deliberate and candid discussion, in some mode, which will unite the Sentiments and Councils of all the States. In the choice of the mode, you Commissioners are of opinion, that a Convention of Deputies from the different states, for the special and sole purpose of entering into this investigation, and digesting a plan for supplying such defects as may be discovered to exist, will be entitled to a preference from considerations, which will occur, without being particularised.

Your Commissioners decline an enumeration of those national circumstances on which their opinion respecting the propriety of a future Convention, with more enlarged powers, is founded; as it would be an useless intrusion of facts and observations, most of which have been frequently the subject of public discussion, and none of which can have escaped the penetration of those to whom they would in this instance be addressed. They are however of a nature so serious, as, in the view of your Commissioners to render the situation of the United States delicate and critical, calling for an exertion of the united virtue and wisdom of all the members of the Confederacy.

Under this impression, Your Commissioners, with the most respectful deference, beg leave to suggest their unanimous conviction, that it may essentially tend to advance the interests of the union, if the States, by whom they have been respectively delegated, would themselves concur, and use their endeavours to procure the concurrence of the other States, in the appointment of Commissioners, to meet at Philadelphia on the second Monday in May next, to take into consideration the situation of the United States, to devise such further provisions as shall appear to them necessary to render the constitution of the Foederal Government adequate to the exigencies of the Union; and to report such an Act for that purpose to the United States in Congress assembled, as when agreed to, by them, and afterwards confirmed by the Legislatures of every State, will effectually provide for the same.

Though your Commissioners could not with propriety address these observations and sentiments to any but the States they have the honor to Represent, they have nevertheless concluded from motives of respect, to transmit Copies of this Report to the United States in Congress assembled, and to the executives of the other States.

By Order of the Commissioners.

Dated at Annapolis

September 14th, 1786

Resolved, that the Chairman sign the aforegoing Report in behalf of the Commissioners.

Then adjourned without day –

New York: Alexander Hamilton, Egbert Benson

New Jersey: Abraham Clarke, William C. Houston, James Schuarman

Pennsylvania: Tenche Coxe

Delaware: George Read, John Dickinson, Richard Bassett

Virginia: Edmund Randolph, James Madison Jr., Saint George Tucker [226]

Appendix 16

Virginia Plan May 29, 1787

1. Resolved that the Articles of Confederation ought to be so corrected and enlarged as to accomplish the objects proposed by their institution; namely, "common defense, security of liberty and general welfare."

2. Resolved therefore that the rights of suffrage in the National Legislature ought to be proportioned to the Quotas of contribution, or to the number of free inhabitants, as the one or the other rule may seem best in different cases.

3. Resolved that the National Legislature ought to consist of two branches.

4. Resolved that the members of the first branch of the National Legislature ought to be elected by the people of the several States every for the term of ; to be of the age of years at least, to receive liberal stipends by which they may be compensated for the devotion of their time to public service; to be ineligible to any office established by a particular State, or under the authority of the United States, except those peculiarly belonging to the functions of the first branch, during the term of service, and for the space of after its expiration; to be incapable of re-election for the space of after the expiration of their term of service, and to be subject to recall.

5. Resolved that the members of the second branch of the National Legislature ought to be elected by those of the first, out of a proper number of persons nominated by the individual Legislatures, to be of the age of years at least; to hold their offices for a term sufficient to ensure their independency; to receive liberal stipends, by which they may be compensated for the devotion of their time to public service; and to be ineligible to any office established by a particular State, or under the authority of the United States, except those peculiarly belonging to the functions of the second branch, during the term of service, and for the space of after the expiration thereof.

6. Resolved that each branch ought to possess the right of originating Acts; that the National Legislature ought to be impowered to enjoy the Legislative Rights vested in Congress by the Confederation and moreover to legislate in all cases to which the separate States are incompetent, or in which the harmony of the United States may be interrupted by the exercise of individual Legislation; to negative all laws passed by the several States, contravening in the opinion of the National Legislature the articles of Union; and to call forth the force of the Union against any member of the Union failing to fulfill its duty under the articles thereof.

7. Resolved that a National Executive be instituted; to be chosen by the National Legislature for the term of years to receive punctually at stated times, a fixed compensation for the services rendered, in which no increase or diminution shall be made so as to affect the Magistracy, existing at the time of increase or diminution, and to be ineligible a second time; and that besides a general authority to execute the National laws, it ought to enjoy the Executive rights vested in Congress by the Confederation.

8. Resolved that the Executive and a convenient number of the National Judiciary, ought to compose a Council of revision with authority to examine every act of the National Legislature before it shall operate, and every act of a particular Legislature before a Negative thereon shall be final; and that the dissent of the said Council shall amount to a rejection, unless the Act of the National Legislature be again passed, or that of a particular Legislature be again negatived by of the members of each branch.

9. Resolved that the National Judiciary be established to consist of one or more supreme tribunals, and of inferior tribunals to be chosen by the National Legislature, to hold their offices during good behavior; and to receive punctually at stated times fixed compensation for their services, in which no increase or diminution shall be made so as to affect the persons actually in office at the time of such increase or diminution. That the jurisdiction of the inferior tribunals shall be to hear and determine in the first instance, and of the supreme tribunal to hear and determine in the [last] resort, all piracies and felonies on the high seas, captures from an enemy; cases in which foreigners or citizens of other States applying to such jurisdictions may be interested, or which respect the collection of the National revenue; impeachments of any National officers, and questions which may involve the national peace and harmony.

10. Resolved that the provision ought to be made for the admission of States lawfully arising within the limits of the United States, whether from a voluntary junction of Government and Territory or otherwise, with the consent of a number of voices in the National Legislature less than the whole.

11. Resolved that a Republican Government and the territory of each State, except in the instance of a voluntary junction of Government and territory, ought to be guaranteed by the United States to each State.

12. Resolved that provision ought to be made for the continuance of Congress and their authorities and privileges, until a given day after the reform of the articles of Union shall be adopted, and for the completion of all their engagements.

13. Resolved that provision ought to be made for the amendment of the Articles of Union whensoever it shall seem necessary, and that the assent of the National Legislature ought not to be required thereto.

14. Resolved that the Legislative Executive and Judiciary powers within the several States ought to be bound by oath to support the articles of union.

15. Resolved that the amendments which shall be offered to the Confederation, by the Convention ought at a proper time, or times, after the approbation of Congress to be submitted to an assembly or assemblies of Representatives, recommended by the several Legislatures to be expressly chosen by the people, to consider and decide thereon.[227]

Appendix 17

New Jersey Plan 1787

1. Resolved that the articles of Confederation ought to be so revised, corrected, & enlarged, as to render the federal Constitution adequate to the exigencies of Government, & the preservation of the Union.

2. Resolved that in addition to the powers vested in the U. States in Congress, by the present existing articles of Confederation, they be authorized to pass acts for raising a revenue, by levying a duty or duties on all goods or merchandizes of foreign growth or manufacture, imported into any part of the U. States, by Stamps on paper, vellum or parchment, and by a postage on all letters or packages passing through the general post-office, to be applied to such federal purposes as they shall deem proper & expedient; to make rules & regulations for the collection thereof; and the same from time to time, to alter & amend in such manner as they shall think proper: to pass Acts for the regulation of trade & commerce as well with foreign nations as with each other: provided that all punishments, fines, forfeitures & penalties to be incurred for contravening such acts rules and regulations shall be adjudged by the Common law Judiciaries of the State in which any offence contrary to the true intent & meaning of such Acts rules & regulations shall have been committed or perpetrated, with liberty of commencing in the first instance all suites & prosecutions for that purpose in the superior common law Judiciary in such State, subject nevertheless, for the correction of all errors, both in law & fact in rendering Judgment, to an appeal to the Judiciary of the U. States.

3. Resolved that whenever requisitions shall be necessary, instead of the rule for making requisitions mentioned in the articles of Confederation, the United States in Congress be authorized to make such requisitions in proportion to the whole number of white & other free citizens & inhabitants of every age sex and condition including those bound to servitude for a term of years & three fifths of all other persons not comprehended in the foregoing description, except Indians not paying taxes; that if such requisitions be not complied with, in the time specified therein, to direct the collection thereof in the non complying States & for that purpose to devise and pass acts directing & authorizing the same; provided that none of the powers hereby vested in the United States in Congress shall be exercised without the consent of at least   States, and in that proportion if the number of Confederated States should hereafter be increased or diminished.

4. Resolved that the United States in Congress be authorized to elect a federal Executive to consist of persons, to continue in office for the term of years, to receive punctually at stated times a fixed compensation for their services, in which no increase or diminution shall be made so as to affect the persons composing the Executive at the time of such increase or diminution, to be paid out of the federal treasury; to be incapable of holding any other office or appointment during their time of service and for years thereafter; to be ineligible a second time, & removeable by Congress on application by a majority of the Executives of the several States; that the Executives besides their general authority to execute the federal acts ought to appoint all federal officers not otherwise provided for, & to direct all military operations; provided that none of the persons composing the federal Executive shall on any occasion take command of any troops, so as personally to conduct any enterprise as General or in other capacity.

5. Resolved that a federal Judiciary be established to consist of a supreme Tribunal the Judges of which to be appointed by the Executive, & to hold their offices during good behaviour, to receive punctually at stated times a fixed compensation for their services in which no increase or diminution shall be made, so as to affect the persons actually in office at the time of such increases or diminution; that the Judiciary so established shall have authority to hear & determine in the first instance on all impeachments of federal officers, & by way of appeal in the dernier resort in all cases touching the rights of Ambassadors, in all cases of captures from an enemy, in all cases of piracies & felonies on the high seas, in all cases in which foreigners may be interested, in the construction of any treaty or treaties, or which may arise on any of the Acts for regulation of trade, or the collection of the federal Revenue: that none of the Judiciary shall during the time they remain in Office be capable of receiving or holding any other office or appointment during their time of service, or for thereafter.

6. Resolved that all Acts of the U. States in Congress made by virtue & in pursuance of the powers hereby & by the articles of Confederation vested in them, and all Treaties made & ratified under the authority of the U. States shall be the supreme law of the respective States so far forth as those Acts or Treaties shall relate to the said States or their Citizens, and that the Judiciary of the several States shall be bound thereby in their decisions, any thing in the respective laws of the Individual States to the contrary notwithstanding; and that if any State, or any body of men in any State shall oppose or prevent the carrying into execution such acts or treaties, the federal Executive shall be authorized to call forth the power of the Confederated States, or so much

thereof as may be necessary to enforce and compel an obedience to such Acts, or an observance of such Treaties.

7. Resolved, that the provision be made for the admission of new states into the Union

8. Resolved, the rule for naturalization ought to be the same in every State.

9. Resolved that a Citizen of one State committing an offense in another State of the Union, shall be deemed guilty of the same offense as if it had been committed by a Citizen of the State in which the offense was committed.[228]

Appendix 18

Hon. Ron Paul House Speech 10/10/2001, HR3074 text, HR3076 text

• Mr. Speaker, I rise to introduce the Air Piracy Reprisal and Capture Act of 2001 and the September 11 Marque and Reprisal Act of 2001. The Air Piracy Reprisal and Capture Act of 2001 updates the federal definition of "piracy" to include acts committed in the skies. The September 11 Marque and Reprisal Act of 2001 provides Congressional authorization for the President to issue letters of marque and reprisal to appropriate parties to seize the person and property of Osama bin Laden and any other individual responsible for the terrorist attacks of September 11. Authority to grant letters of marque and reprisal are provided for in the Constitution as a means of allowing Congress to deal with aggressive actions where a formal declaration of war against a foreign power is problematic. Originally intended to deal with piracy, letters of marque and reprisal represent an appropriate response to the piracy of the twentieth century: hijacking terrorism.

• All of America stood horrified at the brutal attacks of September 11 and all of us stand united in our determination to exact just retribution on the perpetrators of this evil deed. This is why I supported giving the President broad authority to use military power to respond to these attacks. When Congress authorized the use of force to respond to the attacks of September 11 we recognized these attacks were not merely criminal acts but an "unusual and extraordinary threat to the national security."

• Congress must use every means available to fight the terrorists behind this attack if we are to fulfill our constitutional obligations to provide for the common defense of our sovereign nation. Issuance of letters of marque and reprisal are a valuable tool in the struggle to exact just retribution on the perpetrators of the attacks on the World Trade Center and the Pentagon. In fact, they may be among the most effective response available to Congress.

• Since the bombing there has been much discussion of how to respond to warlike acts carried out by private parties. The drafters of the Constitution also had to wrestle with the problem of how to respond to sporadic attacks on American soil and citizens organized by groups not formally affiliated with a government. In order to deal with this situation, the Constitution authorized Congress to issue letters of marque and reprisal. In the early days of the Republic, marque and reprisal were usually used against pirates who, while they may have enjoyed the protection and partnership of governments, where not official representatives of a government.

• Although modern America does not face the threat of piracy on the high seas, we do face the threat of international terrorism. Terrorism has much in common with the piracy of days gone by. Like the pirates of old, today's terrorists are private groups operating to assault the United States government as well as threaten the lives, liberty and property of United States citizens. The only difference is that while pirates sought financial gains, terrorists seek to advance ideological and political agendas through terroristic violence.

• Like the pirates who once terrorized the high seas, terrorists today are also difficult to punish using military means. While bombs and missiles may be sufficient to knock out the military capability and the economic and technological infrastructure of an enemy nation that harbors those who committed the September 11 attacks, traditional military force may not be suitable to destroy the lawless terrorists who are operating in the nations targeted for military force. Instead, those terrorists may simply move to another base before our troops can locate them. It is for these reasons that I believe that, were the drafters of the Constitution with us today, they would counsel in favor of issuing letters of marque and reprisal against the terrorists responsible for this outrageous act.

• Specifically, my legislation authorizes the President to issue letters of marque and reprisal to all appropriate parties to capture Osama bin Laden and other members of al Qaeda or any other persons involved in the September 11 terrorist attacks. The President is also authorized to use part of the $40 billion appropriated by this Congress to respond to the attack, to establish a bounty for the capture of Osama bin Laden. My legislation singles out Osama bin Laden and al Qaeda because the information available to Congress and the American people indicates bin Laden and his organization were responsible for this action. By vesting authority in the President to issue the letters, my legislation ensures that letters of marque and reprisal can be coordinated with the administration's overall strategy to bring the perpetrators of this outrageous act to justice.

• Letters of marque and reprisal resolve one of the most vexing problems facing the country: how do we obtain retribution against the perpetrators of the attacks without inflicting massive damage on the Middle East which could drive moderate Arabs into an allegiance with bin Laden and other terrorists. This is because using letters of marque and reprisal shows the people of the region that we are serious when we say our quarrel is not with them but with Osama bin Laden and all others who would dare commit terrorist acts against the United States.

- Mr, Speaker, I ask that my colleagues join with me in providing the additional "necessary weapon of war" and to help defend our fellow citizens, our sovereign nation, and our liberty by cosponsoring the September 11 Marque and Reprisal Act of 2001 and the Air Piracy Reprisal and Capture Act of 2001.[229]

HR3074

To amend title 18, United States Code, and the Revised Statutes of the United States to provide punishment for, and to authorize the issuance of letters of marque and reprisal against acts of air piracy.

IN THE HOUSE OF REPRESENTATIVES

October 10, 2001

Mr. PAUL introduced the following bill; which was referred to the Committee on the Judiciary

A BILL

To amend title 18, United States Code, and the Revised Statutes of the United States to provide punishment for, and to authorize the issuance of letters of marque and reprisal against acts of air piracy.

Be it enacted by the Senate and House of Representatives of the United States of America in Congress assembled,

SECTION 1. SHORT TITLE.

This Act may be cited as the 'Air Piracy Reprisal and Capture Act of 2001'.

SEC. 2. FINDINGS.

The Congress finds the following:

(1) That the terrorist attacks on September 11, 2001 were acts of air piracy contrary to the law of nations.

(2) That the terrorist attacks were not just criminal actions, but belligerent attacks designed to destroy the sovereign independence of the United States of America contrary to the law of nations.

(3) That the perpetrators of the terrorist attacks were aided and abetted by enemy belligerents contrary to the law of nations.

(4) That similar acts of air piracy are planned for future execution by persons and organizations enjoying safe harbor by nations contrary to the law of nations.

(5) That the lives, liberties, and properties of the American people have been taken, and are threatened to be taken, by acts of air piracy contrary to the law of nations.

(6) That under Article I, section 8 of the United States Constitution, Congress has the power to define and punish piracies and other offenses against the laws of nations.

(7) That under Article I, section 8 of the United States Constitution, Congress has the powers to grant letters of marque and reprisal and to make rules concerning captures on land and water.

SEC. 3. DEFINITIONS.

(1) For the purpose of chapter 81, title 18, United States Code, the term 'piracy as defined by the law of nations' means robbery on the high seas and in the air.

(2) For the purposes of chapter 81, title 18, United States Code, and chapter 7, title 33, United States Code, terms 'vessel' includes 'aircraft' and 'port' include 'airport'.

SEC. 4. PUNISHMENTS FOR PIRACY.

Chapter 81 of title 18, United States Code, is amended--

(1) in section 1651--

(A) by inserting 'or in the skies' after 'on the high seas'; and

(B) by inserting 'or if death results, may be sentenced to death' after 'life';

(2) in section 1652--

(A) by inserting 'or in the skies' after 'on the high seas'; and

(B) by inserting 'or, if death results may be sentenced to death' after 'life';

(3) in section 1653--

(A) by inserting 'on land, or in the sky' after 'on the sea'; and

(B) by inserting 'or, if death results may be sentenced to death' after 'life';

(4) in section 1654--

(A) by inserting ‘or within’ after ‘without’;

(B) by inserting ‘or any individual aboard any such private vessel of war or privateer, whether it be a ship or aircraft’ after ‘privateer’;

(C) by striking ‘fined under this title or’; and

(D) by striking ‘not more than ten years or both.’ and inserting ‘for life.’;

(5) in section 1655--

(A) by inserting ‘or an airman, including steward, stewardess, pilot, copilot or other airplane officer’ after ‘being a seaman’;

(B) by inserting ‘, including the pilot or copilot of an aircraft’ after ‘upon his commander’;

(C) by inserting ‘or persons’ after ‘or goods’; and

(D) by inserting ‘or if death results, may be sentenced to death’ after ‘life’;

(6) in section 1656--

(A) by inserting ‘or being a captain, pilot, or other officer or service member of an aircraft’ after ‘the United States,’;

(B) by inserting ‘or flies’ after ‘runs’; and

(C) by inserting ‘or if death results, may be sentenced to death’ after ‘fined under this title’; and

(7) in section 1657--

(A) by inserting ‘or captain, pilot, copilot or service member’ after ‘mariner’;

(B) by inserting ‘or fly’ after ‘run’;

(C) by inserting ‘or passenger’ after ‘merchandise’;

(D) by inserting ‘or in the skies’ after ‘upon the seas’ both places it appears;

(E) by inserting ‘or being an airman confines the pilot of any aircraft’ after ‘of any vessel’; and

(F) before the dash by striking ‘three’ and inserting ‘ten’.

SEC. 5. SUPPRESSION OF PIRACY.

(a) EXPANSION OF APPLICATION OF PIRACY LAWS- For purposes of sections 4293 through 4299b of the Revised Statutes of the United States, as amended by this Act, each of the terms 'piratical aggressions and depredation' and 'act of piracy' includes all such aggressions, depredations, and other such acts whether committed upon land or sea or in the air in relation to any ship or aircraft.

(b) CONFORMING AMENDMENTS- The Revised Statutes of the United States are amended as follows:

(1) In section 4293 (33 U.S.C. 381)--

(A) by inserting ', including commercial aircraft,' after 'merchant vessels'; and

(B) by inserting ', or of the citizens thereof,' after 'the United States'.

(2) In section 4294 (33 U.S.C. 382), by inserting 'or in the skies' immediately after 'upon the high seas'.

(3) In section 4295 (33 U.S.C. 383)--

(A) by inserting 'and lawful passengers' after 'crew'; and

(B) by inserting ', including commercial aircraft,' after 'merchant vessel'.

(4) In section 4298 (33 U.S.C. 386)--

(A) by striking 'or the commanders of any other suitable vessels,' and inserting 'or the commander or other leader of any other suitable entity operating under the authority of any letters of marque and reprisal granted by Congress'; and

(B) by inserting ', or, whether on the high seas, in the skies or on land, subdue, seize, and take persons and property, using such force as may be necessary to defend the lives, liberties, and property of the citizens of the United States against piratical aggressions and degradations, as authorized by any letter of marque and reprisal granted by Congress' after 'that section'.

(c) TREATMENT OF PROPERTY AND PERSONS IDENTIFIED IN LETTER OF MARQUE AND REPRISAL- The Revised Statutes of the United States are further amended by inserting after section 4299 the following new sections:

'SEC. 4299a. Property identified as subject to seizure under a duly issued letter of marque and reprisal shall be deemed enemy property and subject to confiscation and forfeiture, and further, shall be deemed the property of the captors or of the United States in such proportions as provided for in the letter of marque and reprisal pursuant to which said property was seized.

'SEC. 4299b. Any person identified as subject to seizure under a duly issued letter of marque and reprisal shall be deemed an enemy belligerent of the United States and subject to court-martial jurisdiction thereof for punishment of any violation of the laws of nations, such person to be transferred into the custody of the United States as provided for in the letter of marque and reprisal pursuant to which such person was seized.'.[230]

HR3076

To authorize the President of the United States to issue letters of marque and reprisal with respect to certain acts of air piracy upon the United States on September 11, 2001, and other similar acts of war planned for the future.

IN THE HOUSE OF REPRESENTATIVES

October 10, 2001

Mr. PAUL introduced the following bill; which was referred to the Committee on International Relations

A BILL

To authorize the President of the United States to issue letters of marque and reprisal with respect to certain acts of air piracy upon the United States on September 11, 2001, and other similar acts of war planned for the future.

Be it enacted by the Senate and House of Representatives of the United States of America in Congress assembled,

SECTION 1. SHORT TITLE.

This Act may be cited as the 'September 11 Marque and Reprisal Act of 2001'.

SEC. 2. FINDINGS.

The Congress finds the following:

(1) That the terrorist attacks on September 11, 2001 upon the United States were acts of air piracy contrary to the law of nations.

(2) That the terrorist attacks were acts of war perpetrated by enemy belligerents to destroy the sovereign independence of the United States of America contrary to the law of nations.

(3) That the perpetrators of the terrorist attacks were actively aided and abetted by a conspiracy involving one Osama bin Laden and others known and unknown, either knowingly and actively affiliated with a terrorist organization known as al Qaeda or knowingly and actively conspiring with Osama bin Laden and al Qaeda, both of whom are dedicated to the destruction of the United States of America as a sovereign and independent nation.

(4) That the al Qaeda conspiracy is a continuing one among Osama bin Laden, al Qaeda, and others known and unknown with plans to commit additional acts of air piracy and other similar acts of war upon the United States of America and her people.

(5) That the act of war committed on September 11, 2001, by the al Qaeda conspirators, and the other acts of war planned by the al Qaeda conspirators, are contrary to the law of nations.

(6) That under Article I, Section 8 of the United States Constitution, Congress has the power to grant letters of marque and reprisal to punish, deter, and prevent the piratical aggressions and depredations and other acts of war of the al Qaeda conspirators.

SEC. 3. AUTHORITY OF PRESIDENT.

(a) The President of the United States is authorized and requested to commission, under officially issued letters of marque and reprisal, so many of privately armed and equipped persons and entities as, in his judgment, the service may require, with suitable instructions to the leaders thereof, to employ all means reasonably necessary to seize outside the geographic boundaries of the United States and its territories the person and property of Osama bin Laden, of any al Qaeda co-conspirator, and of any conspirator with Osama bin Laden and al Qaeda who are responsible for the air piratical aggressions and depredations perpetrated upon the United States of America on September 11, 2001, and for any planned future air piratical aggressions and depredations or other acts of war upon the United States of America and her people.

(b) The President of the United States is authorized to place a money bounty, drawn in his discretion from the $40,000,000,000 appropriated on September 14, 2001, in the Emergency Supplemental Appropriations Act for Recovery from and Response to Terrorists Attacks on the United States or from private sources, for the capture, alive or dead, of Osama bin Laden or any other al Qaeda conspirator responsible for the act of air piracy upon the United States on September 11, 2001, under the authority of any letter of marque or reprisal issued under this Act.

(c) No letter of marque and reprisal shall be issued by the President without requiring the posting of a security bond in such amount as the President shall determine is sufficient to ensure that the letter be executed according to the terms and conditions thereof.[231]

Appendix 19

NDAA, Section 1021

NATIONAL DEFENSE AUTHORIZATION ACT FOR FISCAL YEAR 2012

TITLE X - GENERAL PROVISIONS

Subtitle D - Counterterrorism

SEC. 1021. AFFIRMATION OF AUTHORITY OF THE ARMED FORCES OF THE UNITED STATES TO DETAIN COVERED PERSONS PURSUANT TO THE AUTHORIZATION FOR USE OF MILITARY FORCE.

(a) IN GENERAL.—Congress affirms that the authority of the President to use all necessary and appropriate force pursuant to the Authorization for Use of Military Force (Public Law 107–40; 50 U.S.C. 1541 note) includes the authority for the Armed Forces of the United States to detain covered persons (as defined in subsection (b)) pending disposition under the law of war.

(b) COVERED PERSONS.—A covered person under this section is any person as follows:

(1) A person who planned, authorized, committed, or aided the terrorist attacks that occurred on September 11, 2001, or harbored those responsible for those attacks.

(2) A person who was a part of or substantially supported al-Qaeda, the Taliban, or associated forces that are engaged in hostilities against the United States or its coalition partners, including any person who has committed a belligerent act or has directly supported such hostilities in aid of such enemy forces.

(c) DISPOSITION UNDER LAW OF WAR.—The disposition of a person under the law of war as described in subsection (a) may include the following:

(1) Detention under the law of war without trial until the end of the hostilities authorized by the Authorization for Use of Military Force.

(2) Trial under chapter 47A of title 10, United States Code (as amended by the Military Commissions Act of 2009 (title XVIII of Public Law 111–84)).

(3) Transfer for trial by an alternative court or competent tribunal having lawful jurisdiction.

(4) Transfer to the custody or control of the person's country of origin, any other foreign country, or any other foreign entity.

(d) CONSTRUCTION.—Nothing in this section is intended to limit or expand the authority of the President or the scope of the Authorization for Use of Military Force.

(e) AUTHORITIES.—Nothing in this section shall be construed to affect existing law or authorities relating to the detention of United States citizens, lawful resident aliens of the United States, or any other persons who are captured or arrested in the United States.

(f) REQUIREMENT FOR BRIEFINGS OF CONGRESS.—The Secretary of Defense shall regularly brief Congress regarding the application of the authority described in this section, including the organizations, entities, and individuals considered to be "covered persons" for purposes of subsection (b)(2). [232]

Appendix 20

Farewell Address To The People Of The United States

George Washington - September 1796

Friends and Fellow-Citizens:

The period for a new election of a citizen to administer the executive government of the United States being not far distant, and the time actually arrived when your thoughts must be employed in designating the person who is to be clothed with that important trust, it appears to me proper, especially as it may conduce to a more distinct expression of the public voice, that I should now apprize you of the resolution I have formed, to decline being considered among the number of those out of whom the choice is to be made.

I beg you, at the same time, to do me the justice to be assured, that this resolution has not been taken without a strict regard to all the considerations appertaining to the relation which binds a dutiful citizen to his country; and that, in withdrawing the tender of service, which silence in my situation might imply, I am influenced by no diminution of zeal for your future interest; no deficiency of grateful respect for your past kindness; but am supported by a full conviction that the step is compatible with both.

The acceptance of, and continuance hitherto in, the office to which your suffrages have twice called me, have been a uniform sacrifice of inclination to the opinion of duty, and to a deference for what appeared to be your desire. I constantly hoped that it would have been much earlier in my power, consistently with motives which I was not at liberty to disregard, to return to that retirement from which I had been reluctantly drawn. The strength of my inclination to do this, previous to the last election, had even led to the preparation of an address to declare it to you; but mature reflection on the then perplexed and critical posture of affairs with foreign nations, and the unanimous advice of persons entitled to my confidence, impelled me to abandon the idea. I rejoice that the state of your concerns, external as well as internal, no longer renders the pursuit of inclination incompatible with the sentiment of duty or propriety; and am persuaded, whatever partiality may be retained for my services, that, in the present circumstances of our country, you will not disapprove of my determination to retire.

The impressions with which I first undertook the arduous trust, were explained on the proper occasion. In the discharge of this trust, I will only say that I have, with good intentions, contributed towards the organization and administration of the government the best exertions of which a very fallible judgment was capable. Not unconscious, in the outset, of the inferiority of my qualifications, experience in my own eyes, perhaps still more in the eyes of others, has strengthened the motives to diffidence of myself; and, every day, the increasing weight of years admonishes me more and more, that the shade of retirement is as necessary to me as it will be welcome. Satisfied that if any circumstances have given peculiar value to my services, they were temporary, I have the consolation to believe, that while choice and prudence invite me to quit the political scene, patriotism does not forbid it.

In looking forward to the moment which is to terminate the career of my political life, my feelings do not permit me to suspend the deep acknowledgment of that debt of gratitude which I owe to my beloved country for the many honors it has conferred upon me; still more for the steadfast confidence with which it has supported me; and for the opportunities I have thence enjoyed of manifesting my inviolable attachment, by services faithful and persevering, though in usefulness unequal to my zeal. If benefits have resulted to our country from these services, let it always be remembered to your praise, and as an instructive example in our annals, that under circumstances in which the passions, agitated in every direction, were liable to mislead — amidst appearances sometimes dubious — vicissitudes of fortune often discouraging — in situations in which not unfrequently want of success has countenanced the spirit of criticism — the constancy of your support was the essential prop of the efforts, and a guaranty of the plans, by which they were effected. Profoundly penetrated with this idea, I shall carry it with me to the grave, as a strong incitement to unceasing wishes, that Heaven may continue to you the choicest tokens of its beneficence — that your union and brotherly affection may be perpetual — that the free constitution which is the work of your hands may be sacredly maintained — that its administration in every department may be stamped with wisdom and virtue — that, in fine, the happiness of the people of these states, under the auspices of liberty, may be made complete, by so careful a preservation, and so prudent a use of this blessing as will acquire to them the glory of recommending it to the applause, the affection, and adoption of every nation which is yet a stranger to it.

Here, perhaps, I ought to stop. But a solicitude for your welfare, which cannot end but with my life, and the apprehension of danger, natural to that solicitude, urge me, on an occasion like the present, to offer to your solemn contemplation, and to recommend to your frequent review, some sentiments, which are the result of much reflection, of no inconsiderable observation, and which appear to me all-important to the permanency of your felicity as a people. These will be offered to you with the more freedom, as you can only see in them the disinterested warnings of a parting friend, who can possibly have no personal motives to bias his counsel. Nor can I forget, as an encouragement to it, your indulgent reception of my sentiments on a former and not dissimilar occasion.

Interwoven as is the love of liberty with every ligament of our hearts, no recommendation of mine is necessary to fortify or confirm the attachment.

The unity of government, which constitutes you one people, is also now dear to you. It is justly so; for it is a main pillar in the edifice of your real independence; the support of your tranquility at home; your peace abroad; of your safety; of your prosperity; of that very liberty which you so highly prize. But as it is easy to foresee, that, from different causes and from different quarters, much pains will be taken, many artifices employed, to weaken in your minds the conviction of this truth; as this is the point in your political fortress against which the batteries of internal and external enemies will be most constantly and actively (though often covertly and insidiously) directed; it is of infinite moment, that you should properly estimate the immense value of your national union to your collective and individual happiness; that you should cherish a cordial, habitual, and immovable attachment to it; accustoming yourselves to think and to speak of it as a palladium of your political safety and prosperity; watching for its preservation with jealous anxiety; discountenancing whatever may suggest even a suspicion that it can in any event be abandoned; and indignantly frowning upon the first dawning of every attempt to alienate any portion of our country from the rest, or to enfeeble the sacred ties which now link together the various parts.

For this you have every inducement of sympathy and interest. Citizens, by birth or choice, of a common country, that country has a right to concentrate your affections. The name of American, which belongs to you in your national capacity, must always exalt the just pride of patriotism, more than any appellation derived from local discriminations. With slight shades of difference you have the same religion, manners, habits, and political principle. You have, in a common cause, fought and triumphed together; the independence and liberty you possess, are the work of joint councils and joint efforts — of common dangers, sufferings, and success.

But these considerations, however powerfully they address themselves to your sensibility, are greatly outweighed by those which apply more immediately to your interest. Here every portion of our country finds the most commanding motives for carefully guarding and preserving the union of the whole.

The north, in an unrestrained intercourse with the south, protected by the equal laws of a common government, finds in the productions of the latter great additional resources of maritime and commercial enterprise, and precious materials of manufacturing industry. The south, in the same intercourse, benefiting by the same agency of the north, sees its agriculture grow and its commerce expand. Turning partly into its own channels the seamen of the north, it finds its particular navigation invigorated — and while it contributes in different ways to nourish and increase the general mass of the national navigation, it looks forward to the protection of a maritime strength, to which itself is unequally adapted. The east, in like intercourse with the west, already finds, and in the progressive improvement of interior communications by land and water, will more and more find a valuable vent for the commodities which it brings from abroad, or manufactures at home. The west derives from the east supplies requisite to its growth and comfort; and what is perhaps of still greater consequence, it must of necessity owe the secure enjoyment of indispensable outlets for its own productions, to the weight, influence, and the future maritime strength of the Atlantic side of the Union, directed by an indissoluble community of interest as one nation. Any other tenure by which the west can hold this essential advantage, whether derived from its own separate strength, or from an apostate and unnatural connection with any foreign power, must be intrinsically precarious.

While, then, every part of our country thus feels an immediate and particular interest in union, all the parts combined cannot fail to find in the united mass of means and efforts, greater strength, greater resource, proportionably greater security from external danger, a less frequent interruption of their peace by foreign nations; and, what is of inestimable value, they must derive from union an exemption from those broils and wars between themselves, which so frequently afflict neighboring countries, not tied together by the same government, which their own rival- ships alone would be sufficient to produce; but which opposite foreign alliances, attachments, and intrigues, would stimulate and imbitter. Hence, likewise, they will avoid the necessity of those overgrown military establishments, which, under any form of government, are inauspicious to liberty, and which are to be regarded as particularly hostile to republican liberty. In this sense it is, that your union ought to be considered as a main prop of your liberty, and that the love of the one ought to endear to you the preservation of the other.

These considerations speak a persuasive language to every reflecting and virtuous mind, and exhibit the continuance of the union as a primary object of patriotic desire. Is there a doubt whether a common government can embrace so large a sphere? Let experience solve it. To listen to mere speculation in such a case were criminal. We are authorized to hope that a proper organization, of the whole, with the auxiliary agency of governments for the respective subdivisions, will afford a happy issue of the experiment. It is well worth a fair and full experiment. With such powerful and obvious motives to union, affecting all parts of our country, while experience shall not have demonstrated its impracticability, there will always be reason to distrust the patriotism of those who in any quarter may endeavor to weaken its bands.

In contemplating the causes which may disturb our union, it occurs as matter of serious concern that any ground should have been furnished for characterizing parties by geographical discriminations — Northern and Southern; Atlantic and Western; whence designing men may endeavor to excite a belief that there is a real difference of local interests and views. One of the expedients of party to acquire influence within particular districts, is to misrepresent the opinions and aims of other districts. You cannot shield yourselves too much against the jealousies and heart-burnings which spring from these misrepresentations; they tend to render alien to each other those who ought to be bound together by fraternal affection. The inhabitants of our western country have lately had a useful lesson on this head. They have seen in the negotiation by the executive, and in the unanimous ratification by the senate of the treaty with Spain, and in the universal satisfaction at that event throughout the United States, a decisive proof how unfounded were the suspicions propagated among them of a policy in the general government, and in the Atlantic states, unfriendly to their interests in regard to the Mississippi. They have been witnesses to the formation of two treaties, — that with Great Britain, and that with Spain, — which secure to them everything they could desire, in respect to our foreign relations, towards confirming their prosperity. Will it not be their wisdom to rely for the preservation of these advantages on the union by which they were procured? Will they not henceforth be deaf to those advisers, if such there are, who would sever them from their brethren, and connect them with aliens?

To the efficacy and permanency of your union, a government for the whole is indispensable. No alliances, however strict between the parts, can be an adequate substitute; they must inevitably experience the infractions and interruptions which alliances at all times have experienced. Sensible of this momentous truth, you have improved upon your first essay, by the adoption of a constitution of government better calculated than your former for an intimate union, and for the efficacious management of your common concerns. This government, the offspring of your own choice, uninfluenced and unawed; adopted upon full investigation and mature deliberation; completely free in its principles; in the distribution of its powers uniting security with energy, and containing within itself provision for its own amendment, has a just claim to your confidence and your support. Respect for its authority, compliance with its laws, acquiescence in its measures, are duties enjoined by the fundamental maxims of true liberty. The basis of our political system is the right of the people to make and to alter their constitutions of government. But the constitution which at any time exists, until changed by an explicit and authentic act of the whole people, is sacredly obligatory upon all. The very idea of the power and the right of the people to establish government, presupposes the duty of every individual to obey the established government.

All obstructions to the execution of the laws, all combinations and associations, under whatever plausible character, with the real design to direct, control, counteract, or awe, the regular deliberations and action of the constituted authorities, are destructive of this fundamental principle, and of fatal tendency. They serve to organize faction; to give it an artificial and extraordinary force; to put in the place of the delegated will of the nation, the will of party, often a small, but artful and enterprising minority of the community; and according to the alternate triumphs of different parties, to make the public administration the mirror of the ill-concerted and incongruous projects of faction, rather than the organ of consistent and wholesome plans, digested by common counsels and modified by mutual interests.

However combinations or associations of the above description may now and then answer popular ends, they are likely, in the course of time and things, to become potent engines by which cunning, ambitious, and unprincipled men will be enabled to subvert the power of the people, and to usurp for themselves the reins of government; destroying afterwards the very engines which have lifted them to unjust dominion.

Towards the preservation of your government, and the permanency of your present happy state, it is requisite not only that you steadily discountenance irregular opposition to its acknowledged authority, but also that you resist with care the spirit of innovation upon its principles, however specious the pretext. One method of assault may be to effect in the forms of the constitution alterations which will impair the energy of the system, and thus to undermine what cannot be directly overthrown. In all the changes to which you may be invited, remember that time and habit are at least as necessary to fix the true character of governments, as of other human institutions; that experience is the surest standard by which to test the real tendency of the existing constitutions of a country; that facility in changes, upon the credit of mere hypothesis and opinion, exposes to perpetual change, from the endless variety of hypothesis and opinion; and remember especially, that for the efficient management of your common interests, in a country so extensive as ours, a government of as much vigor as is consistent with the perfect security of liberty, is indispensable. Liberty itself will find in such a government, with powers properly distributed and adjusted, its surest guardian. It is, indeed, little else than a name, where the government is too feeble to withstand the enterprises of faction, to confine each member of society within the limits prescribed by the laws, and to maintain all in the secure and tranquil enjoyment of the rights of person and property.

I have already intimated to you the danger of parties in the state, with particular reference to the founding of them upon geographical discriminations. Let me now take a more comprehensive view, and warn you, in the most solemn manner, against the baneful effects of the spirit of party generally.

This spirit, unfortunately, is inseparable from our nature, having its root in the strongest passions of the human mind. It exists under different shapes in all governments, more or less stifled, controlled, or repressed; but in those of the popular form it is seen in its greatest rankness, and is truly their worst enemy.

The alternate domination of one faction over another, sharpened by the spirit of revenge, natural to party dissension, which in different ages and countries has perpetrated the most horrid enormities, is itself a frightful despotism. But this leads at length to a more formal and permanent despotism. The disorders and miseries which result, gradually incline the minds of men to seek security and repose in the absolute power of an individual; and, sooner or later, the chief of some prevailing faction, more able or more fortunate than his competitors, turns this disposition to the purposes of his own elevation on the ruins of the public liberty.

Without looking forward to an extremity of this kind, (which, nevertheless, ought not to be entirely out of sight,) the common and continual mischiefs of the spirit of party are sufficient to make it the interest and duty of a wise people to discourage and restrain it.

It serves always to distract the public councils, and enfeeble the public administration. It agitates the community with ill-founded jealousies and false alarms; kindles the animosity of one part against another; foments occasional riot and insurrection. It opens the door to foreign influence and corruption, which finds a facilitated access to the government itself, through the channels of party passion. Thus the policy and will of one country are subjected to the policy and will of another.

There is an opinion that parties in free countries are useful checks upon the administration of the government, and serve to keep alive the spirit of liberty. This, within certain limits, is probably true; and in governments of a monarchical cast, patriotism may look with indulgence, if not with favor, upon the spirit of party. But in those of the popular character, in governments purely elective, it is a spirit not to be encouraged. From the natural tendency, it is certain there will always be enough of that spirit for every salutary purpose; and there being constant danger of excess, the effort ought to be, by force of public opinion, to mitigate and assuage it. A fire not to be quenched, it demands a uniform vigilance to prevent its bursting into a flame, lest, instead of warming, it should consume.

It is important, likewise, that the habits of thinking, in a free country, should inspire caution, in those intrusted with its administration, to confine themselves within their respective constitutional spheres; avoiding, in the exercise of the powers of one department, to encroach upon another. The spirit of encroachment tends to consolidate the powers of all the departments in one, and thus to create, whatever the form of government, a real despotism. A just estimate of that love of power, and proneness to abuse it, which predominates in the human heart, is sufficient to satisfy us of the truth of this position. The necessity of reciprocal checks in the exercise of political power, by dividing and distributing it into different depositories, and constituting each the guardian of the public weal against invasions of the other, has been evinced by experiments, ancient and modern; some of them in our country, and under our own eyes. To preserve them must be as necessary as to institute them. If, in the opinion of the people, the distribution or modification of the constitutional powers be, in any particular, wrong, let it be corrected by an amendment in the way which the constitution designates. But let there be no change by usurpation; for though this, in one instance, may be the instrument of good, it is the customary weapon by which free governments are destroyed. The precedent must always greatly overbalance, in permanent evil, any partial or transient benefit which the use can at any time yield.

Of all the dispositions and habits which lead to political prosperity, religion and morality are indispensable supports. In vain would that man claim the tribute of patriotism, who should labor to subvert these great pillars of human happiness — these firmest props of the duties of men and citizens. The mere politician, equally with the pious man, ought to respect and to cherish them. A volume could not trace all their connection with private and public felicity. Let it simply be asked, Where is the security for property, for reputation, for life, if the sense of religious obligation desert the oaths, which are the instruments of investigation in courts of justice? And let us with caution indulge the supposition that morality can be maintained without religion. Whatever may be conceded to the influence of refined education on minds of peculiar structure, reason and experience both forbid us to expect that national morality can prevail in exclusion of religious principles.

It is substantially true that virtue or morality is a necessary spring of popular government. The rule, indeed, extends, with more or less force, to every species of free government. Who that is a sincere friend to it can look with indifference upon attempts to shake the foundation of the fabric?

Promote, then, as an object of primary importance, institutions for the general diffusion of knowledge. In proportion as the structure of a government gives force to public opinion, it is essential that public opinion should be enlightened.

As a very important source of strength and security, cherish public credit. One method of preserving it, is to use it as sparingly as possible, avoiding occasions of expense by cultivating peace, but remembering, also, that timely disbursements to prepare for danger, frequently prevent much greater disbursements to repel it; avoiding, likewise, the accumulation of debt, not only by shunning occasions of expense, but by vigorous exertions in time of peace to discharge the debts which unavoidable wars have occasioned, not ungenerously throwing upon posterity the burdens which we ourselves ought to bear. The execution of these maxims belongs to your representatives; but it is necessary that public opinion should cooperate. To facilitate to them the performance of their duty, it is essential that you should practically bear in mind, that towards the payment of debts there must be revenue; that to have revenue there must be taxes; that no taxes can be devised which are not more or less inconvenient and unpleasant; that the intrinsic embarrassment, inseparable from the selection of the proper objects, (which is always a choice of difficulties,) ought to be a decisive motive for a candid construction of the conduct of the government in making it, and for a spirit of acquiescence in the measures for obtaining revenue which the public exigencies may at any time dictate.

Observe good faith and justice towards all nations; cultivate peace and harmony with all; religion and morality enjoin this conduct; and can it be that good policy does not equally enjoin it? It will be worthy of a free, enlightened, and, at no distant period, a great nation, to give to mankind the magnanimous and too novel example of a people always guided by an exalted justice and benevolence. Who can doubt but that, in the course of time and things, the fruits of such a plan would richly repay any temporary advantages which might be lost by a steady adherence to it? Can it be that Providence has connected the permanent felicity of a nation with its virtue? The experiment, at least, is recommended by every sentiment which ennobles human nature. Alas! it is rendered impossible by its vices!

In the execution of such a plan, nothing is more essential than that permanent, inveterate antipathies against particular nations, and passionate attachment for others, should be excluded; and that, in the place of them, just and amicable feelings towards all should be cultivated. The nation which indulges towards another an habitual hatred, or an habitual fondness, is, in some degree, a slave. It is a slave to its animosity or to its affection, either of which is sufficient to lead it astray from its duty and its interest. Antipathy in one nation against another, disposes each more readily to offer insult and injury, to lay hold of slight causes of umbrage, and to be naughty and intractable when accidental or trifling occasions of dispute occur.

Hence frequent collisions, obstinate, envenomed, and bloody contests. The nation, prompted by ill-will and resentment, sometimes impels to war the government, contrary to the best calculations of policy. The government sometimes participates in the national propensity, and adopts, through passion, what reason would reject; at other times, it makes the animosity of the nation subservient to the projects of hostility, instigated by pride, ambition, and other sinister and pernicious motives. The peace often, sometimes, perhaps, the liberty of nations has been the victim.

So, likewise, a passionate attachment of one nation for another produces a variety of evils. Sympathy for the favorite nation, facilitating the illusion of an imaginary common interest in cases where no real common interest exists, and infusing into one the enmities of the other, betrays the former into a participation in the quarrels and the wars of the latter, without adequate inducements or justification. It leads, also, to concessions to the favorite nation of privileges denied to others, which are apt doubly to injure the nation making the concessions, by unnecessarily parting with what ought to have been retained, and by exciting jealousy, ill-will, and a disposition to retaliate in the parties from whom equal privileges are withheld; and it gives to ambitious, corrupt, or deluded citizens, (who devote themselves to the favorite nation,) facility to betray or sacrifice the interests of their own country without odium, sometimes even with popularity; gilding with the appearances of a virtuous sense of obligation to a commendable deference for public opinion, or a laudable zeal for public good, the base or foolish compliances of ambition, corruption, or infatuation.

As avenues to foreign influence, in innumerable ways, such attachments are particularly alarming to the truly enlightened and independent patriot. How many opportunities do they afford to tamper with domestic factions, to practise the art of seduction, to mislead public opinion, to influence or awe the public councils! Such an attachment of a small or weak, towards a great and powerful nation, dooms the former to be the satellite of the latter. Against the insidious wiles of foreign influence, (I con jure you to believe me, fellow-citizens,) the jealousy of a free people ought to be constantly awake, since history and experience prove that foreign influence is one of the most baneful foes of republican government. But that jealousy, too, to be useful, must be impartial, else it becomes the instrument of the very influence to be avoided, instead of a defence against it. Excessive partiality for one foreign nation, and excessive dislike for another, cause those whom they actuate to see danger only on one side, and serve to veil and even second the arts of influence on the other. Real patriots, who may resist the intrigues of the favorite, are liable to become suspected and odious; while its tools and dupes usurp the applause and confidence of the people to surrender their interests.

The great rule of conduct for us, in regard to foreign nations, is, in extending our commercial relations, to have with them as little political connection as possible. So far as we have already formed engagements, let them be fulfilled with perfect good faith. Here let us stop.

Europe has a set of primary interests, which to us have none, or a very remote relation. Hence, she must be engaged in frequent controversies, the causes of which are essentially foreign to our concerns. Hence, therefore, it must be unwise in us to implicate ourselves, by artificial ties, in the ordinary vicissitude of her politics, or the ordinary combinations and collisions of her friendships or enmities.

Our detached and distant situation invites and enables us to pursue a different course. If we remain one people, under an efficient government, the period is not far off when we may defy material injury from external annoyance; when we may take such an attitude as will cause the neutrality we may at any time resolve upon, to be scrupulously respected; when belligerent nations, under the impossibility of making acquisitions upon us, will not lightly hazard the giving us provocation; when we may choose peace or war, as our interest, guided by justice, shall counsel.

Why forego the advantages of so peculiar a situation? Why quit our own to stand upon foreign ground? Why, by interweaving our destiny with that of any part of Europe, entangle our peace and prosperity in the toils of European ambition, rivalship, interest, humor, or caprice?

It is our true policy to steer clear of permanent alliances with any portion of the foreign world; so far, I mean, as we are now at liberty to do it; for let me not be under stood as capable of patronizing infidelity to existing engagements. I hold the maxim no less applicable to public than to private affairs, that honesty is always the best policy. I repeat, therefore, let those engagements be observed in their genuine sense. But, in my opinion, it is unnecessary, and would be unwise, to extend them.

Taking care always to keep ourselves, by suitable establishments, on a respectable defensive posture, we may safely trust to temporary alliances for extraordinary emergencies.

Harmony, and a liberal intercourse with all nations, are recommended by policy, humanity, and interest. But even our commercial policy should hold an equal and impartial hand; neither seeking nor granting exclusive favors or preferences; consulting the natural course of things; diffusing and diversifying by gentle means the stream of commerce, but forcing nothing; establishing with powers so disposed, in order to give trade a stable course, to define the rights of our merchants, and to enable the government to support them, conventional rules of intercourse, the best that present circumstances and natural opinion will permit, but temporary, and liable to be, from time to time, abandoned or varied, as experience and circumstances shall dictate; constantly keeping in view that it is folly in one nation to look for disinterested favors from another; that it must pay with a portion of its independence for whatever it may accept under that character; that by such acceptance, it may place itself in the condition of having given equivalents for nominal favors, and yet of being reproached with ingratitude for not giving, more. There can be no greater error than to expect or calculate upon real favors from nation to nation. It is an illusion which experience must cure, which a just pride ought to discard.

In offering to you, my countrymen, these counsels of an old, affectionate friend, I dare not hope they will make the strong and lasting impression I could wish — that they will control the usual current of the passions, or prevent our nation from running the course which has hitherto marked the destiny of nations. But if I may even flatter myself that they may be productive of some partial benefit, some occasional good; that they may now and then recur to moderate the fury of party spirit; to warn against the mischiefs of foreign intrigue; to guard against the impostures of pretended patriotism; this hope will be a full recompense for the solicitude for your welfare by which they have been dictated.

How far, in the discharge of my official duties, I have been guided by the principles which have been delineated, the public records and other evidences of my conduct must witness to you and to the world. To myself, the assurance of my own conscience is, that I have at least believed myself to be guided by them.

In relation to the still subsisting war in Europe, my proclamation of the 22d of April, 1793, is the index to my plan. Sanctioned by your approving voice, and by that of your representatives in both houses of Congress, the spirit of that measure has continually governed me, uninfluenced by any attempts to deter or divert me from it.

After deliberate examination, with the aids of the best lights I could obtain, I was well satisfied that our country, under all the circumstances of the case, had a right to take, and was bound in duty and interest to take, a neutral position. Having taken it, I determined, as far as should depend upon me, to maintain it with moderation, perseverance, and firmness.

The considerations which respect the right to hold this conduct, it is not necessary on this occasion to detail. I will only observe, that, according to my understanding of the matter, that right, so far from being denied by any of the belligerent powers, has been virtually admitted by all.

The duty of holding a neutral conduct may be inferred, without anything more, from the obligation which justice and humanity impose on every nation, in cases in which it is free to act, to maintain inviolate the relations of peace and amity towards other nations.

The inducements of interest for observing that conduct, will best be referred to your own reflections and experience. With me, a predominant motive has been to endeavor to gain time to our country, to settle and mature its yet recent institutions, and to progress, without interruption, to that degree of strength and constancy, which is necessary to give it, humanly speaking, the command of its own fortune.

Though, in reviewing the incidents of my administration, I am unconscious of intentional error, I am, nevertheless, too sensible of my defects not to think it probable that I may have committed many errors. Whatever they may be, I fervently beseech the Almighty to avert or mitigate the evils to which they may tend. I shall also carry with me the hope that my country will never cease to view them with indulgence; and that, after forty-five years of my life dedicated to its service, with an upright zeal, the faults of incompetent abilities will be consigned to oblivion, as myself must soon be to the mansions of rest.

Relying on its kindness in this as in other things, and actuated by that fervent love towards it, which is so natural to a man who views in it the native soil of himself and his progenitors for several generations, — I anticipate, with pleasing expectation, that retreat, in which I promise myself to realize, without alloy, the sweet enjoyment of partaking, in the midst of my fellow-citizens, the benign influence of good laws, under a free government — the ever favorite object of my heart, and the happy reward, as I trust, of our mutual cares, labors, and dangers.[233]

Appendix 21

Thomas Jefferson Second Inaugural

March 4, 1805

Proceeding, fellow citizens, to that qualification which the constitution requires, before my entrance on the charge again conferred upon me, it is my duty to express the deep sense I entertain of this new proof of confidence from my fellow citizens at large, and the zeal with which it inspires me, so to conduct myself as may best satisfy their just expectations.

On taking this station on a former occasion, I declared the principles on which I believed it my duty to administer the affairs of our commonwealth. My conscience tells me that I have, on every occasion, acted up to that declaration, according to its obvious import, and to the understanding of every candid mind.

In the transaction of your foreign affairs, we have endeavored to cultivate the friendship of all nations, and especially of those with which we have the most important relations. We have done them justice on all occasions, favored where favor was lawful, and cherished mutual interests and intercourse on fair and equal terms. We are firmly convinced, and we act on that conviction, that with nations, as with individuals, our interests soundly calculated, will ever be found inseparable from our moral duties; and history bears witness to the fact, that a just nation is taken on its word, when recourse is had to armaments and wars to bridle others.

At home, fellow citizens, you best know whether we have done well or ill. The suppression of unnecessary offices, of use less establishments and expenses, enabled us to discontinue our internal taxes. These covering our land with officers, and opening our doors to their intrusions, had already begun that process of domiciliary vexation which, once entered, is scarcely to be restrained from - reaching successively every article of produce and property. If among these taxes some minor ones fell which had not been inconvenient, it was because their amount would not have paid the officers who collected them, and because, if they had any merit, the state authorities might adopt them, instead of others less approved.

The remaining revenue on the consumption of foreign articles, is paid cheerfully by those who can afford to add foreign luxuries to domestic comforts, being collected on our seaboards and frontiers only, and incorporated with the transactions of our mercantile citizens, it may be the pleasure and pride of an American to ask, what farmer, what mechanic, what laborer, ever sees a tax-gatherer of the United States? These contributions enable us to support the current expenses of the government, to fulfil contracts with foreign nations, to extinguish the native right of soil within our limits, to extend those limits, and to apply such a surplus to our public debts, as places at a short day their final redemption, and that redemption once effected, the revenue thereby liberated may, by a just repartition among the states, and a corresponding amendment of the constitution, be applied, in time of peace, to rivers, canals, roads, arts, manufactures, education, and other great objects within each state. In time of war, if injustice, by ourselves or others, must sometimes produce war, increased as the same revenue will be increased by population and consumption, and aided by other resources reserved for that crisis, it may meet within the year all the expenses of the year, without encroaching on the rights of future generations, by burdening them with the debts of the past. War will then be but a suspension of useful works, and a return to a state of peace, a return to the progress of improvement.

I have said, fellow citizens, that the income reserved had enabled us to extend our limits; but that extension may possibly pay for itself before we are called on, and in the meantime, may keep down the accruing interest; in all events, it will repay the advances we have made. I know that the acquisition of Louisiana has been disapproved by some, from a candid apprehension that the enlargement of our territory would endanger its union. But who can limit the extent to which the federative principle may operate effectively? The larger our association, the less will it be shaken by local passions; and in any view, is it not better that the opposite bank of the Mississippi should be settled by our own brethren and children, than by strangers of another family? With which shall we be most likely to live in harmony and friendly intercourse?

In matters of religion, I have considered that its free exercise is placed by the constitution independent of the powers of the general government. I have therefore undertaken, on no occasion, to prescribe the religious exercises suited to it; but have left them, as the constitution found them, under the direction and discipline of state or church authorities acknowledged by the several religious societies.

The aboriginal inhabitants of these countries I have regarded with the commiseration their history inspires. Endowed with the faculties and the rights of men, breathing an ardent love of liberty and independence, and occupying a country which left them no desire but to be undisturbed, the stream of overflowing population from other regions' directed itself on these shores; without power to divert, or habits to contend against, they have been overwhelmed by the current, or driven before it; now reduced within limits too narrow for the hunter's state, humanity enjoins us to teach them agriculture and the domestic arts; to encourage them to that industry which alone can enable them to maintain their place in existence, and to prepare them in time for that state of society, which to bodily comforts adds the improvement of the mind and morals. We have therefore liberally furnished them with the implements of husbandry and house hold use; we have placed among them instructors in the arts of first necessity; and they are covered with the aegis of the law against aggressors from among ourselves.

But the endeavors to enlighten them on the fate which awaits their present course of life, to induce them to exercise their reason, follow its dictates, and change their pursuits with the change of circumstances, have powerful obstacles to encounter; they are combated by the habits of their bodies, prejudice of their minds, ignorance, pride, and the influence of interested and crafty individuals among them, who feel themselves something in the present order of things, and fear to become nothing in any other. These persons inculcate a sanctimonious reverence for the customs of their ancestors; that whatsoever they did, must be done through all time; that reason is a false guide, and to advance under its counsel, in their physical, moral, or political condition, is perilous innovation; that their duty is to remain as their Creator made them, ignorance being safety, and knowledge full of danger; in short, my friends, among them is seen the action and counteraction of good sense and bigotry; they, too, have their anti-philosophers, who find an interest in keeping things in their present state, who dread reformation, and exert all their faculties to maintain the ascendency of habit over the duty of improving our reason, and obeying its mandates.

In giving these outlines, I do not mean, fellow citizens, to arrogate to myself the merit of the measures; that is due, in the first place, to the reflecting character of our citizens at large, who, by the weight of public opinion, influence and strengthen the public measures; it is due to the sound discretion with which they select from among themselves those to whom they confide the legislative duties; it is due to the zeal and wisdom of the characters thus selected, who lay the foundations of public happiness in wholesome laws, the execution of which alone remains for others; and it is due to the able and faithful auxiliaries, whose patriotism has associated with me in the executive functions.

During this course of administration, and in order to disturb it, the artillery of the press has been levelled against us, charged with whatsoever its licentiousness could devise or dare. These abuses of an institution so important to freedom and science, are deeply to be regretted, inasmuch as they tend to lessen its usefulness, and to sap its safety; they might, indeed, have been corrected by the wholesome punishments reserved and provided by the laws of the several States against falsehood and defamation; but public duties more urgent press on the time of public servants, and the offenders have therefore been left to find their punishment in the public indignation.

Nor was it uninteresting to the world, that an experiment should be fairly and fully made, whether freedom of discussion, unaided by power, is not sufficient for the propagation and protection of truth — whether a government, conducting itself in the true spirit of its constitution, with zeal and purity, and doing no act which it would be unwilling the whole world should wit ness, can be written down by falsehood and defamation. The experiment has been tried; you have witnessed the scene; our fellow citizens have looked on, cool and collected; they saw the latent source from which these outrages proceeded; they gathered around their public functionaries, and when the constitution called them to the decision by suffrage, they pronounced their verdict, honorable to those who had served them, and consolatory to the friend of man, who believes he may be intrusted with his own affairs.

No inference is here intended, that the laws, provided by the State against false and defamatory publications, should not be enforced; he who has time, renders a service to public morals and public tranquility, in reforming these abuses by the salutary coercions of the law; but the experiment is noted, to prove that, since truth and reason have maintained their ground against false opinions in league with false facts, the press, confined to truth, needs no other legal restraint; the public judgment will correct false reasonings and opinions, on a full hearing of all parties; and no other definite line can be drawn between the inestimable liberty of the press and its demoralizing licentiousness. If there be still improprieties which this rule would not restrain, its supplement must be sought in the censorship of public opinion.

Contemplating the union of sentiment now manifested so generally, as auguring harmony and happiness to our future course, I offer to our country sincere congratulations. With those, too, not yet rallied to the same point, the disposition to do so is gaining strength; facts are piercing through the veil drawn over them; and our doubting brethren will at length see, that the mass of their fellow citizens, with whom they cannot yet resolve to act, as to principles and measures, think as they think, and desire what they desire; that our wish, as well as theirs, is, that the public efforts may be directed honestly to the public good, that peace be cultivated, civil and religious liberty unassailed, law and order preserved, equality of rights maintained, and that state of property, equal or unequal, which results to every man from his own industry, or that of his fathers. When satisfied of these views, it is not in human nature that they should not approve and support them; in the meantime, let us cherish them with patient affection; let us do them justice, and more than justice, in all competitions of interest; and we need not doubt that truth, reason, and their own interests, will at length prevail, will gather them into the fold of their country, and will complete their entire union of opinion, which gives to a nation the blessing of harmony, and the benefit of all its strength.

I shall now enter on the duties to which my fellow citizens have again called me, and shall proceed in the spirit of those principles which they have approved. I fear not that any motives of interest may lead me astray; I am sensible of no passion which could seduce me knowingly from the path of justice; but the weakness of human nature, and the limits of my own understanding, will produce errors of judgment sometimes injurious to your interests. I shall need, therefore, all the indulgence I have heretofore experienced — the want of it will certainly not lessen with increasing years. I shall need, too, the favor of that Being in whose hands we are, who led our forefathers, as Israel of old, from their native land, and planted them in a country flowing with all the necessaries and comforts of life; who has covered our infancy with his providence, and our riper years with his wisdom and power; and to whose goodness I ask you to join with me in supplications, that he will so enlighten the minds of your servants, guide their councils, and prosper their measures, that whatsoever they do, shall result in your good, and shall secure to you the peace, friendship, and approbation of all nations.[234]

Appendix 22

James Madison First Inaugural

March 4, 1809

Unwilling to depart from examples, of the most revered authority, I avail myself of the occasion now presented, to express the profound impression made on me, by the call of my Country to the station, to the duties of which I am about to pledge myself, by the most solemn of sanctions. So distinguished a mark of confidence, proceeding from the deliberate and tranquil suffrage of a free and virtuous nation, would, under any circumstances, have commanded my gratitude and devotion; as well as filled me with an awful sense of the trust to be assumed. Under the various circumstances which give peculiar solemnity to the existing period, I feel that both the honor and the responsibility allotted to me, are inexpressibly enhanced.

The present situation of the world is indeed without a parallel; and that of our own Country full of difficulties. The pressure of these too is the more severely felt, because they have fallen upon us at a moment, when the national prosperity being at a height not before attained, the contrast resulting from the change, has been rendered the more striking. Under the benign influence of our Republican institutions, and the maintenance of peace with all nations, whilst so many of them were engaged in bloody and wasteful wars, the fruits of a just policy were enjoyed in an unrivaled growth of our faculties and resources. Proofs of this were seen in the improvements of agriculture; in the successful enterprises of commerce; in the progress of manufacturers, and useful arts; in the increase of the public revenue, and the use made of it in reducing the public debt; and in the valuable works and establishments everywhere multiplying over the face of our land.

It is a precious reflection that the transition from this prosperous condition of our Country, to the scene which has for some time been distressing us, is not chargeable on any unwarrantable views, nor, as I trust, on any involuntary errors, in the public Councils. Indulging no passions which trespass on the rights or the repose of other nations, it has been the true glory of the United States to cultivate peace by observing justice, and to entitle themselves to the respect of the nations at war, by fulfilling their neutral obligations, with the most scrupulous impartiality. If there be candor in the world, the truth of these assertions, will not be questioned. Posterity at least will do justice to them.

This unexceptionable course could not avail against the injustice and violence of the Belligerent powers. In their rage against each other, or impelled by more direct motives, principles of retaliation have been introduced, equally contrary to universal reason, and acknowledged law. How long their arbitrary edicts will be continued, in spite of the demonstrations that not even a pretext for them has been given by the United States, and of the fair and liberal attempt to induce a revocation of them, can not be anticipated. Assuring myself, that under every vicissitude, the determined spirit and united Councils of the nation, will be safeguards to its honor and its essential interests, I repair to the post assigned me, with no other discouragement, than what springs from my own inadequacy to its high duties. If I do not sink under the weight of this deep conviction, it is because I find some support in a consciousness of the purposes, and a confidence in the principles which I bring with me into this arduous service.

To cherish peace and friendly intercourse with all nations having correspondent dispositions; to maintain sincere neutrality toward belligerent nations; to prefer in all cases, amicable discussion and reasonable accommodation of differences, to a decision of them by an appeal to Arms; to exclude foreign intrigues and foreign partialities, so degrading to all Countries, and so baneful to free ones; to foster a spirit of independence too just to invade the rights of others, too proud to surrender our own, too liberal to indulge unworthy prejudices ourselves, and too elevated not to look down upon them in others; to hold the Union of the States as the basis of their peace and happiness; to support the Constitution, which is the cement of the Union, as well in its limitations as in its authorities; to respect the rights and authorities reserved to the States and to the people, as equally incorporated with, and essential to the success of, the general system; to avoid the slightest interference with the rights of conscience, or the functions of religion so wisely exempted from civil jurisdiction; to preserve in their full energy, the other salutary provisions in behalf of private and personal rights, and of the freedom of the press; to observe economy in public expenditures; to liberate the public resources by an honorable discharge of the public debts; to keep within the requisite limits a standing military force, always remembering, that an Armed and trained militia is the firmest bulwark of Republics; that without standing Armies their liberty can never be in danger; nor with large ones, safe; to promote by authorized means, improvements friendly to agriculture, to manufactures, and to external as well as internal commerce; to favor, in like manner, the advancement of science and the diffusion of information as the best aliment to true liberty; to carry on the benevolent plans which have been so meritoriously applied to the conversion of our aboriginal neighbours from the degradation and wretchedness of savage life, to a participation of the improvements of which the human mind and manners are susceptible in a civilized state: As far as sentiments and intentions such as these can aid the fulfillment of my duty, they will be a resource which can not fail me.

It is my good fortune, moreover, to have the path in which I am to tread, lighted by examples of illustrious services, successfully rendered in the most trying difficulties, by those who have marched before me. Of those of my immediate predecessor, it might least become me here to speak. I may however, be pardoned for not suppressing the sympathy with which my heart is full, in the rich reward he enjoys in the benedictions of a beloved Country, gratefully bestowed or exalted talents, zealously devoted, thro' a long career, to the advancement of its highest interest and happiness.

But the source to which I look for the aids which alone can supply my deficiencies, is in the well tried intelligence and virtue of my fellow Citizens, and in the Councils of those representing, them in the other Departments associated in the care of the national interests. In these my confidence will, under every difficulty be best placed; next to that which we have all been encouraged to feel in the guardianship and guidance of that Almighty Being whose power regulates the destiny of nations, whose blessings have been so conspicuously dispensed to this rising Republic, and to whom we are bound to address our devout gratitude for the past, as well as our fervent supplications and best hopes for the future.[235]

NOTES

[1] Todd & Curti, *Rise of the American Nation* (New York: Harcourt, Brace & World, Inc., 1964), p. 21

[2] William Bradford, *of Plymouth Plantation* (Rendered into Modern English by Harold Paget 1909, republished by Vision Forum, San Antonio, TX, 1998) p. 21

[3] Frances Dillon, *A Place For Habitation- The Pilgrim Fathers & Their Quest* (London: Hutchinson & Co, 1973) p. 118

[4] Benjamin W. Labaree, "Colonial Life", *Encyclopedia Americana*, (1992) Vol. 7, p. 283

[5] Southworth & Southworth, *Early Days In America* (Syracuse, New York: Iroquois Publishing Co, 1944) p. 412

[6] Olga W. Hall-Quest, *Guardians of Liberty- Sam Adams & John Hancock* (New York: E.P. Dutton & Co, 1963), pp. 44-46

[7] Donald S. Lutz, "The Relative Influence of European Writers on Late Eighteenth Century American Political Thought," *American Political Science Review,* Vol. 78 (1984): pp. 189-97, cited by John Eidsmoe, *Christianity and the Constitution* (Grand Rapids, Michigan: Baker Academic, 1987), pp. 51-54

[8] John Eidsmoe,*Christianity and the Constitution* (Grand Rapids, Michigan: Baker Academic, 1987), p. 56

[9] John Locke, *Two Treatises of Government,* (London: Millar, Woodfall, et.al., 1764 ed.) Ch. IX, Sec. 123

[10] William J. Federer, *America's God and Country - Encyclopedia of Quotations* (St. Louis, MO: Amerisearch, 2000), p. 51

[11] Sir William Blackstone, *Commentaries on the Laws of England* (Oxford: Clarendon Press, 1765, 7th edition) p. 39

[12] Ibid., pp.41-42

[13] Ibid.

[14] Ibid., p. 54

[15] Ibid., p. 129

[16] Thomas Paine, *Thomas Paine – Common Sense and Other Writings*, ed. by George Stade (New York: Barnes & Noble Books, 2005), p.46 * Note- This is my source book for Paine's Common Sense essay and quotes

[17] Joyce Appleby, Introduction to *Thomas Paine – Common Sense and Other Writings* (New York: Barnes & Noble Books, 2005), pp. xxiv-xxv

[18] Paine, *Common Sense*, p.17

[19] James Madison, *The Federalist No.51, The Federalist Papers,* ed. by Clinton Rossiter (New York: Signet Classic Edition, published by Penguin Group USA, 2003) p.319

[20] Paine, *Common Sense,* p. 17

[21] W. Cleon Skousen, *5000 Year Leap*, (Malta, ID: National Center for Constitutional Studies, 2006) pp. 174-175

[22] Paine, *Common Sense,* p.19

[23] Ibid., p.17

[24] Thomas Jefferson, Letter to Gideon Granger Aug. 13, 1800, *Thomas Jefferson – Writings*, ed. by Merrill D. Peterson (New York: Literary Classics of the United States Inc., 1984), p. 1079

[25] Paine, *Common Sense*, p.30

[26] Ibid., p. 22

[27] Ibid., p. 26

[28] Ibid., p 37

[29] Ibid., p. 35

[30] Thomas Jefferson, *Inaugural Address,* March 4, 1801; M. Sears, *The American Politician* (Boston: E. Leland and W. J. Whiting, 1842) p. 66

[31] Dr. Ron Paul, speech in the U.S. House of Representatives, 9/5/2002, reprinted in; *A Foreign Policy of Freedom* (Lake Jackson, TX: Foundation for Rational Economics and Education , Inc., 2007), pp. 207-218

[32] Paine, *Common Sense*, p. 35

[33] Ibid., p. 35

[34] Ibid., p. 38

[35] Ibid., p. 45

[36] Ibid., p. 46

[37] Ibid., p. 46

[38] Ibid., p. 52

[39] Ibid., p. 51

[40] John Adams, July 3, 1776 letter to Abigail Adams; quoted by Federer, *America's God and Country, p. 9*

[41] Ibid.

[42] Locke, *Two Treatises of Government,* Ch. XI, Sec. 135

[43] Blackstone, *Commentaries on the Laws of England*, pp. 39-41

[44] Locke, *Two Treatises of Government,* Ch. II, Sec. 6

[45] Blackstone, *Commentaries on the Laws of England*, p. 54

[46] John Adams, *The Political Writings of John Adams,* ed. by George A. Peek Jr. (New York: Liberal Arts Press, 1954) p. 96, cited by Skousen, *5000 Year Leap*, p. 127

[47] John Adams, *The Works of John Adams,* 10 vols., ed. by Charles Francis Adams (Boston: Little, Brown and Company, 1850-1856) p. 6:9, 280, cited by Skousen, *5000 Year Leap*, p. 174

[48] Frederic Bastiat, *The Law*, originally published 1850(Illinois, USA: BN Publishing, 2007), p. 9

[49] James Madison, *Property*; National Gazette, March 29, 1792, printed in *Madison-*Writings, ed. by Jack N. Rakove (New York: Literary Classics of the United States, 1999) p. 515

[50] Alexander Hamilton, *The Federalist No.22, The Federalist Papers,* ed. by Clinton Rossiter (New York: Signet Classic Edition, published by Penguin Group USA, 2003) p.319

[51] Madison, *The FederalistNo. 39*, p. 148

[52] Locke, *Two Treatises of Government*, Ch. XIX, Sec. 222

[53] Locke, *Two Treatises of Government*, Ch. XVIII, sec. 208-209

[54] Hall-Quest, *Guardians of Liberty- Sam Adams & John Hancock,* p.101

[55] Paul C. Bowers Jr., "American Revolution", *Encyclopedia Americana* (1992), Vol. 1, pp. 714-733

[56] Roger Sherman, June 26, 1787; *The Anti-Federalist Papers*, ed. by Ralph Ketcham (New York: Penguin Putnam, 2003 printing) p. 91

[57] Articles of Confederation - *Documents Illustrative of the Formation of the Union of the American States* (Washington D.C., Government Printing Office- Library of Congress, 1927), edited by Charles C. Tansill, pp. 27-37

[58] Alexander Hamilton, *Letter to James Duane- September 3, 1780.* Jack Rakove, ed., *Founding America – Documents from the Revolution to the Bill of Rights,* (New York: Barnes & Noble Books, 2006), pp. 176-193

[59] Alexander Hamilton, *Address of the Annapolis Convention – September 14, 1786.* Charles C. Tansill, ed., *Documents Illustrative of the Formation of the Union of the American States* (Washington D.C., Government Printing Office- Library of Congress, 1927), pp. 40-43

[60] Ibid.

[61] Ibid.

[62] Ibid.

[63] Report of proceedings in Congress, Feb 21, 1787, printed in *Documents Illustrative of the Formation of the Union of the American States,* pp. 44-46

[64] Patrick Henry, quoted in, *Miracle at Philadelphia – The Story of the Constitutional Convention May to September 1787.* Catherine Drinker Bowen, (New York: Little, Brown and Co, 1966), p. 18

[65] Drinker Bowen, *Miracle at Philadelphia,* pp. 41-43

[66] Drinker Bowen, *Miracle at Philadelphia,* p.43

[67] Ibid., p. 41

[68] Ibid., p. 43

[69] Alexander Hamilton, *The Federalist*, No. 9, p. 71

[70] Charles Kesler, *The Federalist Papers*, introduction p. X, (New York: Signet Classic Edition, published by Penguin Group USA, 2003)

[71] Alexander Hamilton, quoted by Drinker Bowen, *Miracle at Philadelphia,* p.201

[72] Ibid., p. 112

[73] John Dickinson, quoted by, Drinker-Bowen, *Miracle at Philadelphia*, p. 58

[74] George Mason, quoted by, Drinker-Bowen, *Miracle at Philadelphia*, p. 262

[75] Skousen, *5000 Year Leap,* pp. 155-161

[76] Madison, *The Federalist No. 10*, p. 76

[77] Madison, *The Federalist No. 39*, p. 237

[78] Baron Charles de Montesquieu, *The Spirit of the Laws,* Great Books of the Western World, vol. 38 (Chicago: Encyclopedia Britannica, Inc., 1952), p. 70, cited by Skousen, *5000 Year Leap,* p. 197

[79] Ibid.

[80] Samuel Adams, *An Oration Delivered at the State-House, In Philadelphia, To A Very Numerous Audience; On Thursday the 1st of August, 1776 (London: J. Johnson, 1776) pp. 3-4*

[81] Benjamin Rush, *Address to the People of the United States June 3, 1786,:* Rakove, ed., *Founding America- Documents from the Revolution to the Bill of Rights*, p. 310

[82] Blackstone, *Commentaries on the Laws of England*, pp. 46-49

[83] Hamilton, *The Federalist No. 9*, p. 71

[84] Hamilton, *The Federalist No. 32,* p. 194

[85] Madison, *The Federalist No. 39*, p. 239

[86] Ibid., p. 240

[87] Madison, *The Federalist No. 45,* p.286

[88] Madison, *The Federalist No. 40,* p. 247

[89] Hamilton, *The Federalist No. 22*, p. 148

[90] Joseph Andrews, *A Guide for Learning and Teaching the Declaration of Independence and the U.S. Constitution* (USA: The Center For Teaching The Constitution, 2010), p. 191

[91] Madison, *The Federalist No. 52*, p. 324

[92] Ibid., p. 327

[93] Ibid., p. 323

[94] Samuel Adams, "*Loyalty and Sedition",* Public Advertiser. 1748; also quoted in *America's God and Country* by William J. Federer (St. Louis: Amerisearch Inc., 2000) p. 23

[95] Madison, *The Federalist No.* 52, pp. 323-324

[96] Madison, *The Federalist No. 54*, p. 338

[97] Madison, *The Federalist No. 45*, pp. 286-287

[98] Madison, *The Federalist No. 39*, p. 240

[99] Hamilton, *The Federalist No. 9*, p. 71

[100] Brandon Stewart, *The Foundry,* blog of The Heritage Foundation, accessed 11/19/2012; http://blog.heritage.org/2011/01/17/list-of-states-suing-over-obamacare/

[101] Thomas Jefferson letter to Gideon Granger Aug 13, 1800, *Writings,* pp. 1078-1080

[102] Hamilton, *The Federalist No. 22*, p. 148

[103] Madison, *The Federalist No. 45*, p. 289

[104] Hamilton, *The Federalist No. 12*, p. 91

[105] Hamilton, *The Federalist No. 33*, p. 198

[106] Hamilton, *The Federalist No. 36*, pp. 219-220

[107] Hamilton, *The Federalist No. 30*, p. 184

[108] Hamilton, *The Federalist No. 34*, p. 203

[109] Hamilton, *The Federalist No. 30*, p. 186

[110] Madison, *The Federalist No. 45*, pp. 288-289

[111] Hamilton, *The Federalist No. 35*, p. 213

[112] Madison, *The Federalist No. 45,* p. 288

[113] Thomas Jefferson letter to Gideon Granger Aug 13, 1800, *Writings,* pp. 1078-1080

[114] Patrick Henry, speech during Virginia Ratifying Convention June 7, 1788; *The Anti-Federalist Papers*, p. 212

[115] "John DeWitt" Oct. 27, 1787; *The Anti-Federalist Papers,* p. 197

[116] Ibid.

[117] "The Centinel" No. 1, Oct. 5, 1787; *The Anti-Federalist Papers*, p. 232

[118] The Address and Reasons of Dissent of the Minority of the Convention of Pennsylvania to their Constituents, Dec. 18, 1787; *The Anti-Federalist Papers,* p. 243

[119] Ibid., pp. 252-253

[120] "Brutus" No. 1 Oct. 18, 1787; *The Anti-Federalist Papers,* p. 273

[121] Tansill, *Documents Illustrative of the Formation of the Union of the American States, p. 1039*

[122] http://en.wikipedia.org/wiki/IRS, accessed 2/20/2013

[123] Bureau of Labor Statistics, U.S. Department of Labor, *Occupational Outlook Handbook, 2012-13 Edition*, Military Careers, on the Internet at http://www.bls.gov/ooh/military/military-careers.htm (visited *December 27, 2012*).

[124] Madison, *The Federalist No. 45*, p. 289

[125] Summary of Wickard v. Filburn, http://www.lawnix.com/cases/wickard-filburn.html, accessed 3/8/2013

[126] Hamilton, *The Federalist No. 22*, p. 139

[127] Ibid.

[128] Madison, *The Federalist No. 42,* p. 264

[129] Joseph Story, L.L.D., *The Constitutional Class Book; Being A Brief Exposition of the Constitution of the United States* (Boston: Hilliard, Gray & Company, 1834), p. 80

[130] Alexander Hamilton quoted by, Dr. Ron Paul, *Gold, Peace, and Prosperity* (Auburn, AL: Ludwig von Mises Institute, 2011), p. 56

[131] Madison, *The Federalist No. 44*, p. 278

[132] Thomas Jefferson quoted by Dr. Ron Paul, *Gold, Peace, and Prosperity*, p. 15

[133] Daniel Webster quoted by Ibid., p. 16

[134] Madison, *The Federalist No. 45,* p. 289

[135] Edwin Meese III, *"The Constitution and Crime",* Sep. 15, 2010, http://www.heritage.org/research/commentary/2010/09/the-constitution, accessed 11/25/2012

[136] Madison, *The Federalist No. 41*, p. 252

[137] Madison, *The Federalist No. 41*, p. 255

[138] Ibid. p. 257

[139] John Quincy Adams, July 4, 1821 foreign policy speech, http://www.presidentialrhetoric.com/historicspeeches/adams_jq/foreignpolicy.html, accessed 2/20/2013

[140] Hamilton, *The Federalist No. 29*, p. 181

[141] Hamilton, *The Federalist No. 33,* p. 199

[142] Ibid.

[143] George Mason; quoted by Drinker Bowen, *Miracle at Philadelphia,* p. 203

[144] John Dickinson, quoted by Ibid. p. 204

[145] Richard Beeman, *The Penguin Guide to the United States Constitution* (New York: The Penguin Group, 2010), p.37

[146] John Rutledge; quoted by Drinker Bowen, *Miracle at Philadelphia*, p. 202

[147] Madison, *The Federalist No. 42*, pp. 262-263

[148] Sir William Blackstone, *Commentaries on the Laws of England,* quoted by Alexander Hamilton, The Federalist No. 84, p. 511

[149] Hamilton, *The Federalist No. 36*, p. 219

[150] Hamilton, *The Federalist No. 21*, pp. 138-139

[151] David McCullough, *John Adams* (New York: Simon & Schuster, 2001) p. 507; for more detail on the Federal Property Tax of 1798 see essays by Dr. Bill Long at, http://www.drbilllong.com/LegalHistoryII/TaxII.html

[152] Hamilton, *The Federalist no. 84*, p. 511

[153] Madison, *The Federalist no. 45*, p. 287-288

[154] John Jay, *The Federalist No. 64*, p. 389

[155] Ibid.

[156] Beeman, *Penguin Guide to the US Constitution*, p. 43

[157] John Bingham, Congressional Globe, House of Representatives, 37th Congress, 2nd Session1862; http://memory.loc.gov/cgi-bin/ampage?collId=llcg&fileName=059/llcg059.db&recNum=680

[158] John Bingham, Congressional Globe, House of Representatives, 39th Congress, 1st Session 1866; http://memory.loc.gov/cgi-bin/ampage?collId=llcg&fileName=071/llcg071.db&recNum=332

[159] Emmerich de Vattel, *The Law of Nations or the Principles of Natural Law* (London:1797 ed.), Book 1, Ch. 19, Section 212

[160] Franklin letter to Dumas, quoted in; Introduction to The Law of Nations by Albert de Lapradelle (Washington: Carnegie Institution of Washington, 1916), p. xxx

[161] Ibid., p. xxxv

[162] Jerome Corsi. "Rubio Autobiography Proves He's Not Eligible For VP?" 6/18/2012 <http://www.wnd.com/2012/06/rubio-autobiography-proves-hes-not-eligible-for-vp/> accessed 1/13/2013

[163] Beeman, *Penguin Guide to the US Constitution*, p. 44

[164] Hamilton, *The Federalist No. 74*, p. 446

[165] Hamilton, *The Federalist No. 78*, p. 464; The text notes for this essay indicate that Montesquieu, in *Spirit of Laws*, said, "Of the three powers mentioned, the JUDICIARY is next to nothing."

[166] Ibid.

[167] Ibid., p. 465

[168] Ibid., p. 469

[169] Hamilton, *The Federalist No. 79*, p. 471

[170] Ibid., p. 472

[171] Hamilton, *The Federalist No. 80*, p. 478

[172] Madison, *The Federalist No. 39*, p. 237

[173] Ibid., p. 236

[174] Andrews, *A Guide for Learning and Teaching the Declaration of Independence and the U.S. Constitution*, p. 267

[175] Madison, *The Federalist No. 43, p. 274*

[176] Hamilton, *The Federalist No. 33,* p. 197

[177] Ibid., p. 200

[178] Madison, *The Federalist No. 44*, p. 284

[179] Ibid., *Federalist No. 39*, p. 240

[180] George Washington, *Farewell Address September 17, 1796*; This address was delivered to Congress at Philadelphia and was also published in newspapers throughout the country; printed in *The American Politician,* by M. Sears, pp. 44-45

[181] John Adams, *Letter to the officers of the First Brigade of the Third Division of the Militia of Massachusetts, October 11, 1798*, quoted by Federer, America's God and Country, pp. 10-11

[182] John Quincy Adams *April 27, 1837 letter, The Historical Magazine*, July 1860 (New York: Charles B. Richardson & Co., 1860) pp. 193-194

[183] Samuel Adams, *Letter to James Warren, February 12, 1779*, quoted by Federer, America's God and Country, p. 23

[184] Benjamin Rush, *Essays*, *Literary, Moral, & Philosophical* (Philadelphia: printed by Thomas & William Bradford, 1806, second edition), p. 8

[185] Alexis de Tocqueville, *Democracy In America* (New York: Bantam Dell, 2004; first published 1835) pp. 352-353

[186] Ibid., p. 353

[187] Ibid., p. 355

[188] Ibid., p. 357

[189] Ibid., p. 358

[190] Ibid.

[191] Ibid., p. 366

[192] Jefferson, Writings, pp. 519-520

[193] Joseph Story, *Commentaries on the Constitution of the United States*, 3rd ed., 2 vols. (Boston: Little, Brown and Company, 1858), 2:666-67, art. 1879, cited by Skousen, 5000 Year Leap, p. 87

[194] Madison, June 12, 1788 speech in VA Ratifying Convention, *Writings,* p. 382

[195] Library of Congress Exhibit, http://www.loc.gov/exhibits/religion/rel06-2.html, accessed 2/25/2013; also cited by William J. Federer, *Backfired- A Nation Born for Religious Tolerance No Longer Tolerates Religion (St. Louis: Amerisearch Inc., 2007), p. 240*

[196] Federer, *Backfired,* pp. 233-234

[197] Ibid., p. 234

[198] Madison, *Writings,* p. 682

[199] Virginia proposed amendments, June 27, 1788 as cited in; *The Anti-Federalist Papers,* p. 221

[200] George Mason June 14, 1788 in Virginia ratifying debates, David Robertson, *Debates and Other Proceedings of the Convention of Virginia* (Richmond, VA: Enquirer Press for Ritchie & Worsley and Augustine Davis, 1805), p. 270

[201] Samuel Adams *The Rights of the Colonists* – November 1772, cited by Verna M. Hall, *The Christian History of the Constitution* (San Francisco: The Foundation for American Christian Education, 1966), p. 365

[202] George Mason June 14, 1788, *Debates and Other Proceedings of the Convention of Virginia,* p. 271

[203] James Madison, *The Federalist No. 46*, pp. 295-297

[204] Andrew Napolitano. "Individuals Are Sovereign, Not The Government". 1/9/2013. <http://www.wnd.com/2013/01/individuals-are-sovereign-not-the-government/> accessed 1/13/2013

[205] John Adams, quoted by McCullough in *John Adams,* p. 62

[206] Hamilton, *The Federalist No. 83,* pp.498-499

[207] Ibid., p. 500

[208] Hamilton, *The Federalist No. 84*, p. 512

[209] Ibid., p. 513

[210] Ibid., p. 514

[211] Center for Responsive Politics; http://www.opensecrets.org/bigpicture/reelect.php, accessed 2/21/2012

[212] *Mayflower Compact,*Nov. 11, 1620,Source text: *The Federal and State Constitutions, Colonial Charters, and Other Organic Laws of the United States,* comp. by Benjamin Perley Poore (Washington: Government Printing Office, 1877), p. 931

[213] *Fundamental Orders of Connecticut*, Source text: Connecticut Comptroller's Office, *The Three Constitutions of Connecticut*, comp. by A. Chamberlain (Hartford, CT: Hartford Press, 1901) pp. 7-16

[214] *Declaration of Rights and Grievances,* Oct 1765, Source text: *The Origin and Growth of the American Constitution*, by Hannis Taylor (Boston: Houghton Mifflin Co, 1911) pp. 495-496

[215] *Suffolk* Resolves, September 1774, Source text: Supplement to the Massachusetts Gazette, Sep., 15, 1774

[216] *Declaration and Resolves – 1st Continental Congress,* Source text: Tansill, *Documents Illustrative of the Formation of the Union of the American States*, 1927, pp. 1-5

[217] Patrick Henry, March 23, 1775, Source text: *American Statesmen – The Revolutionary Period*, vol. 3 of 32, ed. by John T. Morse Jr., *Patrick Henry* text by Moses Coit Tyler (Boston: Houghton, Mifflin and Company, 1898) pp. 140-145

[218] *Olive Branch Petition,* July 8, 1775, Source text: *Journals of the Continental Congress, Vol. II- 1775,* Worthington Chauncey Ford, Chief – Div. of Manuscripts (Washington: Government Printing Office, 1905), pp. 158-162

[219] *Declaration of the Causes and Necessity of Taking Up Arms,* July 6, 1775, Source text: Tansill, *Documents Illustrative of the Formation of the Union of the American States*, pp. 10-17

[220] Thomas Jefferson, Aug. 13, 1800 letter to Gideon Granger, source text: *Jefferson – Writings*, ed. by MerrillD. Peterson (New York: Literary Classics of the United States, 1984) pp. 1078-1080

[221] Thomas Jefferson, *First Inaugural* Address, March 4, 1801, Source text: M. Sears, *The American Politician*, pp. 64-68

[222] James Madison, "Property", National Gazette, March 29, 1792; source text: *Madison-Writings*, ed. by Jack N. Rakove (New York: Literary Classics of the United States, 1999), pp. 515-517

[223] *Virginia Declaration of Rights,* June 12, 1776, Source text: *Founding America – Documents from the Revolution to the Bill of Rights,* ed. by Jack N. Rakove, pp. 88-90

[224] *Summary View of the Rights of British America,* 1774, Source text: *Jefferson – Writings,* ed. by Peterson, pp. 105-122

[225] *Massachusetts Circular* Letter, Feb. 11, 1768, Source text: *Journals of the House of Representatives of Massachusetts* (Boston: Green and Russell, 1767-1768); http://www.masshist.org/revolution/doc-viewer.php?old=1&mode=nav&item_id=289

[226] *Address of the Annapolis Convention,* September 14, 1786, Source text: Tansill, *Documents Illustrative of the Formation of the Union of the American States*, pp. 40-43

[227] *Virginia Plan,* Source text: *The Anti-Federalist Papers, ed.* by Ralph Ketcham, pp.37-39

[228] *New Jersey Plan,* Source text: Tansill, *Documents Illustrative of the Formation of the Union of the American States*, pp. 967-970

[229] Source text: Hon. Dr. Ron Paul Air Piracy Reprisaland Capture Actof 2001Extended Remarks House of Representatives 10/20/2001, http://thomas.loc.gov/cgi-bin/query/D?r107:9:./temp/~r107PkwgrF, accessed 2/22/2013

[230] Source text: H.R. 3074 Air Piracy Reprisal and Capture Act of 2001, http://thomas.loc.gov/cgi-bin/query/z?c107:H.R.3074, accessed 2/22/2013

[231] Source text: H.R. 3076 September 11 Marque and Reprisal Act of 2001, http://thomas.loc.gov/cgi-bin/query/z?c107:H.R.3076:, accessed 2/22/2013

[232] NDAA, Section 1021, http://www.gpo.gov/fdsys/pkg/BILLS-112hr1540enr/pdf/BILLS-112hr1540enr.pdf, accessed 2/22/2013

[233] George Washington, *Farewell Address,* 1796, Source text: M. Sears, *The American Politician*, pp.35-51

[234] Source text: *The Writings of Thomas Jefferson,* vol. 3, ed. by H.A. Washington (Philadelphia: J.B. Lippincott & Co., 1864), pp. 40-45

[235] James Madison, *First Inaugural,* March 4, 1809, Source text: M. Sears, *The American Politician*, pp. 77-80

Bibliography

Adams, John Quincy. "Stray Leaves From An Autograph Collection." *The Historical Magazine and Notes and Queries Concerning the Antiquities, History and Biography of America, Vol IV* July 1860: 193-194.

Adams, Samuel. *An Oration Delivered at the State-House, In Philadelphia, To A Very Numerous Audience; On Thursday the 1st of August, 1776.* London: J. Johnson, 1776.

Andrews, Joseph. *A Guide for Learning and Teaching the Declaration of Independence and the U.S. Constitution.* The Center for Teaching the Constitution, 2010 edition.

Athearn, Robert G. *The American Heritage New Illustrated History of the United States, Volumes 1,2,3.* New York: Dell Publishing Co., 1963.

Bastiat, Frederic. *The Law.* Illinois: BN Publishing, 1850 (2007 printing).

Beeman, Richard. *The Penguin Guide to the United States Constitution.* New York: Penguin Group, 2010.

Blackstone, William. *Commentaries On The Laws of England.* Oxford: Clarendon Press, 1765.

Bowers Jr., Paul C. "American Revolution." *Encyclopedia Americana* (1992).

Bradford, William. *of Plymouth Plantation, 1909 edition.* San Antonio: Vision Forum, 1998.

Connecticut, State of, Comptroller. *The Three Constitutions of Connecticut.* Hartford: Hartford Press, 1901.

Corsi, Jerome. *"Rubio Autobiography Proves He's Not Eligible For VP?"* 18 June 2012. *World Net Daily (www.wnd.com).*

Curti, Lewis Paul Todd & Merle. *Rise of the American Nation.* New York: Harcourt, Brace and World, Inc., 1964.

Dillon, Frances. *A Place for Habitation - The Pilgrim Fathers.* London: Hutchison & Co, 1973.

Drinker Bowen, Caroline. *Miracle at Philadelphia - The Story of the Constitutional Convention May to September 1787.* New York: Little, Brown, and Company, 1966.

Eidsmoe, John. *Christianity and the Constitution.* Grand Rapids: Baker Academic, 1987.

Federer, William J. *America's God and Country - Encyclopedia of Quotations.* St. Louis: Amerisearch Inc., 2000.

Backfired - A Nation Born for Religious Tolerance No Longer Tolerates Religion. St. Louis: Amerisearch Inc., 2007.

Ford, Worthington. *Journals of the Continental Congress.* Washington: Government Printing Office- Library of Congress, 1905.

Garner and Bryan A. Ed. in Chief. *Black's Law Dictionary - Pocket Edition.* West Group, 1996.

Globe, Congressional. "37th Congress, 2nd Session." Washington D.C., 1862.

—. "39th Congress, 1st Session." Washington D.C., 1866.

Hall, Verna M. *The Christian History of the Constitution.* San Francisco: Foundation for American Christian Education, 1966

Hall-Quest, Olga W. *Guardians of Liberty - Sam Adams & John Hancock.* New York: E.P. Dutton & Company, 1963.

Hamilton, Alexander, John Jay, James Madison, ed. by Clinton Rossiter. *The Federalist Papers*. New York: Penguin Group, 2003.

III, Edwin Meese. "The Constitution and Crime." 15 9 2010. *Heritage Foundation, www.heritage.org*. 25 11 2012.

Jefferson, Thomas. *The Writings of Thomas Jefferson, vol. III, ed. by H.A. Washington*. Ed. H.A. Washington. Philadelphia: J.B. Lippincott & Co., 1864.

—. *Writings, ed. by Merrill D. Peterson*. New York: Literary Classics of the United States Inc., 1984.

Ketcham, Ralph. *The Anti-Federalist Papers*. New York: Penguin Putnam, 1986 (2003 printing).

Labaree, Benjamin W. "Colonial Life." *Encyclopedia Americana* (1992).

lawnix.com. Summary of Wickard v. Filburn, http://www.lawnix.com/cases/wickard-filburn.html. n.d. 8 March 2013.

Locke, John. *Two Treatises of Government*. London: A. Millar, H. Woodfall, I. Whiston and B. White, et al, 1764 edition.

Long, Dr. Bill. *www.drbilllong.com*. n.d. 28 November 2012.

Madison, James. *Writings, ed. by Jack N. Rakove*. New York: Literary Classics of the United States, 1999.

Massachusetts, House of Representatives. "Massachusetts Circular Letter - February 11, 1768." *Journal of the House of Representatives of Massachusetts*. Boston: Green and Russell, 1768. 288.

McCullough, David. *John Adams*. New York: Simon & Schuster, 2001.

Napolitano, Andrew. *"Individuals Are Soverign, Not the Government."* 9 January 2013. *World Net Daily (www.wnd.com)*. 13 January 2013.

Paine, Thomas. *Common Sense and Other Writings*. New York: Barnes & Noble Books, 2005.

Paul, Ron. *A Foreign Policy of Freedom*. Lake Jackson, TX: Foundation For Rational Economics and Education Inc., 2007.

—. *Gold, Peace, and Prosperity - The Birth of a New Currency; 2nd ed.* Auburn, AL: Ludwig von Mises Institute, 2011.

Poore, Benjamin Perley. *The Federal and State Constitutions, Colonial Charters, and Other Organic Laws of the United States*. Washington: Government Printing Office, 1877.

Rakove, John. *Founding America - Documents From the Revolution to the Bill of Rights*. New York: Barnes & Noble Books, 2006.

Randall, Mary Hoehling and Betty. *For Life and Liberty*. New York: Julian Messner, 1969.

Robertson, David. *Debates and Other Proceedings of the Convention of Virginia*. Richmond, VA: Enquirer Press (for Ritchie & Worsley and Augustine Davis), 1805

Rush, Benjamin. *Essays, Literary, Moral, & Philosophical*. Philadelphia: Thomas & Samuel F. Bradford, 1798.

Sears, M. *The American Politician; Containing the Declaration of Independence, the Constitution of the United States, the Inaugural and First Annual Addresses and*

Messages of All the Presidents, and Other Important State Papers. Boston: E. Leland and W. J. Whiting, 1842.

Skousen, W. Cleon. *The 5000 Year Leap*. Malta, ID: National Center For Constitutional Studies, 2006.

Southworth, Gertrude Van Duyn and Southworth, John Van Duyn. *Early Days In America*. Syracuse: Iroquois Publishing Company, 1944.

Stewart, Brandon. *"List of 27 States Suing Over Obamacare."* 17 1 2011. *Heritage Foundation Blog, www.blog.heritage.org.* 19 11 2012.

Story L.L.D., Joseph. *The Constitutional Class Book; Being A Brief Exposition of the Constitution of the United States.* Boston: Hilliard, Gray & Company, 1834

Tansill, Charles C. editor. *Documents Illustrative of the Formation of the Union of the American States*. Washington D.C.: Library of Congress, 1927.

Taylor, Hannis. *The Origin and Growth of the American Constitution*. Boston: Houghton Mifflin Co, 1911.

"The Congressional Globe." Washington: F. & J. Rives, 1862, 1866.

Tocqueville, Alexis de. *Democracy In America*. New York: Bantam Dell, 1835 (2004 edition).

Tyler, Moses Coit. *Patrick Henry - American Statesmen - The Revolutionary Period vol.3*. Boston: Houghton, Mifflin and Company, 1898.

Vattel, Emmerich de. *The Law of Nations*. Philadelphia: T. & J.W. Johnson & Co; Law Booksellers, 1758 (1863 edition).

—. *The Law of Nations*. New York: Carnegie Institution, 1758 (1916 edition).

Warren, Joseph. "Suffolk Resolves." *Massachusetts Gazette - Supplement* 15 September 1774: 1.

Webster, Noah. *An American Dictionary Of The English Language*. Chesapeake, VA: Foundation for American Christian Education (2010 printing), 1828.

Webster 1828 Dictionary online: www.1828-dictionary.com.
*note this site also contains the 1913 Webster dictionary definitions